GLIMPSES OF
HEAVEN

Dream Visitations from the Afterlife—
and a Visit to Eternity

THOMAS HARDESTY

GLIMPSES OF HEAVEN
DREAM VISITATIONS FROM THE AFTERLIFE—
AND A VISIT TO ETERNITY

Scripture quotations from the Holy Bible, King James Version (Authorized Version). First published in 1611. Quoted from the KJV Classic Reference Bible.f

iUniverse books may be ordered through booksellers or by contacting:

iUniverse
1663 Liberty Drive
Bloomington, IN 47403
www.iuniverse.com
1-800-Authors (1-800-288-4677)

ISBN: 978-1-5320-6483-8 (sc)
ISBN: 978-1-5320-6485-2 (hc)
ISBN: 978-1-5320-6484-5 (e)

Library of Congress Control Number: 2019900389

Print information available on the last page.

iUniverse rev. date: 01/30/2019

To Dad
See you on the Other Side.
Again.

CONTENTS

Acknowledgements...ix

Preface...xi

Introduction xv

Chapter 1   Goodbye, Dad...1

Chapter 2   Clar Clar.. 12

Chapter 3   Grandma.. 26

Chapter 4   Gramps... 61

Chapter 5   Uncle Billy... 77

Chapter 6   Sylvia 82

Chapter 7   Uncle Denny.. 100

Chapter 8   Dad.. 118

Chapter 9   Dad's Third Visitation: A Walk in Eternity................ 149

Chapter 10   A Matter of Faith 167

Epilogue... 187

A Final Note 197

ACKNOWLEDGEMENTS

When I decided to finally sit down and begin writing this book after considering it for a few years, I had no idea what I was getting myself into. Although I had 30 years of print journalism under my belt and had written thousands of published newspaper articles, this was my first book project. To say it was a completely different animal would be a gross understatement.

First of all, those 30 years of newspaper experience were in sports. This was my first endeavor writing something outside my "comfort zone" of football fields, basketball gymnasiums and baseball diamonds.

Secondly, due to the deeply personal nature of this book, it turned out to be an intensely emotional endeavor. After all, it's not easy reliving the deaths of loved ones, let alone detailing those deaths in writing.

And finally, I was clueless on how long it would take to complete this project. When I started it in December 2017, I figured I could finish it in three months, four tops.

Not even close.

After more than a year of hunkering down at the laptop in our family room, it's finished. Thanks go out to more people than I can mention who not only helped in this process but supported and guided me throughout my journalism career, making this book possible in the first place:

—First and foremost, my wife Kim, who spent countless hours reading and rereading this book as it took shape from just a few pages to the finished product you see now. Her many suggestions and keen eye for detail made this a much better book than it ever would have been without her input.

—My good friend Tom Kessler, who was kind enough to devote a good chunk of his time to editing this book. There isn't a better copy editor or proofreader on the planet. Period.

—iUniverse designers Neriza Kate Neri (cover) and Angelie Rose Granados (interior), whose talents brought my vision for the cover magnificently to life and gave the entire book a clean, reader-friendly presentation.

—The editorial staff at iUniverse, whose recommendations were invaluable for a first-time book author.

—My colleagues throughout my journalism career, particularly my mentors, former University of Akron communications instructor Lori Noernberg and the late Dave Richardson, owner and publisher of the *Barberton (Ohio) Herald* newspaper and my first boss. Without their knowledge, expertise and commitment to my professional development, my journalism career would not have been possible.

—The late Jack Heldreth, my English teacher at Mogadore High School. Mr. Heldreth accomplished the impossible with his students: He made English class fun and interesting. His gentle, patient style of teaching and compelling coursework planted the first seeds of authoring a book in my mind.

—And last but certainly not least, our fur babies past and present: cats Sylvia, Halen, Nookie, Boo, Roxy, Morrie and Ashton and our dog Noel, for enriching my life in ways that cannot be measured. I love you all.

PREFACE

We are surrounded by death.

We can't get away from it. Whether on the news, in movies or in our personal relationships, death is all around us. It is a constant in our lives. Death is as much a part of life as life itself.

And it's waiting for us. Someday, it will be our turn to experience the most mysterious, the most feared and the least understood aspect of human existence. Death could happen tomorrow, next week, next month, next year, or not for several decades. Or it could be just hours, minutes or even seconds away.

That "when" is part of our innate fear of death: We don't know when it will happen. The "when" is always in the back of our minds, inexorably creeping toward the front as we get older. We know that with each flip of the calendar from one month to the next, from one year to the next, we are getting closer to death. Time seems to quicken as we age, because we know it's running out. We can see the sands slipping through the hourglass of our lives, and when we hit the age of fifty—which I am now—we know that, almost certainly, more of our life sits in the bottom of that glass than in the top. Probably a lot more. And as the years click by and we pass more of those milestone ages, we know our time on Earth is growing short. We just don't know how short.

The "how" is another part of our fear: Will death happen suddenly? Will I know when it's about to happen? Will I know when it's actually under way? Will I suffer first? Will I be terrified? What does it feel like to die? Does it hurt? Is it just like falling asleep, and we are unaware of that exact moment when our body shuts down forever, the same way we are unaware of that exact moment when our conscious mind shuts down for the night? Will I know I am dying, if even for a millisecond, as it happens? Death is the ultimate fear of the unknown.

And the last part of this fear is the "what": What comes after death? Anything? Some kind of an afterlife? Nothing at all? Are we unaware that our life is over, the same way we were unaware that our life was about to begin just prior to our birth?

We live our lives knowing that somehow, somewhere, at some point, our lives will end. We will die. We know this. We prepare for it even when it seems far off: We prepare mentally, we prepare emotionally, we prepare financially. It comes to the forefront of our minds every time we stand at the casket of a deceased loved one and gaze down at their lifeless, embalmed body, never to rise again, knowing someday that will be us in that suit or dress with our head propped up on that little pillow and the open coffin lid hanging ominously over our body, waiting to be closed and latched to hide our physical shell in darkness for eternity.

When we walk out of that funeral home, or head back to our car following that graveside service at the cemetery, we hope that our turn in the ground, the crypt or the urn is far off in the future. We hope there are still a lot of miles ahead of us before they close that lid and throw that dirt on us. But we know death is coming for us all the same, and it's only a matter of time before it finds us.

Yet while we fear death, we are also fascinated by it. We look for any kernel of information that might give us some insight into the nature of death. We want to know as much as we can about it. We hunger for the tiniest nugget that will bring just a little more understanding to it. We read and hear about near-death experiences; we are told of coroners' and doctors' viewpoints on the subject; even ghost hunters, mediums and psychics may be able to shed just a little more light on what awaits after our heart stops beating, our blood stops flowing and our brain activity ceases.

Death is immersed in our popular culture. Hollywood has helped to set the pace with countless films dedicated to the topic, and we even go all-out in celebration of a day dedicated to all things horror and death: Halloween. Drive through any neighborhood throughout the month of October, and you will be treated to elaborate yard displays featuring all manner of ghosts, skeletons, vampires, coffins and tombstones. We fear death, yet we pay homage to it.

Why? It's the most consistent and the most unstoppable force in our existence. Nobody will escape it. We all know that death is in our future, the last thing we will experience on this Earth. From the moment we are born, the grim specter of death shadows us. As legendary poet T.S. Eliot so famously wrote: "And I have seen the eternal Footman hold my coat, and snicker." Death, indeed, is always waiting.

But we don't know what comes afterward, which is the root of our fascination with death. Religions have their various beliefs; science tells us that death is the end, there is no afterlife, move along folks, nothing to see here; agnostics are somewhere in between, hoping our souls live forever but waiting to see evidence to that effect.

In the end, nobody of any belief system knows for sure what awaits the instant following death. We're going to find out, though.

And I believe I already have.

INTRODUCTION

Heaven is real.

Can I say I know this for a fact? No. Nobody can say they know, for a fact, that Heaven exists. And nobody can say they know, for a fact, that it doesn't.

You either believe it exists, or you don't. It's a matter of faith either way.

But it helps if you've seen Heaven. And I have.

No, I didn't have a near-death experience. At least I don't think so. All I did was go to bed one night and wake up the next morning.

But in between, while I slept, my dad showed me Heaven. Some may say he came to me in a dream, but I call it a visitation within the dream state, of which I've experienced many from my deceased loved ones. Dreams don't make sense. They are fuzzy, garbled images and themes from your subconscious that your sleeping mind tries to piece together like a jigsaw puzzle, and the result is what that puzzle would look like if a three-year-old had assembled it. You would have no idea what the picture was supposed to be. The puzzle would only consist of nonsensical fragments that seemed to bear no correlation to one another—just like images and information in a dream.

But the visitations from my dead loved ones have always been crystal clear and made perfect sense. The information my dead loved ones passed along to me in these visitations was contemporary. They have relayed messages, delivered dire warnings that soon came to pass and offered reassurance.

And, in the case of my dad, showed me Heaven. In full color. And he didn't just show me Heaven. He took me there with him.

Yes, I was there. I was in Heaven with my dad—at least, as much of Heaven as I was allowed to see and experience since I wasn't actually dead. Dad and I walked side by side in Heaven. While my sleeping body lay peacefully in bed in Stow, Ohio, my soul traveled to Heaven with my dad. Of this I am sure.

I didn't see God. I didn't meet Christ. But they were there because I could feel their amazing love. A love that does not exist in this Earthly plane of existence, but a love that exists all the same. It's waiting for us.

I know, because I felt it. The same way I believe Heaven exists because I saw it. Because I was there, if only briefly.

I used to fear death, for the same reason anyone fears death: Because we don't know what happens when we die. Is it the great darkness? The great nothingness? Ashes to ashes, dust to dust? Are we in a casket or an urn and that's it, lights out, it's all over? Or is there something more? Does our soul, our consciousness, survive the body's physical death? Do we have eternal life?

It's the single greatest question facing humanity: What happens when we die?

I no longer fear death, because I know the answer to that question thanks to my dad. And while I can't prove Heaven exists, I know what I saw.

And seeing is believing.

So why did I write this book? The answer to that question is simple: I had to. What I experienced with Dad in Heaven, what I have experienced in the many other visitations I have received from my deceased loved ones, have been so profound and so life-changing that I had no recourse other than to write it. I knew I was going to write this book, someday, the instant I returned to this plane of existence and woke up from the dream state—the altered state—that had served as the vehicle to connect with my father somewhere between my dimension and his. It was just too compelling a journey not to tell.

Yes, I am a Christian. I believe in the basic principles of Christianity, but I am not what you would call "devout." I can't remember the last time I attended a church service—my absence is measured in decades—and while I have read portions of the Bible, I have come nowhere close to even reading half of it. But I believe that God is the Creator, our Heavenly Father, and Jesus is the Son of

God, our Savior who died on the cross for our sins so that we would have a path to Heaven. While naysayers and non-believers will point to that and insist my Christian bent has steered my conscious mind in a biased direction and caused my unconscious mind to create an artificial concept of Heaven in the dream state, I know what I saw, I know how I felt and I know what I experienced. I know how deeply it affected me. I know how it changed my outlook on life. I know how it changed my outlook on death. It altered my entire paradigm. That comes from something stronger than a simple dream or a religious or philosophical belief system. That comes from conviction—conviction rooted in an intensely real, palpable, personal experience.

I can't prove any of it, but then again, scientists can't prove how the universe began. Science has offered up the Big Bang Theory, which is exactly that: A theory. They say there is substantial evidence to that effect due to the nature and behavior of the matter that comprises the universe. They say this with conviction (there's that word again) based on the knowledge, research and expertise they possess in their respective scientific disciplines.

What scientists are talking about when they discuss the Big Bang Theory is, of course, creation; the creation of everything—the same thing that is described in the Book of Genesis in the Bible. Science says that just prior to the Big Bang, the entire universe was the size of a subatomic particle, an idea known as the initial singularity. Which begs the obvious question: How did the universe in that subatomic form, perhaps smaller than a quark (regarded as the smallest particle currently known to humanity), come into existence? It wasn't always there, it had to start somehow, so what was there before the initial singularity and how did *that* come into being? To simply say that nothing existed before the universe, and that the universe somehow just got itself under way from that nothing, is not a scientific explanation. If there was nothing—no atoms, no molecules, no mass, no space-time, not even the universe itself—how, then, did material come into existence to make the universe? Magic? That's the fundamental problem facing science: At some point, it has to prove that something started from nothing and became everything. That issue has to be reconciled by science, and it can't.

Scientists also tell us the universe is still expanding and that they can prove it. Fine, but expanding into what? Inherent in the idea of expansion is that there is literally an edge of the universe, with something else on the other side of that edge that the universe is expanding into. What's on the other side of the universe?

Which brings us back to science's basic conundrum: Again, at some point, it has to prove how the pre-Big Bang singularity started. Something had to create that and set it in motion, because before that occurred there was nothing, not even the empty, black vacuum of space. What—or who—created that singularity and kicked it into motion? After all, nothing is the absence of anything. So it's common sense that the universe didn't just begin from nothing—unless it had help. There was nothing before the universe existed, and then the universe began, but there's a vital step missing in that birthing process: How the universe was actually conceived. It began from nothing, and you don't get energy from nothing.

We also hear scientists talk about multiple universes, multiple dimensions and the like, all of which may someday be proven to exist. But even if they are, there had to be a starting point for them—a genesis, if you will. And regardless of how many universes and dimensions there might be, all of them would have started from nothing. We have only proven the existence of one universe at the moment, the one we reside in, and it obviously hasn't existed forever in time because scientists actually know its age: approximately 13.8 billion years old. By assigning an age to the universe, scientists are issuing a de facto admission that nothing existed before it.

The only logical, reasonable conclusion is that the universe was created.

It's almost impossible—in fact, it might be impossible—to imagine *nothing* in your mind's eye since it's, well, nothing. Nothing doesn't look like anything. So when you close your eyes and try to picture nothing, you can't. Trying to imagine nothing existing before the universe came into existence can be overwhelming and even frightening.

When Dad and I would lay awake late at night and discuss these heavy topics, I would ask him what if nothing had ever existed? There would be no him, no me, no Earth, no Moon, no Sun, no galaxies, not even the universe. I would close my eyes and imagine it, imagine nothing having ever existed and what that would look like, and it would blow my mind. It made me feel so small, so insignificant, so vulnerable, and waves of fear would wash over me to the point where I could literally feel my blood start to run cold. It all seemed so fragile. What if there had never been anything and, more importantly in my mind, *why* was there anything? It would have been so easy for nothing to have ever existed at all, yet here we are. Why? Why do we need to be here, why does anything need to be here?

I would ask Dad these pressing questions and, sensing his young son's angst and anxiety, he would say in a soothing voice: "But we are here, Bear. That's all that matters." ("Bear" was my parents' nickname for me, shortened from "Grumpy Bear" when I was little due to my less-than-pleasant personality in the morning. I wasn't a morning person then, and I'm not a morning person now.) Dad's words and the tone of his voice comforted me, and I would realize I was safe in my home, lying next to my father, and all was right with the world.

Yes, we were here, and that indeed was all that mattered.

A space documentary I once saw on television (I'm a huge fan of all things space and astronomy, I can't get enough of it because "Are we alone?" is second only to "What happens when we die?" on the list of great questions facing humanity) featured a theoretical physicist who answered the question of "What was here before the Big Bang?" by saying nothing was here, the Big Bang is simply when time began. In other words, he unwittingly endorsed the Book of Genesis: There was nothing, and then there was everything. He essentially was saying that the Big Bang was created, and that represented the beginning of time. The Bible says almost the same thing, only it doesn't mention the Big Bang per se, it says: "In the beginning, God created the heavens and the earth."

In fact, even Albert Einstein's theory of relativity fits nicely into the creation model. According to Einstein's theory, the expansion of the singularity—the Big Bang—is when time started. So when scientists talk about the Big Bang, and the Bible talks about God creating the heavens and the earth, they are talking about the exact same thing: The moment of creation. The Big Bang Theory, then, in many ways is the scientific application of the Book of Genesis.

This, of course, rankles scientists of every stripe, most of whom are unabashedly atheist or antitheist. It's perfectly understandable and acceptable why science can't take things on faith; after all, science is in the business of replicability and proven fact, and faith is the opposite of that. To know our place in the universe requires exploration and discovery, and exploration and discovery require evidence and authenticity, not gospel. Science can't guess or assume; it has to know, it has to confirm. But that doesn't mean things that are taken on faith don't exist, it just means that things taken on faith haven't been vetted by science—yet. And to that end, science has anointed itself judge and jury on what is and what isn't. It has crowned itself master and commander of all that exists and all that doesn't exist. Science has, in a very real sense, assumed the mantle of God.

And many—if not most—scientists are unapologetic in their biased, parochial approach to defining humanity's place in the universe. It's a religious dogma all its own. Scientists take it on faith that God does not exist, dismissing out of hand the possibility of a Creator simply because they don't believe in one. Their paradigm doesn't allow for it. However, it's often not enough for science to merely close its mind to all possibilities; sadly, "skeptics" and non-believers often take to sophomoric denigration of those who have the audacity to believe that there is more to this life, this existence, than meets our five senses. Those who embrace religion are often labeled as superstitious, illogical or flat-out ignorant, when real ignorance lies in those who are afraid to seek the truth wherever it may be and in whatever form it may take. This openly hostile stance taken by secularists against religion is rooted in the fact that they are humanists as much as they are atheists and antitheists; that is to say, in the dogmatic world of science, since there is no God, Creator or deity of any form, science alone is the undisputed authority of this existence—an authority which science does not enjoy having challenged. The very idea of God is a threat to science and that authority.

Science doesn't have all the answers, and it never will. In fact, science has often been wrong—sometimes spectacularly so—on a wide range of issues throughout history, many of its theories and predictions going by the wayside when new information is learned. In these instances, science simply picks itself back up, dusts itself off, shrugs its shoulders and says, "OK, so we were wrong. Now we know." And then proceeds to explain that that's how science works: You come up with a theory, make a prediction based on your modeling of that theory, and wait to be proven right or wrong. Yet despite this litany of surprises through the centuries, science unfailingly and arrogantly assumes it will be right even when there is zero evidence to support that assumption. You would think that an institution that has been so wrong so often would be a little more open to the possibilities. Yet when a religious explanation or perspective doesn't rise to the level of scientific proof—which it usually does not because of the reliance on faith—science eagerly rips it to shreds and scatters it to the wind while haughtily claiming the intellectual high ground. This hypocrisy on the part of science is hard to ignore. Science treats religious teachings and beliefs as fairy tales due to the lack of supporting scientific proof. But just because science can't prove something doesn't mean it's not real.

Science claims it is in the business of finding answers. If that's the case, then it should be searching all avenues to procure those answers, not just the avenues of its choosing based on its own narrow set of beliefs. How are we as a species supposed to get answers when those charged with finding the answers refuse to ask the right questions? The painful truth is, science is too dogmatic to be trusted to deliver all the answers, and it shouldn't be that way. Science should be humanity's vanguard in the grand quest for higher truth, not a censor to hide that truth. What individual scientists do or do not believe should have no bearing on the science they perform; it's not so much that they don't believe in God as much as they hope God does not exist. They don't want God to be real, so their starting point is to marginalize the very concept of God and anyone who believes in Him so as to put it in the category of fantasy and therefore not worthy of serious research. Perhaps most galling is that atheists and antitheists often present their view that there is no God as incontrovertible fact, which it manifestly is not; it's only their belief—or wish—that God does not exist. Just as Christians and those of other faiths cannot prove that God exists, neither can non-believers prove that He doesn't. The only way to get all the answers and discover all the higher truths is to pursue them honestly and fully, and science does neither.

By itself, science possesses unlimited potential for discovery; science is the vehicle that allows mankind to confirm what had been just a theory, or what was unknown altogether. Science is how we know things for certain. It is man's application of science that keeps it in a box and restricts its awesome power—a power that many scientists seem afraid to fully unleash for fear of what it might find—and prove. Because if, as many scientists claim, science will someday unravel all the mysteries of the universe and that everything can and will be explained by the laws of physics, then, in the ultimate twist of irony, science itself might well prove the concept of intelligent design and the existence of a divine Creator.

In fact, who's to say that the laws of physics themselves aren't actually divine in nature, that the equations of physics, taken collectively, aren't in fact the mind of God?

This book isn't about science vs. religion or evolution vs. Creation, and it's not my intent to put science on a golf tee, pull my favorite driver out of the bag and hit it a Tiger Woods mile. It may not sound like it, but I love science. I appreciate and respect what science has done for humanity; I'm only suggesting that it release its dogmatic shackles and freely search for the answers regardless of where they might lead.

I'm actually a science junkie. I subscribe to the daily email updates from NASA's Jet Propulsion Laboratory in Pasadena, California; every day, I anxiously await the latest news from JPL to land in my inbox. These hot-off-the-press releases are chock full of information on remarkable robotic space missions, incredible cosmological discoveries and cutting-edge technologies that turn science fiction into science fact. I devour the endless space documentaries on the Discovery and Science channels, and I can sit for hours, mesmerized, watching as astronauts float in the zero gravity of the International Space Station on NASA TV. I also own an extensive library of books and videos dedicated to all things science, particularly my passion, space science.

In short, I am a space nerd. And I officially became a space nerd in the early morning hours of December 7, 1972, when Mom excitedly raced into my darkened bedroom and shook me awake to watch the dazzling night launch of the final lunar landing mission, Apollo 17. "Tommy! Get up, Tommy!" Mom said eagerly. "The astronauts are about to go to the Moon! Hurry and get up or you're going to miss it!" It was almost 12:30 in the morning. Bleary-eyed, I stumbled out to the living room of our little one-floor apartment in east Akron and was greeted with an awe-inspiring sight on our floor-model color television: The giant Saturn V rocket, its magnificent white shell gleaming brilliantly under the intense lighting of the launch pad, contrasting dramatically against the pitch-black background of the Florida night. It was almost too much for my four-year-old brain to process. The scene was beautiful and eerie at the same time. I sat on the couch with Mom and Dad as we anxiously listened to the countdown, then moments later watched in wonder as the engines of the behemoth ignited in a giant ball of flame—adding to the astonishing ambiance of the nighttime spectacle. We continued to watch as the massive rocket cleared the gantry, climbed into the night sky and soared toward the Moon.

I was awestruck—and I was hooked. In honor of the occasion, Mom and Dad bought me a Moon-landing model kit depicting the lunar service module floating over the cratered surface of the Moon. I wasted little time in assembling and proudly displaying the model on my bedroom dresser.

I have been a space science enthusiast ever since that unforgettable night.

While I haven't held back in my frustration with science's maddening provinciality, scientists are actually some of my greatest heroes, with beautiful minds like theoretical physicist Dr. Michio Kaku, planetary scientist and engineer Dr. Alan Stern, and theoretical physicist and cosmologist Dr. Lawrence Krauss topping that list. I can listen to those three men speak for hours, hanging on their every word, and I often have. I marvel at their brilliance and ambition. We owe a debt of gratitude to the diligence, devotion and dedication of the men and women in science who have gladly turned their lives over to stretching the boundaries of humanity and expanding its horizons, their thirst for knowledge and quest for discovery inexorably pushing the human condition forward.

I'm also not in lockstep with all the principles of Christianity. I believe in ghosts, reincarnation and intelligent life elsewhere in the universe—all of which fly in the face of established Christian doctrine. As I have said, I consider myself a Christian, but I also cannot and will not ignore what I have experienced in my life. Certain things I have witnessed run counter to Christian teachings, yet neither can they be proven or replicated by science. But they happened and they're real. I know that, because I was there. I saw these things happen. I experienced them firsthand in real time. I don't need dogma—religious or scientific—to tell me what I saw, if I saw anything at all, or if my experiences were real. I know damn well they were real, as real as me sitting here writing this right now. Religion, science and skeptics don't get to define our existence. We don't have to check our brains at the door and let others do our thinking for us. We don't have to rely on their belief systems to make sense of the world and universe around us. God gave us brains and free will with the expectation that we use both. And if we use both and we're honest with ourselves, we know that reality can't be defined by what religious and secular institutions would like it to be. Shakespeare himself wrote: "There are more things in heaven and earth, Horatio, than are dreamt of in your philosophy."

I know God exists because I have felt His presence. I can't prove it, but I know it to be so. I also know evil exists because I have been in its presence as well. Those dark forces are real, and when they're near you the feeling of dread and despair is palpable. True evil is extremely powerful and can destroy you. It preys on the weak, the confused and the angry. It can grab hold of you without you even realizing it, and by the time you do it's too late. I have sensed evil many, many times. I have also felt it. I rarely talk about those instances, any part of them, because I believe that doing so empowers the dark entities and opens a door for them to enter our realm. And once they're here, they may not leave.

When you are in the presence of real evil, it is unmistakable. It is unambiguous. And if you're not careful, it can begin to control you or even possess you. I know that I have felt evil, and I never want to feel it again. I know Satan exists and Hell is real. I can't prove this, but I know the evil I felt was not of this world. Satan wishes to destroy God's creatures and creation, and he can use you to perform his task. If your mind is not strong, he can trick you into feeling helpless and unloved, putting you in a mental and psychological position to do his bidding. This evil feeds on human frailty, and we are all susceptible to it. I instinctively sensed that the evil I felt was trying to consume me and ruin me. Even kill me.

This brings up a litany of questions commonly asked by atheists and antitheists: What kind of God would allow His own children to be manipulated so terribly by such a dark force? Couldn't an all-powerful God prevent that from happening? And what kind of loving God permits His children to suffer so much pain and misery on this planet? Why do bad guys so often win and good guys so often lose? Why do so many wonderful people have such awful things happen to them?

These are legitimate questions. It can often seem like Earth is, in fact, Hell. I have witnessed such abject suffering in places like hospitals and nursing homes that, at times, I myself have actually questioned the existence of a supreme being. When I walk down the halls of a nursing home and see people sitting along the walls in wheelchairs talking to imaginary friends, bawling for no apparent reason, slumped over unaware of their surroundings and having no idea what day, month or year it is, I can't help but question why any god would allow this cruelty to occur. Or when I walk through a hospital and see countless poor souls of all ages chained to their beds by all manner of wires and tubes that connect them to all manner of monitors and machines—and I know that some of these people have no hope of leaving the hospital alive—I wonder why any god would allow this indignity to happen. Christian doctrine says that since Jesus suffered, we must suffer as He suffered. Suffering is part of the human experience, we're told. But while Christ was immortal, we are not, so we are not built to handle suffering the way Christ was. Therefore, I don't subscribe to the notion that we are supposed to suffer simply because Christ suffered. I think it is grossly unfair to hold a mortal being to the same standard as an immortal deity. Suffering is the Christian explanation—you could say justification—for having to live in a hell on Earth, but to my way of thinking it's not a very good one.

But then, I don't have an explanation for any of the terrible things we see or experience on a regular basis. I can't explain a bus full of schoolchildren plunging off a cliff. I can't explain someone's grandmother stepping off a curb and into the path of a city bus. I can't explain a family of five getting slaughtered in their home by a demented killer. I can't explain a father having to find a way to tell his young children that their mother was raped and killed, or law enforcement officials solemnly telling parents that their missing child was found dead. I can't explain a 747 falling out of the sky and killing everyone on board. I can't explain a doctor having to tell a mother and father that their two-year-old child has brain cancer. I can't explain or make sense of any of it, why God would allow such appalling things to happen so routinely. As Christians, we are taught that everything we do and experience, no matter how good or bad, is because God gave us free will, but I believe that the human brain is not wired to fully comprehend why such abhorrent things occur—and especially why a loving God would allow such tragedies to take place considering that He has the power to prevent them from happening. As I often say to my wife, Kim: "When I get to the Pearly Gates, St. Peter has some 'splaining to do." I'm only half-joking when I say this, because it would be nice to get concrete answers at some point. And maybe we will.

However, while atheists and non-believers like to point to scenarios such as those detailed above as proof that their theory is correct, the fact is none of it negates the existence of God. Just because humanity can't understand or explain why terrible things happen does not mean there is no God; it just means that, as human beings, we don't possess the ability to understand or explain these things. Put another way, trying to define God and assign a probability to His existence in human terms isn't possible, because if we can't understand why God allows human tragedy, then by definition we can't understand God. He is outside of mind and time, whereas our human existence is mired in both.

Therefore, there is only one way for us to truly understand God: Join Him in His realm. And we will.

Which brings me back to the concept of Heaven. If the Big Bang Theory is real and can be modeled scientifically, and the Big Bang is another way of saying Creation, then it's literally not a leap of faith to suggest that Heaven, too, is real. The Big Bang may never be proven by science. But even if it can, it will be much easier to prove than the existence of Heaven. That realm will always remain ethereal, because there's only one way to find out if it actually exists.

Or in my case, two ways.

I'm far from the only person to experience Heaven prior to dying. Untold millions of people have claimed to have seen it, usually during near-death experiences and often accompanied by loved ones who have died. Seeing Heaven and receiving visitations from deceased friends and family members in the dream state are not modern concepts; in fact, belief in an afterlife and contact with the dead pre-dates Christianity by thousands of years. The Greeks and Romans of antiquity strongly believed that dreams were actually messages from the dead. The ancient Mesopotamians and Chinese believed that the soul, or at least part of it, could actually visit people and travel to other places in the dream realm. So this belief—this experience—of the soul journeying to other dimensions and realities during physical slumber cuts across all cultures, races, religions, philosophies and epochs.

As such, dreams have been seen throughout human history as the lifting of the veil between this Earthly physical realm and other planes of existence, including the Hereafter. As the body shuts down for its night's sleep, the unconscious mind takes possession of the brain and becomes a receptor in the spiritual world, an oscillator sifting through frequencies the way an AM receiver picks up radio waves. The unconscious mind—uninhibited by the sleeping conscious mind—is free to lock on to any signal anywhere in the spiritual matrix. And like a radio whose dial is tuned to a person's favorite station, this unconscious receptor is often locked on to the most familiar of signals:

Departed loved ones.

With the veil between dimensions lifted as a person sleeps, loved ones who have passed on are free to communicate with that person's unconscious mind. While some see these interactions as mere dreams, others view them as actual communication with the dead.

I firmly believe the latter. The visitations I have experienced in the dream state always contain at least one, and usually more, of three primary common denominators that reinforce my belief that these are not just the workings of my sleeping brain, but rather spiritual contact with my deceased loved ones through my unconscious mind:

1. They are happy, healthy and safe where they are.
2. They are always with me.
3. We will be reunited soon.

While these visitations shared many similarities—their unmistakable messages, their remarkable clarity and their impact on me chief among them—one primary difference has been the length of time, or my perception of the length of time, these visitations lasted. Some were lengthy and involved, some were brief and simplistic. The longer visitations were complex and often involved several people. The shorter visitations were basic and involved few people—sometimes just myself and my deceased loved one. As such, my retelling of these visitations will vary accordingly; some were simply more detailed and intricate than others.

And while most of these visitations occurred in the dream state, not all of them have. Two of those that I will cover in this book happened while I was very much awake, unfolding right in front of me in this dimension. No, I didn't see an apparition, I didn't hear strange noises and I wasn't physically touched in any way, but they were physical nonetheless—as you will read later. Visitations of this manner are also common and have been very well-documented throughout history.

Therefore, another reason for this book is the hope that those reading it can relate to my experiences. It's not an easy thing for someone to disclose, because there is a significant segment of the population that not only doesn't believe in any of this whatsoever, but will mentally fit you with a tinfoil hat upon hearing your story, complete with eye-rolls, snickers and snarky comments. They feel threatened by these experiences because the idea of any kind of afterlife offends their sensibilities. Their entire world view is challenged, so they strike back out of fear. Sadly, as a result, many people only tell these experiences to their closest, most trusted loved ones, and many never tell anyone at all for fear of harming personal relationships or even their chances of gaining or retaining employment.

But I worked in the media as a sports writer for over thirty years. I'm accustomed to getting eviscerated for things I have written, but that never stopped me from telling it like it is. Truth cannot be allowed to be bullied into silence by those who wish to hide it. Therefore, I'm not afraid or ashamed to tell this story, for two reasons: It involves many of my deceased loved ones, whom you will "meet" later in this book; and I know that what I experienced with them is real, even if there are some who can't accept that. This book isn't meant to convince anyone of anything or to change minds, it's just a recounting of events—you could call them supernatural events—that I experienced and maybe you have experienced, too. Make of it what you will.

And the experiences that I will detail in this book are far from the only ones I've had. Many fall squarely in the realm of the paranormal, things that cannot be explained by science and are not accepted by religion, but that happened to me nonetheless that I will not and cannot forget—another book all by itself. There are enigmas in our world that we do not understand and cannot explain, phenomena that give us a fleeting glimpse into another world which exists all around us that we can occasionally see, hear or feel if we are paying attention, like when you suddenly get goosebumps and don't know why or you are alone in a room and get the overwhelming feeling that you are being watched. I've seen objects suddenly move across flat surfaces—indoors with the windows closed—without being touched; I have felt a hand squeeze my shoulder when I was the only person in the room; I've seen several of our cats, in individual instances, clearly track someone or something that I could not see walking across the room; and, on countless occasions, I've even felt the unmistakable touch of one of our deceased cats rubbing up against my legs, pressing their soft fur and warm body against me with enough force to cause me to look down to see which of our living cats was greeting me, only to see nothing.

These experiences were real, as were those with my dead loved ones. To better understand their visitations, I will describe who they were in life so you have insight into their actions in death. I could write volumes on each of these wonderful, unique people. All of them helped shape me into the person I am today. In fact, the most challenging aspect of this book was deciding what to include and what to leave out when discussing them, because how do you tell the story of a human being in a single chapter of a book? You can't, so the only way to do them justice is to paint a portrait of them with an anecdotal brush so that you, the reader, feel as if you knew them yourself.

I will say this: The manner in which some of my loved ones died seriously challenged my belief system at the time. Why God would allow such good people to endure such incredible suffering made no sense whatsoever. As I said earlier, I have a basic understanding of the Christian ideal of suffering, based on Christ's suffering just prior to and during His crucifixion. But Christ was an immortal. He knew who He was and where He was going after He was crucified; He knew He was not going to actually die. We mortals don't know that. We hope for it, we believe it, we have faith in it, but we don't know it for one-hundred percent fact, and we certainly aren't equipped to handle suffering the same way as an immortal. So it didn't seem fair to me that several of my loved ones had to suffer so terribly before taking their last breath.

I still don't understand it completely, but knowing what I know now from my loved ones' visitations, I am able to make better sense of it: We suffer as Christ suffered because Christ is within us and we are going to join Him in His kingdom after physical death. We are one with Him, and suffering is a part of that.

I miss my departed loved ones terribly. Every day, something will remind me of them: A song on the radio, a show on TV, driving down a particular roadway, the time of year; it could be anything. I miss them all. But while their time on Earth with me has ended, our time together has not.

These are my glimpses of Heaven.

CHAPTER 1

GOODBYE, DAD

All I could see of my dad was his tousled salt-and-pepper hair. He was on the floor in the living room of his house, the rest of his body hidden from my view by the love seat he lay in front of. But even from my obstructed angle from the kitchen, it was obvious that Dad was on his back. Motionless.

My dad, Doug Hardesty, was dead, the victim of a massive heart attack. Gone at the age of sixty-three, just like his father before him.

My wife Kim and I had gotten the mournful call from my mother around 7 that evening, when the phone rang in our house and interrupted the tranquility of an otherwise beautiful July day, the rich pastels of an early-evening sky about to give way to the constellation-filled velvety blackness of night. We didn't answer the phone, choosing instead to let the voice mail handle the call. We were relaxing in our family room and figured it was just another telemarketer. A few minutes later, I glanced at the caller ID and saw that it was my mom and she had left a message. I dialed into our voice mail, and I instantly could tell something was wrong.

Terribly, horribly wrong.

She was difficult to understand, trying to formulate words through a mouth quivering with emotion. Still, the shaky voice on the other end of the line was unmistakable: "Tommy, call me back immediately. Something's happened to your dad."

I hadn't heard my mother's voice sound like this since the morning her mother died on Nov. 1, 1985, when I was seventeen years old and a senior in high school. On that particular morning, a Friday, the normal routine of me getting ready for school and Mom and Dad getting ready for work was interrupted by the shrill ring of the telephone. I was in the kitchen at the time, right next to the phone on the wall, and the ringing at that odd hour startled me. I picked it up. It was one of my aunts, an older sister of Mom's. "Tommy, is your mom there?" she asked. Her voice was weak and unsteady. She obviously had been crying.

All the energy instantly left my body. I knew what this call was for. Grandma had been battling cancer for a little over a year and had gone downhill in recent weeks. Death had not seemed imminent, but then again, with cancer, death is always around the next corner, a lesson I have painfully learned with the passing of each loved one to the dreaded disease. "Yeah," I replied, "she's getting ready for work. Hang on."

"Mom," I said loudly to cover the distance from the kitchen to my parents' bedroom on the other end of the house, "pick up the phone. It's for you." I put the receiver back to my ear and waited for the familiar click of the bedroom phone being picked up. Mom answered. "Hello?"

I hung up the kitchen phone before I could hear another word. I knew what was coming next. And I didn't have to wait long.

"SHE'S GONE. SHE'S GONE," Mom wailed from her bedroom seconds later. "OHHH, SHE'S GONE." I could hear her heavy footsteps coming down the hallway toward the dining room and kitchen, sobbing loudly as she walked. I began to cry in the kitchen. My mother was never the same after that moment. Something changed inside her. Something died inside her. She was still my mother, but she never again was the person I had known. Grandma's death crushed my mom's spirit, made her an inherently unhappy person, even, eventually, sapping her own will to live. As her only child, I instinctively sensed this. From that day forward, she put on a façade to hide the searing emotional pain she felt inside each and every day that her mother was gone. Mom never recovered from Grandma's death.

Now, nearly twenty years later on July 1, 2005, my mother's quaking voice was back, this time on my voice mail, and it could only mean one thing: Death.

I swallowed hard and dialed the phone. Mom picked up immediately. "Hello?" she said heavily. "Mom, what's wrong?" I asked, knowing full well the answer I was about to receive.

"Tommy, your dad died," she said through a heaving voice, each syllable uttered through a heavy breath as when a sobbing child tries to explain how he injured himself. "He's gone. The paramedics are here. Please come over right now."

"OK, Mom, we'll be right over," I told her, and hung up. I was numb. I felt nothing, physically or emotionally. I had just been told my dad was dead, and my body and mind were unable to process the information. All I could do was go to the top of the family room stairs and say to Kim, who was on the couch: "Hey, hon, we have to go to Mom's right now. My dad just died."

"What?!" Kim exclaimed as she bolted off the couch.

"Yeah, he's gone. We have to go now. Mom's waiting for us."

"What happened?" Kim asked.

"I don't know," I replied. "Mom just said he died and the paramedics are there."

We jumped in the car and made the half-hour trip from Stow to Mogadore, me trying to make sense of what was happening, Kim doing her best to keep me calm as I drove. I was in shock, still processing the news, when we arrived at their house. Oddly enough, it was the first time I had ever been there. They had bought the house the previous year, but due to our somewhat estranged relationship with them, we had not been there. Dad and I had recently begun repairing our relationship and had made tentative plans for Kim and me to come over and visit. Then this happens.

Just two days earlier, Dad and I had had a pleasant, lengthy conversation on the phone, just catching up on things. He sounded happy, his voice strong. At sixty-three, Dad looked great for his age. But then again, he had always appeared much younger than his actual age. Like all Hardesty men, he had to keep a close eye on his heart health, particularly his blood pressure, but he always kept his weight down and seemed in reasonably good shape. Toward the end of our conversation, he said, "There was something else I was going to tell you, but I can't remember what it was now. Oh well, I'll just tell you the next time we talk."

There was no next time. Dad was dead forty-eight hours later.

The paramedics were still at Mom's house when we got there, looking at Kim and I sympathetically as we walked through the door.

"He's over there on the floor," Mom sobbed, pointing toward the love seat in the living room. Mom was a petite woman, standing around 5-foot-4 (just a couple inches shorter than Dad) with platinum blonde hair that fell just past her shoulders; she was a pretty woman, but at this moment in the kitchen, she appeared tired, haggard and defeated as Dad lay dead just a few feet away from her.

I could see the very top of his head, just a few inches of his salt-and-pepper hair, but nothing more. I didn't want to see more. I had seen all I needed to see.

Mom filled me in on the day's events in their house. Dad had woken up not feeling well, complaining of pain in his back and soaking T-shirt after T-shirt with sweat. He turned down offers of being taken to the hospital, opting instead for back rubs and his favorite malady drink, ginger ale.

He did not improve as the day wore on. When the ginger ale ran out, he asked Mom to make a quick run to the store in Mogadore to pick up more, a trip that would take no more than a few minutes. When she returned, Dad was sitting on the love seat, facing the television with his back to her, only the back of his head visible from her viewpoint. She announced her arrival and said she had gotten more ginger ale.

He didn't answer.

Figuring he was either engrossed in the TV program or had fallen asleep, she walked around to the front of the love seat to get his attention. He appeared to have dozed off sitting upright, his head slumped slightly downward. Dad could fall asleep any time, anywhere, without warning. His naps were the stuff of legend in our family, so the fact that he had fallen asleep on the love seat in front of the television was not alarming.

"Doug!" Mom said again, louder this time. "I got your ginger ale."

Still nothing.

She gently shook him, but he didn't budge. It was then she noticed that his eyes were slightly open, staring downward, something she hadn't noticed earlier due to the tilted angle of his head.

"Doug!" she shouted.

Again, nothing.

He was gone.

Mom immediately called 9-1-1, then me. And there he lay on the floor when I arrived, put there by the paramedics.

By this time, other family members began arriving at the house. I had retreated to a chair in Dad's study at the front of the house, trying to come to grips with what had just occurred. It didn't seem real.

Aunt Betsy, Mom's younger sister, entered the study. "Tom, the paramedics are taking your dad out to the ambulance," she told me. "Do you want to go out and say goodbye?"

"No," I said. "I don't want to remember him that way."

It was the same reason why I didn't step around to the front of the love seat when we first arrived: Seeing my father's lifeless body was too much to bear. Whether he was on the floor or on a gurney, I simply was not prepared for that sight so soon. I knew I would get my chance to see him again in a few days, when I had time to mentally steel myself for his funeral.

So there I sat in his study as the EMTs wheeled him out of his house, his dream house, the house he had waited nearly his entire life to buy and proudly call his own. But he got less than a year to enjoy it before he was rolled out of it with a sheet over his body. He was only sixty-three, the same age as his dad when he had died nearly three decades earlier. I had thirty-seven years with my dad, and they went by in the blink of an eye. And as I sat in that chair, the setting sun serving as a somber metaphor for the day's sad events, one thought dominated my shocked, confused mind: I'll never see Dad again.

I was wrong.

Dad wasn't religious, but he was very spiritual. By definition he was a Protestant Christian, but not a practicing one. He rarely attended church, but he believed in the basic tenets of the Bible—God the Almighty, Jesus Christ the Savior, Heaven and Hell—but he was far more likely to be found napping in front of the television on Sundays than sitting in a church pew.

Still, Dad was a strong believer in the afterlife. He took an "anything is possible" approach to our existence, and that included all things paranormal and supernatural. He kept an open mind to all of it, because, as far as he was concerned, nobody knew the truth and there was only one way to find out. And nobody is in a hurry to discover that truth.

But Dad was absolutely convinced of one thing: Our soul survives physical death. Where the soul ended up was another matter. Heaven? Hell? Purgatory? Earth? Another dimension? Dad and I had engaged in countless conversations on this subject over the years—usually lasting deep into the night—where we pondered life, death, and what it all means. Many of these conversations took place in the wee hours on Christmas Eve, Dad's favorite night of the year. He and I would sit by the Christmas tree, Mom having gone to sleep in their bedroom hours earlier, and discuss the birth of Christ and everything else associated with Christmas. It would be dead silent outside, most of the houses in the neighborhood having long since gone dark as families prepared to rise earlier than usual the next morning to tear into their presents, yet Dad and I would be up burning the proverbial midnight oil delving into these heavy topics. Dad would often say, "If there is no Heaven and our spirit doesn't live on, then what's the point of all this? We have to live on. It's the only thing that makes sense."

And Dad lives on. Of this I am certain.

DAD'S FIRST VISITATION

July 3, 2005.

Dad had departed this Earthly realm less than forty-eight hours earlier, and Kim and I were preparing to head back over to Mom's house in Mogadore to pick her up and go to the funeral home to make arrangements for Dad's services. We had spent the night with Mom at her house the night Dad died, spent the next day with her, then returned to our home in Stow the night of July 2 to take care of our cats and get a much-needed good night's sleep in our own bed. It had been a nightmarish twenty-four hours and none of us had anything left. We were mentally tapped out.

The next morning, I took a shower in our main bathroom. It was all I could do to shampoo my hair and soap my body as I braced myself for what, without question, would be the most difficult day of my life: Taking my wife and mother to the funeral home to pick out the coffin that would forever house my dad's body.

I had lost many loved ones before, but this was different. This was my dad, the person who helped give me life. In many ways, I was my dad. It was largely because of him that I am passionate about sports, music, history, geography and current events. Some of my absolute favorite things in life—Ohio State football, the British rock band Def Leppard and legendary late-night radio talk show host Art Bell—are directly attributable to Dad. He got me interested in all of them. His influence on me and my life to this day is immeasurable.

And on the morning of July 3, 2005, I was preparing to help make the arrangements where I would say goodbye to him forever.

My head had been spinning for more than twenty-four hours. I had found it difficult to concentrate with so many things weighing so heavily on my mind, and as I stood in the shower I was barely cognizant of the fact that Kim was on the other side of the curtain, standing three feet away from me in front of the mirror as she got ready to go to Mom's. The hot water washing over my body relaxed me. I positioned my body so that the stream of water beat against the back of my neck, drooping my head to expose more of my neck area to the steady rhythm of the water. I closed my eyes, soaking in the calming effects of the shower. I could literally feel my muscles start to loosen—they had been bound as tightly as a snare drum since the moment Mom told me that Dad was dead. It was cleansing my mind as well, allowing me a brief respite from the maelstrom of emotions that had overtaken me. For a couple minutes, anyway, I was finally able to find some semblance of peace. My mind started to drift, mesmerized by the warmth and solitude of the shower.

Suddenly, I was jolted alert by an overwhelming aroma. It was right in my face, and it wasn't there even two seconds ago. Its appearance was immediate. It wasn't soap or shampoo—I knew what those smelled like, plus I hadn't started using either yet. I figured it was Kim's perfume. And it was right under my nose.

"Hon, are you spraying perfume or something?" I said loudly over the steady sounds of the bathroom fan and shower. "It smells really strong in here."

"No," she replied. "I haven't sprayed anything. Are you sure you're not smelling the soap or shampoo in there?"

"No, it's definitely not that. I'm not even using any yet," I said. "This smell is different. It's really strong. You haven't put any perfume on or sprayed your hair or anything?"

"No," she reiterated.

"Can you smell it?" I asked.

"No," she said, "I don't smell anything."

This struck me as odd: Something I smelled so strongly in the shower was non-existent to Kim at the bathroom sink three feet away.

"That doesn't make any sense," I said, perplexed. "It's *really* strong in here. I can't believe you can't smell it."

I then took a step forward in the bathtub to reach for the shampoo, the water from the shower head beating against my back—and the smell was gone. It must have dissipated, I thought. But it sure had dissipated quickly. Definitely weird.

Curious, I took a step backward toward the shower head—and stepped right back into the fragrant smell, still as strong as ever. I stepped forward again; the smell was gone. I stepped back; there it was again. This was behaving like no aroma I had experienced before. It existed only within a very tight boundary, basically limited to the area directly under my nose and extending a few inches forward and to the sides, and no more. It did not permeate the bathroom or even the entire shower area itself. It didn't move, and it didn't dissipate. It remained stationary in one tiny area, almost as if it was being physically constrained by … something.

I began to wash my hair, and the familiar smell of the shampoo wafted past my nose—but the unidentified fragrance remained, mingling with the odor of the shampoo. I rinsed, and the smell of the shampoo dissipated. The fragrant smell did not.

I soaped up, and that familiar smell entered the shower area. But the strong fragrance did not.

I wracked my brain trying to think of what could be causing this smell. It was nothing I was using in the shower, nothing Kim was using at the sink, nothing I could identify. Whatever it was, it had come out of nowhere and it was pleasing to the nose.

Then, in an instant, the smell disappeared. Under my nose one second, gone the next. I moved about in the shower to see if the fragrance had finally begun to drift, but there was no indication of it at all, not even the slightest hint.

"Now it's gone," I said to Kim, the soap rinsing from my body. "It was here a second ago, then it left just like that. I can't smell it at all anymore."

About a minute later I turned the shower off, stepped out of the bathtub and began to towel off. The smell was nowhere to be found. I chalked it up to one of life's little mysteries and went on with the dreadful business of getting ready to go to the funeral home.

By the time we arrived at Mom's house, I had forgotten all about the mystery smell. After all, there were more pressing things to worry about.

We weren't at Mom's house long, and we only needed to drive about ten minutes to the funeral home in the Ellet neighborhood of east Akron to meet with the funeral director and make the arrangements for Dad's services. Still, I figured I'd better hit the bathroom real quick before we left. The bathroom that Dad used in their house was located in the hallway adjacent to his bedroom (my parents slept in separate bedrooms, not an unusual occurrence over the course of their marriage), which was the most convenient bathroom for visitors to access.

Once in the bathroom, my attention was directed to Dad's personal hygiene products clustered on the counter around the sink. If I hadn't known better, I would have thought he had just used them five minutes earlier. A couple of the items had pop-up lids that were still conveniently in the "up" position for future use. The overwhelming sadness of the moment washed over me. The sink area was exactly as he had left it, his personal effects sitting there waiting for the return of an owner who was never coming back. Dad's eyes had gazed upon this very scene not forty-eight hours earlier.

Tears filled my eyes as I picked up a couple of the items and smelled their contents. Shaving cream, cologne, aftershave. One by one, I smelled them, picking them up, putting them to my nose, then setting them back down. It was heart-wrenching and soothing at the same time. It drove home the fact that I would never see him again, yet it made me feel closer to him.

After a minute or two, there were only a couple bottles that I hadn't smelled. I grabbed a small, gray plastic bottle of aftershave lotion that had one of those pop-up lids that was still open. I put it to my nose and sniffed.

Instantly, my blood ran cold. I pulled the bottle of aftershave away from my nose, and for several seconds I could do nothing but stare at the bottle in my hand. I couldn't move, I almost couldn't breathe. It was like I was suffering some sort of paralysis.

Because I knew that smell.

"Oh my God," I was finally able to whisper to myself. "This is it. This is *it!*"

Incredibly, the aroma wafting from the open nozzle of that bottle was the exact same aroma that I had smelled so strongly in the shower about an hour earlier back home. It was unmistakable.

My blood continued to run cold as I stood there, stunned, staring in disbelief at the bottle of aftershave in my hand.

I smelled the bottle several more times to confirm that it was, indeed, the same thing I had smelled in the shower. It was. There was absolutely no mistaking it. None whatsoever.

A feeling of peace then washed over me. I now knew what had happened earlier in the shower:

Dad had come to say goodbye.

I knew it in my heart and felt it in my soul. While I was in the shower, Dad had paid his only child one last visit before moving on. And the aftershave was the perfect conduit. It was something I could readily connect to him because of its unique smell and my easy access to the bottle in his bathroom. It was genius on Dad's part.

He had come to say he was OK.

I glanced around the tiny bathroom. "Thanks, Dad," I said. I knew he could hear me.

And with that, I opened the door, walked out of the bathroom and prepared to head over to the funeral home. As horrible and heartbreaking as the day was about to become, it now felt just the slightest bit different and I felt just the slightest bit better. Even though we were about to pick out a casket for Dad's body, I knew his soul was elsewhere.

Because he had come to say he lived on.

I had just experienced my first visitation from my father. But it would hardly be the last.

CHAPTER 2

CLAR CLAR

My first real experience with death occurred on Oct. 18, 1977. I was nine years old, a fourth-grader at Somers Elementary School in Mogadore. My paternal grandfather, Clarance Hardesty, had fallen ill a few weeks earlier and ended up in the hospital battling pneumonia, sending my grandmother Dolores (known as "Dee Dee" to friends and family) into an emotional tailspin. After all, they had been together since their early teenage years.

"Clar Clar" (pronounced as Claire Claire), as he was known to the family, had just turned sixty-three. The family assumed Clar Clar would recover and soon be safely back in his home in the Kenmore neighborhood of southwest Akron.

Instead, he never saw home again.

Pneumonia turned into double pneumonia, followed by a heart attack and stroke that left him barely able to speak or sit upright in the chair in his hospital room. He had great difficulty chewing his food and often would stare off into space, unable to focus or comprehend what was said to him. He was near death.

Dad chose not to let me in on any of this at the time, sparing his young son the sad details of his dying grandfather. All the facts of Clar Clar's demise

I learned later in life. I had no idea at the time that Clar Clar was in bad shape. All I knew was that Dad drove to the hospital to visit Clar Clar nearly every day, and he always came back with the same report: Clar Clar was holding his own.

But he wasn't holding his own. He was dying.

Still, despite his grave condition, Clar Clar briefly started to show signs of slight improvement, giving the family hope that he would overcome this avalanche of ailments and somehow survive.

Tuesday, Oct. 18, 1977, was just like any other weekday morning in our apartment in Mogadore. Mom and Dad busily scurried about getting ready for work, Cleveland radio station WMMS 101 FM blaring out of the clock radio next to their bed and filling the upper floor of our apartment with rock hits, news and weather, while I prepared for another day in Mrs. Spires' fourth-grade class at Somers.

Then the phone rang. Mom was in the kitchen and answered the phone on the wall. She was sitting at the kitchen table as I walked through the living room toward her to see who was calling at such an early and unusual hour. This was strange, and I just had to know what was going on. Something was wrong. Something had to be wrong for a phone call at this time of the morning.

Mom's voice was soft and low as she spoke to the person on the other end of the line. It was difficult to discern what she was saying, but I had never heard her sound so subdued. This isn't good, I thought. After a minute or two, she hung up the phone, put her head in her hand and began sobbing.

"What's wrong, Mom?" I asked, though I sensed the sickening answer that was about to come.

She looked up at me through tear-filled eyes. "Clar Clar died, Tommy."

It felt like a piano had just fallen out of a building and landed on my soul. I fell into her arms and began to sob.

My first close loved one had died. My grandfather, my friend, the man who inspired my passion for history and sports and passed down an unbridled love of Ohio State football, the man whom my personality emulates the most among all my relatives, was gone.

My nine-year-old brain could barely process what was happening. It didn't seem real. I was overcome with grief and just wanted to wake up from this nightmare. My mind couldn't make sense of it. All I could think was that Clar Clar was gone and I would never see him again.

I was wrong.

—

Clar Clar was a quiet, reserved man and, to me, looked a lot like President Lyndon Johnson. Maybe not a spitting image, but pretty close in my eyes. And the fact that he bore a resemblance to a United States president was perfect considering Clar Clar's love of anything to do with history. He had an encyclopedia set of world history going back to before the Greeks, and I would implore him to go through those books with me and tell me all about the Egyptians, the Romans, Napoleon, etc., and he would happily oblige, sitting down with his young grandson and going over historical details that would bore a lot of people stiff. But I hung on every word.

Part of it was I just loved history, and part of it was I just loved being with Dee Dee and Clar Clar; Dee Dee was a diminutive woman, a shade under five feet tall, and her platinum blonde, coiffed hair and devotion to style (she would often dress up in her best outfits and jewelry just to wear around the house) gave her an elegant appearance on the order of the Gabor sisters—contrasting nicely with Clar Clar's far more conservative, low-key demeanor. As a young boy, there was nothing like spending the weekend at their house—especially with my three Hardesty cousins. Staying the night at Dee Dee and Clar Clar's in the 1970s was like living in an alternate universe for us four grandkids. It was an oasis of fun, a place where we were guaranteed rest and relaxation beginning when our parents dropped us off on Friday nights and lasting until our parents picked us back up on Sunday afternoons, free from the stress and demands of the school week. The tiny house atop Kenmore hill was like a mini-resort to us, somewhere we could "get away from it all," even if for me "getting away" meant going from Mogadore to Kenmore, a drive of less than twenty minutes from the east side of Akron to the west. It was an even shorter trip for my cousins, who also lived in Kenmore. But it may as well have been on the Moon. Dee Dee and Clar Clar's house was a sanctuary, and every Sunday when Dad picked me up to take me back home, I immediately began looking forward to my return the next weekend. In between, the school week dragged on endlessly, and the thought of all the fun and good times that were waiting for me at Dee Dee and Clar Clar's was never far from my mind. It was truly a special place.

I spent countless weekends with my cousins at Dee Dee and Clar Clar's over the years, and each and every one was pure magic. We regularly awoke to the comforting sounds of Dee Dee preparing breakfast in the kitchen, the strong aroma of bacon and eggs permeating the little bungalow on 8th Street Southwest. The pleasing smells never failed to rouse us grandchildren, who could be found sleeping in the adjacent living room, sprawled among pillows and blankets on the couch, love seat, or on the floor inside a makeshift tent of bedsheets stretched across the entire room. By the time we sleepily staggered into the kitchen, Clar Clar was already there, occupying his usual place at the table as Dee Dee busily served up the goodies, softly humming her favorite tunes—often the classic "It Had to Be You," sung by Ginger Rogers and Danny Thomas, among others—as she went.

And no weekend was complete without an impromptu piano lesson from Clar Clar. With a grandchild sitting on either side of him, he would teach us a song one finger at a time. Clar Clar would take my right index finger in his hand and guide it from one key to the next as I did my best to commit each key and its sound to memory. This is how I learned to play parts of "The Entertainer" and "The Star Spangled Banner" at a very young age. I never learned to play much else, but it's a testament to Clar Clar's acumen at the piano that I learned to play anything at all.

At night it was time for the TV shows: Carol Burnett, Donny and Marie, Police Woman, Mary Tyler Moore, All in the Family, Sanford and Son, Love Boat, Fantasy Island. And, of course, Clar Clar's favorite: Lawrence Welk. I'm told I regularly stood in front of the television in the living room and mimicked the tap-dancers on the Lawrence Welk Show, my legs "going a hundred miles an hour" according to Dee Dee, but I always found it difficult to believe since I have no ability to dance, and no interest in dancing, whatsoever. However, if

Dee Dee said it, then it's gospel because a more decent, humble, honest human being has never walked the face of the Earth. If ever there was a living human angel, it was my father's mother, Dolores Hardesty.

Spending New Year's at Dee Dee and Clar Clar's was the pinnacle of my existence back then. My parents would drop me off at their house early on New Year's Eve (Mom and Dad had an ulterior motive: Clearing their docket for some serious party time with their friends later that night). Dee Dee immediately would set about making preparations for the evening's festivities, which always culminated with us standing on the front porch at the stroke of midnight with me banging on pots and pans and shouting "Happy New Year!" at the top of my lungs. The neighbors must have loved us.

The next day was football, football, and more football. I would sit next to Clar Clar on the living room couch and watch the college bowl games all day long. The Cotton Bowl. The Sugar Bowl. The Orange Bowl. And especially the Rose Bowl, which usually featured our beloved Ohio State Buckeyes against, usually, the Southern California Trojans—ending in, usually, a loss for our Bucks. Night fell on many a wintry New Year's Day in the 1970s with Ohio State on the short end of the scoreboard in Pasadena, California (with the wonderful exception of Jan. 1, 1974, when our Buckeyes got the best of the Trojans 42-21). But getting to share those times with Clar Clar—as disappointed as we were when the Buckeyes lost—are priceless memories that I will cherish until my dying day. In fact, "bowl day" remains a de facto religious holiday in our house, and it goes back to watching the New Year's Day bowl games with Clar Clar on his couch in Kenmore in the early to mid-1970s.

Something else I cherish: Clar Clar's clever pranks. He was always pulling a fast one on the grandkids. One of his favorites was throwing snowballs at the kitchen window as we sat at the table watching him shovel the driveway and back patio. He would pack the snow softly so that it splattered against the window in a white puff rather than have the window shatter in a thousand pieces in our faces. But, of course, that was the crux of the prank, because the window shattering in our faces is exactly what we feared was going to happen. We would watch as he put the shovel down, carefully fashion a snowball in his gloves—making sure that we noticed—and, with a devilish grin, heave it at the window. We would go flying in all directions to avoid what we were sure was going to be glass shattering all over the kitchen, diving under the table or hiding behind a chair, then poof, the snowball would hit the window and disintegrate. Of course, there were times we didn't know the snowball was coming. We would be sitting at the table, when suddenly the thud of a snowball hitting the window inches from our faces would nearly levitate us straight up out of our chairs—and leave Clar Clar howling with laughter outside.

Another of his favorite pranks was "the bug." I would sit on his lap in his favorite chair in the living room, and he would draw pictures for me on a piece of paper, with a book or magazine under it for stability. I would laugh and giggle as he drew funny pictures, then suddenly he would look at me with a concerned expression on his face and draw a bug at one end of the paper. Then another bug next to the first one. Then another. And another. It was a crude drawing, usually just several stick legs protruding from a round bug body, but to a young child it looked menacing all the same. The bug would inexorably "crawl" across the paper toward my arm, which was suddenly dangerously exposed to the advancing bug. He would draw another bug, look me in the eye with a worried face, draw another one, point at it and look at me again, and so on until the bug nearly reached the other side of the paper. When it had almost reached my arm, he would draw one last bug and make a quick motion with his pencil as if the bug was scurrying off the paper and exclaim, "There it goes! It's on you!!" And I would bolt out of the chair, shrieking my way out of the living room to the safety of Dee Dee, who would promptly march into the living room and jokingly admonish Clar Clar. "Clarance, are you scaring Tom Tom again?" Which, of course, would be met with howls of laughter from Clar Clar, still sitting in the chair with the "bug paper" in his lap. He loved it. And so did I.

Yet another of Clar Clar's pranks was tied to the Old Maid card game. The basic idea of the game is to not be the Old Maid. You pick a card out of the other player's hand to try and match it with another in your hand, then the other player draws out of your hand, and on it goes. Clar Clar would hold his cards out in front of him, the cards fanned out all nice and neat except for one, which would stick up prominently over the others. It was a Jedi mind trick: Clar Clar wanted to make it obvious that I should pick that card, but I would think he was trying to fool me into taking a different card, so I would pick the raised one. And it would be the Old Maid—every time. Of course, that was his plan all along: To make me out-think myself. The look on my face when I pulled the card from his hand and saw that it was the Old Maid would send Clar Clar into fits of laughter.

How I continually fell for this, even at that young age is, quite frankly, disturbing.

I had never seen a dead body until I attended Clar Clar's services.

It had been nearly a month since I had last seen him, in late September. This was now late October, and I was about to attend my first calling hours and funeral. I didn't know what to expect. All I knew was that I was going to see Clar Clar, but he was dead. I had no context for what awaited me.

When I walked through the doors of the funeral home with Mom and Dad, I could see the casket up ahead at the end of the next room, about thirty feet away. We had to walk through one room to get to the room where Clar Clar was laid out, and as we got closer, I could see his head elevated on the pillow at the left end of the casket, the side with the lid raised for viewing; the lower half of the lid was closed over his legs. It was my first glimpse of a dead body, my first glimpse of ... death. The first thing I noticed specifically as we neared the casket was that the angle of his head on the pillow didn't seem right; it appeared odd to me, like the angle was too sharp. In fact, from this distance all I could see was his head on the pillow; the rest of his body was shielded from view by the side of the casket. I was unnerved.

As we reached the coffin, his body finally came into complete view. I was in a sort of shock looking at my dead grandfather for the first time. I solemnly stood at his side with my parents for several quiet seconds, maybe even a minute or so, before I noticed my dad gazing down forlornly at his own deceased father. Dad wore an expression on his face that I had never seen before. His eyes seemed almost lifeless, no light in them whatsoever, and he looked completely defeated. He just stared down at Clar Clar, his face exuding sorrow. Finally, he said softly, "Hi, Clar Clar. You were a great man." It was the first time in my life that I had seen my father appear vulnerable.

At first, I didn't want to be that close to the coffin. It made me uneasy. The imposing visuals—from the ominous appearance of the casket itself, to the satin lining inside the casket, to Clar Clar's lifeless body adorned in a suit, to the placement of his hands over his abdomen and the positioning of his fingers—were too much for my nine-year-old senses. Nothing about it looked natural, looked right. I hadn't known what to expect, but I certainly hadn't expected this. The optics of seeing Clar Clar's dead body in a casket was overwhelming. I began to feel dizzy.

The whole scene was unbearably sad, peculiar, distressing and, to be brutally honest, creepy. Everything about it looked so cold, so anesthetized, so sterile. Everything looked so … final. I wasn't prepared for any of it. And the embalmed body in the coffin didn't look like the Clar Clar that I had known; it looked more like a mannequin. His skin looked synthetic and the coloring wasn't quite right. Even his closed eyes didn't look right; they seemed much too rounded and raised under their lids.

Then something odd began to happen: The longer I stood there, the more comfortable I felt. After standing by his head for a while, I somehow gathered the courage to reach in and touch his hair—which had seemed to be the only thing on his body that appeared as it did in life; the color, cut and texture all were correct. I held my breath as I slowly reached toward his head, not sure what to expect, not sure that reaching into a coffin to touch a dead body was even a good idea at all. My fingers made contact with his hair, and … it was soft. I was relieved; it actually felt natural. I stroked his hair from the top of his forehead back as far as I could, stopping where the back of his head rested on the casket pillow. His gray hair was combed straight back as it had been in life. I continued to gently stroke his hair as people made their way to the casket to pay their respects, smiling politely at me as I stood at one end of the coffin.

Stroking my grandfather's hair comforted me. It made me feel closer to him. In periods where I was the only person standing at the casket, I felt that I was providing Clar Clar with some company. I didn't want him to be alone, so I made it my duty to make sure he wasn't. Whereas earlier I had stood at the casket almost in fear, now I was there in complete peace. At Clar Clar's side is where I belonged.

When I had to leave his side, I wasn't gone long. I would go sit down for a quick break or meet yet another long-lost relative who expressed shock over how big I had gotten since the last time they had seen me, then make my way back to the casket and continue stroking his hair. I was with Clar Clar again, and there was no place else I would rather be. Whereas earlier I had only seen a dead body lying in that casket, I now saw my grandfather, my dad's dad, a man I deeply loved and admired, a man with whom I shared so many traits and interests, a man who even then I knew had made a tremendous impact on my life despite our short time together and whose influence affects me to this day.

I stared at Clar Clar's face as I stroked his hair, thinking back to all those fun times we had when we played Old Maid, watched football games on TV in the living room, walked partway down the hill and set up lawn chairs in a neighbor's gravel driveway that overlooked the Kenmore High School football stadium to watch the Cardinals play home games on crisp Saturday afternoons in the fall, sat at the piano together, and all the other countless grandfather-grandson moments that had come to a premature end. It didn't seem fair; I felt like Clar Clar had been stolen from us, gone too soon, and we had been cheated out of so many good years and good times with him. I was thankful that, for this short time at least, I could stand at his casket and spend these final moments with my grandfather and friend before we had to go our separate ways forever. I cherished every second we had together in that funeral parlor, me dressed in a little suit that Mom put together for me, Clar Clar adorned in his burial suit that Dee Dee picked out for him. I never wanted to leave his side.

I didn't get that same opportunity at the funeral the next day. Everything seemed to happen so fast, and everything was so final. Unlike the calling hours the day before, the funeral didn't leave much time for viewing. We went up to the casket briefly before the service started, then once it did, that was it. My time with Clar Clar was done forever. We were seated in a section that was situated behind the front end of the casket, so all I could see during the service was the back of Clar Clar's head—the same area that I had stroked continuously the day before. It was my first funeral, so all the sights and sounds were new to me: The sniffles, the red eyes, the minister reading from the Bible (particularly Psalm 23:4-6; I will never forget his voice as he spoke the words, "Yea, though

I walk through the valley of the shadow of death, I will fear no evil: for thou art with me; thy rod and thy staff they comfort me." I can hear these words in my head as clearly today as when I heard them in the funeral home that late October day in 1977. That was the sentence that brought the finality of Clar Clar's death home to me; that it really was over and he really was gone forever. That verse will always haunt me).

When the minister finished performing the service, everyone lined up and walked past the open casket one last time as the organ played its mournful music (I was in line next to Clar Clar's younger brother Frank, who reached into the casket as we filed past, placed his right hand over Clar Clar's right hand and, without saying a word, gave it a squeeze in a somber gesture of goodbye), then we walked out of the funeral home and that was it. The service was over.

It was the last time I ever saw Clar Clar's body. But it wasn't the last time I saw him.

CLAR CLAR'S SECOND VISITATION

Clar Clar has visited me twice since his death in 1977, and I will detail his second visitation first for reasons you will see later in this book. The two visitations were vastly different in nature, yet the messages they delivered were both conspicuous and contemporary.

After Clar Clar died, a heartbroken Dee Dee embarked on the gut-wrenching task of parceling out some of his belongings to family members. This was done piecemeal over a period of several years; Dee Dee had a fear of living alone, so following Clar Clar's death she lived with family members for several months, then began living with roommates at her house. Over time, she gradually was able to dole out Clar Clar's belongings to the family, each person receiving items that best suited their interests or that they had specifically requested.

One day while at her house, several years after Clar Clar had died, Dee Dee beckoned me into the tiny hallway that served as the main thoroughfare connecting her bedroom, the spare bedroom, the bathroom, the kitchen, the living room and the stairs to the attic. It was the nerve center of the house, and it was only a few feet long. On the small section of wall that separated her bedroom from the spare room was a cabinet with drawers underneath it. Dee Dee had one of the drawers pulled open and was digging through it when I arrived in the hallway. She turned toward me, holding something in her hand, but I couldn't see what it was.

"Here, Tom Tom, I want you to have this," she said in a subdued, almost melancholy, tone. (Dee Dee almost always called me Tom Tom, even in my adult years. She had a pet nickname for every family member, and Tom Tom was mine, which I found comforting and endearing.) She held out her hand to reveal a shiny metal watch. "This was one of Clarance's. It doesn't work anymore, honey, but it's something of his that you can remember him by. It will be a keepsake for you."

I knew the watch well. I had seen him wear it, and others like it, for as long as I could remember. It had a large face and a silver metallic band that pulled out like an accordion to fit any size wrist—the kind that could rip the hair off your wrist if it got caught in the twists of the band. I held the watch in my hand, delighted to have this treasure of Clar Clar's even though I couldn't actually use it to keep time. I took it home with me, and for the next several decades it moved from one dresser drawer to another as I got older and moved from one house to another. It was one of my prized possessions, and I always knew exactly where it was. I would pull it out of a dresser drawer from time to time just to look at it and feel it in my hands, thinking about Clar Clar as I did so. It made me feel closer to him.

The watch never worked; the battery had been dead long before Dee Dee gave it to me. I never bothered to get a replacement battery for the watch, for a few reasons: I wasn't planning on wearing it for fear of something happening to it, so it wasn't necessary for the watch to keep time; I wasn't sure I could even track down a compatible battery for such an old watch; and when Dee Dee said the watch didn't work anymore, I assumed she meant that it literally no longer worked, battery or no battery. So the watch sat silently in my dresser drawers, inactive for decades. But that didn't matter to me. It was a tangible piece of Clar Clar, something I could actually see and feel. In a very real sense, the watch helped bridge the gap between his dimension and mine.

In the years following his death, I had tried to get to the mausoleum in southwest Akron where he was interred—the cemetery was actually just a few minutes from where he had lived in Kenmore—as often as I could, usually on or around the anniversary of his death as well as the big holidays. Dad and I used to go to the cemetery together, often late at night when it was just the two of us standing in front of the mausoleum, its imposing façade bathed in the eerie glow of the building's exterior lights. We would quietly stare at his plot, situated at eye level to us, often tracing our fingers over his metal nameplate. Neither of us would say a word, but I could often hear Dad's soft sniffles as he fought back tears while he stood there. After a few minutes of quiet reflection, our visits always ended the same way: Dad would pat Clar Clar's slab a couple times and say, "Thanks, Clar Clar. You were a good man." That moment always struck me, because that was the rare time when I saw Dad's soul laid bare, the pain of losing his father still evident in his watery eyes all those years, all those decades, later. As his son and his only child, I was extremely saddened to see my dad in such a state. We would then turn and walk solemnly back to the car, often driving home without a word being said.

Several years ago, Kim and I made one of those trips to the mausoleum, close to the anniversary of Clar Clar's death as usual. Only now, with Dad gone, I was the one who was the most deeply affected, standing in front of Clar Clar's plot in quiet introspection as I had done with Dad so many times before, and I was the one who patted the grave slab and said, "Thanks, Clar Clar. You were a good man." It's funny how your place in life evolves and you assume the roles of those who have passed on, picking up the family mantle and carrying on as previous generations did before you were born and future generations will do long after you die. It's the cycle of life. And death.

On this particular occasion, upon arriving home from the cemetery, I went upstairs to our bedroom to change into my "comfy clothes," which always consists of a tank top and shorts for bumming around the house. As I opened one of my dresser drawers, I felt an intense urge to grab Clar Clar's watch. I pulled it out of the drawer and held it in my hand, contemplating the fact that this watch, at one time, had been on Clar Clar's wrist. I looked at it resting in my hand, studying its features and thinking about Clar Clar.

And then I noticed something—something unbelievable, something nonsensical, something impossible:

It was working!

I was overcome with excitement. This couldn't be. It absolutely, positively *could not be.* This watch had not worked for more than thirty years. It had never worked the entire time that I owned it. Its battery had been dead for several decades.

But sure enough, the tiny second hand at the bottom of the watch was inexplicably moving, silently circling around its miniature face within the larger watch face. I tried to grasp the fact that the watch was working with a long-dead battery inside it, but I just couldn't wrap my mind around it. It shouldn't have been working, there was no reason for it to be working, but yet it was. I stood in disbelief in our bedroom, staring in stunned silence at the watch as the little second hand defiantly motored around its miniature face. I was speechless. A watch with a dead battery that hadn't worked for decades suddenly working defied logic.

My hair stood on end as I studied the watch. My lungs felt devoid of air. I couldn't even blink. I was in shock.

I wasn't sure what to do next. On a whim, I decided to reset the time on the watch, pulling up the knob that controls the larger hands and turning it until they reflected the current time. I then held the watch for a few minutes, watching intently to see if the hands moved and if they kept pace with the time. To my utter amazement, they did. I excitedly called for Kim to come into the bedroom, partly to show her this astonishing development and partly to prove to myself that I wasn't hallucinating. She looked at it closely and verified that, indeed, the watch was working.

"This isn't possible," I said to her. "There's no way this can happen. The battery has been dead forever."

"Well, it's definitely working," Kim said as she examined the watch. "The hands are moving plain as day."

After marveling at the watch for several more minutes, I put it back in the drawer. My plan was to leave it there overnight and check it the next day to see if it was still working. As I crawled into bed later that night, I knew I was experiencing a miracle. And I knew who was orchestrating it.

I checked the watch the next day. It was still working. I continued to check it every few hours for the next few days and, sure enough, the watch with a dead battery that hadn't worked in decades was keeping perfect time. There was no explanation for it.

Well, actually there was one explanation, and only one explanation: Clar Clar was letting me know that he was there with me in the house and he was OK.

After a couple more days of keeping perfect time, the watch suddenly stopped working. Just like that. I had begun to think that the watch may work indefinitely; after all, if it could run on a dead battery, then theoretically it could run forever. So the day I pulled it out of the drawer and saw that its hands were motionless once more, literally frozen in time, I became wracked with disappointment. I stared at the watch, hoping that it was only a brief hiccup and waited a minute or two for it to resume working, but it didn't. I reluctantly put it back in the drawer and checked the next day. The hands were still idle. I checked the following day, and the day after that, and the day after that. Each time, the hands were still. The watch was dead again.

I couldn't shake the disappointment. Yes, I had wanted the watch to continue to work, but more than that, the fact that it no longer did meant, to me anyway, that Clar Clar was gone. I had enjoyed his presence those last several days; seeing the watch working again had made me feel close to him, and now that it wasn't, the house felt just a little bit emptier.

The last time I pulled the watch out of the drawer (just to make sure), I looked at it for a few more moments—and then I smiled as the magnitude of what had happened hit me. My disappointment vanished and was replaced by an inner peace. Clar Clar had given me a tremendous gift, in a manner that only I would recognize: By springing his watch back to life again on the anniversary of his death after I had just visited his grave.

In showing himself to me in that manner, he was also showing me— proving to me—that life is eternal. That watch has never worked since, but Clar Clar had delivered his message loud and clear.

For the second time.

CHAPTER 3

GRANDMA

I have never met a tougher woman than my maternal grandmother. No, check that. I have never met a tougher *person* than my maternal grandmother. All my grandparents were children of the Great Depression, and they learned to make the most of a tough situation at a very young age. Not much fazed them. They had grown up in a period of American history that had required monumental individual sacrifice, when having food on the table every day and a roof over your head was almost considered a luxury. Those stark conditions had made my grandparents strong and resilient, taught them to appreciate the little things, gave them a perspective on life that future generations couldn't hope to grasp.

But even in this light, Grandma was cut from a different cloth. She was a country woman, having lived her entire life in rural Northeast Ohio. As such, Grandma was a strong, wise, independent woman. I spent many weekends in my formative years at Grandma and Grandpa's house, which sat on a large property in Brimfield, Ohio, that featured an impressive garden behind the house and a tract of land extending tens of acres past the garden, much of it wooded (more on the house and property shortly). I can vividly remember stumbling out of bed to an empty house many a weekend morning when I was growing up, wondering where everyone went, only to look out a back window and see Grandma toiling away in her beloved garden. I would quickly get dressed and join her in the garden, where I was often greeted with Grandma turning to look at me and cheerfully saying, "It's about time you got up. I thought you were going to sleep all day!" And it would only be eight o'clock in the morning; she had already been out there since sunrise. Grandma would then give me a task to do in the garden, usually picking vegetables, and my day would begin—hours after she had already started hers. She was a tireless worker with a laser-like focus.

But as tough as Grandma was, she was also one of the sweetest people I've ever met. From her soft eyes that peered out from behind her glasses to her warm smile and hearty laugh, Grandma exuded a tenderness that belied her no-nonsense style. She was also very talented in a wide array of disciplines—everything from gardening, to cooking, to knitting (I still have a little footie that she made for me when I was very young), to sewing and crafts (she made a little puppy dog stuffed animal for me when I was a baby, which I also still have and know exactly where it is), to even the handling of firearms—she knew her way around rifles and shotguns. She was an amazing woman.

Grandma also didn't suffer fools, and that included her at-times rambunctious grandchildren—me, the oldest, and my three Eddy cousins, Shelley, Jeff and Pam, the children of Mom's older sister Sue. We often played the fool, racing through their large colonial farmhouse playing tag or hide and seek or—my personal favorite—going to the top of the long flight of carpeted stairs at the second level of the house and careening back down to the bottom, feet first, on my belly. I'll say this: Once you got going past the first few steps at the top, you could pick up some serious speed as you slid to the bottom. It was a rush for young kids like us.

This clown show never lasted long, however. Grandma made sure of it. My belly slides down the stairs often ended with me sliding right into Grandma's waiting arms at the bottom—a shocking turn of events indeed, considering my face was inches from the carpet and I had no idea Grandma would be standing there. And that would bring an unceremonious end to the carpet-slide festivities, because when Grandma told you to stop doing something, you stopped. Immediately. It wasn't a negotiation, it wasn't a democracy, there was no bargaining or compromise. It was game, set, match, Grandma.

And you knew it. Her voice had conviction; you knew she meant what she said, the rules were the rules, and you didn't want to test her rules. Of course, that doesn't mean we didn't test her on occasion—after all, we were kids and, as such, just couldn't help ourselves at times. But when we did, whatever bright idea we had put into motion was stopped in its tracks. As for what happened when she had to tell us something a third time, I have no idea. There were no third times.

Just underneath Grandma's tough exterior, though, was a heart of gold. She was a sweet, warm, caring person who set an endearing example for her five children and four grandchildren. Her hearty country dinners were always a highlight of any weekend stay, as were my futile attempts to sneak a cookie out of her beloved cookie jar on the kitchen counter. Grandma would be in the living room, located down the hallway from the kitchen, sitting in her rocking chair, located at the far end of the living room from the hallway entrance, watching TV. In other words, I was completely out of sight from her and, for any normal human being, out of earshot. But Grandma was no ordinary human being. She had radar-quality hearing. Regardless of how carefully I tried to remove the lid of her ceramic cookie jar, it inevitably always made the slightest "clink" sound as the lid slid off the container—sometimes so softly I could barely hear it myself—and, with my hand literally in the cookie jar, a voice would bellow from the living room: "Who's in the cookie jar?!" Of course, she knew it was me. I would freeze in place, hand in jar, wondering how on Earth she could have possibly heard the lid come off the jar when she was so far away and had the television on.

I think it was as much a game for Grandma as it was for me: She didn't really care if I had a cookie; she just wanted to let me know that I could not slip anything past her—and I couldn't.

This was never more clearly illustrated than the time I wet the bed. I don't remember exactly what age I was when this occurred; I was pretty young but old enough to be embarrassed that it happened, so I'm guessing that I was around eight or nine years old, maybe even ten. It wasn't a problem I had, just a good old-fashioned accident. It actually woke me up in the middle of the night as it was in progress, and I was at a loss as to what to do about it. There wasn't much I could do at that point since it was the middle of the night, so I did my best to avoid the affected area of the bed for the rest of my sleep—which wasn't easy. When I woke up, I knew I had to act fast if I was going to successfully cover up the crime scene: Grandma would be coming into the room to make up the bed as soon as she heard me stirring. The clock was ticking.

So I hatched a plan: I would make up the bed for her, thus hiding the wet evidence underneath the covers. By bedtime that night, I figured, the sheets should be dry and I would be in the clear. My plan was foolproof. And with that, I quietly slid out of bed, trying mightily to tread as softly on the carpeted floor as humanly possible so as to not alert Grandma that I was awake (her hearing was not of this world). With no sound of Grandma approaching the room, I stealthily made up the bed, pulling the covers up over the pillows and smoothing everything out.

When I finished, I stepped back and admired my maid service-quality bed-making effort. Perfect!

Moments later, Grandma entered the room—and stopped dead in her tracks at the sight of the neatly made-up bed. I stood next to it, beaming with pride.

"Wow, look at that!" she said.

I continued to smile from ear to ear, glancing from her to the bed and back to her. Mission accomplished, I thought. My plan had gone off without a hitch; if I wasn't the smartest kid in the world, I at least had to be in the conversation.

"That looks great, Tommy," Grandma said.

I felt a huge sense of relief. In my mind I was too old to be wetting the bed, so I couldn't imagine the embarrassment I would have felt if she had discovered my nighttime transgression. I was in the clear.

And then I wasn't. For reasons I couldn't immediately discern, Grandma stepped around to the side of the bed. *Why is she doing that?* I thought. *She just said I did a great job. She should be leaving the room, not walking further into it.*

This was bad.

And it got worse when, to my horror, she reached down, grabbed the top of the bedspread and yanked it down past the middle of the bed. She stared for a few seconds, studying the blanket underneath. The evidence was still covered. All she has to do, I thought, was just pull that bedspread back up where it belonged and we could go happily about our day.

Instead, she ripped the blanket and top sheet down—and there, exposed by the bright morning light streaming through the windows, was the large round patch of soaking-wet bedsheet. I thought I might die.

"AHA!!" Grandma exclaimed. "I knew it!"

"I'm sorry, Grandma," I said sheepishly. "I couldn't help it. It happened during my sleep." I was so ashamed.

She stood for a moment, then without a word reached down and went to work stripping the bed. She wasn't nearly as affected by the incident as I was. In fact, she was surprisingly unfazed.

But I had to know. "What made you look under the covers, Grandma?" I asked.

She stopped what she was doing and straightened up, then turned and eyed me through her glasses. "I knew something was wrong," she said with a smirk, "because you've never made the bed in your life."

Then she promptly went back to changing out the bed.

Clearly, I did not think my plan through. This was a woman who had raised five children; there was nothing under the sun that she hadn't seen. Surely there had been bed-wetting incidents from at least some of her kids, probably including my own mother.

Sneaking cookies, concealing urine-stained sheets or anything else, it didn't matter. Trying to pull something over on Grandma was pure folly.

I can't properly introduce you, the reader, to Grandma and Grandpa without also introducing you to their rustic house in the southern Portage County countryside, so I will give a visual tour and a little background here before I go any further. Their house was an integral part of their personalities and psyche; it was a style of living as much as it was a home, so to fully understand my maternal grandparents, it is necessary to paint a clear picture of where and how they lived. Their house is also a big part of me; in a very real sense I grew up in that house, spending much of my childhood there on weekend visits and extended stays in the summer. It was a place of respite and solitude, somewhere to slow down, kick my feet up and escape the hustle and bustle of city life. I loved it there; it was a wonderful change of pace to what I was accustomed to in my normally hectic day-to-day routine during the school week, and I always looked forward to Mom and Dad dropping me off at Grandma and Grandpa's on Friday nights for a weekend of R&R in the great outdoors.

I'll try not to get too bogged down in the minutiae of their house and property, but since both were large and the house featured many interesting—even mysterious—nooks and crannies that contributed greatly to its ambiance, I will provide a detailed snapshot of their beautiful, elegant home and its pastoral setting amidst the rolling farmland of Portage County.

Also, I will call their house a "farmhouse" for descriptive purposes, although technically theirs wasn't a farmhouse per se (actually, the house still stands and is occupied by my aunt and uncle, my aunt having been raised in the house); Grandma and Grandpa didn't actually farm the land other than to plant and tend to a very large garden in the back, and they did not keep animals on the property except for dogs. I label it a farmhouse primarily because it has the classic appearance of one and sits in a rural area (I'll describe the house itself in more detail shortly).

As I stated earlier, the property they owned was fairly large—around eighty-some acres—and was rather isolated other than a smattering of houses spaced out along their quiet country road. To a city boy like me, though, Grandma and Grandpa's house seemed like it was out in the middle of nowhere compared to the congested neighborhoods where we had lived in Akron and Mogadore, where the distance to our neighbors was measured in feet. Their house sat virtually alone; from their property, you could see exactly two other houses: one adjacent to theirs to the east but separated by Grandma and Grandpa's large side yard and secondary driveway to their barn, as well as several big trees; and another house that sat cater-corner from theirs on the other side of the road and was bordered by a large cornfield that was situated directly across the street from Grandma and Grandpa's house. Stretching behind and next to the cornfield were thick woods that extended several hundred yards to a half-mile or more; we would often grab the binoculars around dusk to watch the deer emerge from that wood line to forage for food. Grandma and Grandpa somehow could spot the deer with their naked eye, even though the distance from their house to the woods behind the cornfield was between a quarter- and a half-mile, and the tan coats of the deer often blended in with the trees in the low lighting of dusk. They would excitedly beckon their young grandson over to one of the front windows and point in the direction of the deer, and I would peer intently through the glass and see nothing but cornstalks and trees; not until I put the binoculars up to my face could I see the animals. I have since come to learn that people who live out in the country often have exceptionally fine-tuned senses, borne out of necessity for living in isolated rural areas—a survival instinct as much as anything else.

Everything about Grandma and Grandpa's property was big, especially to my young eyes: The house was big, the yards were big, the garden was big, the trees were big, the woods were big, the open spaces were big, even the sky seemed bigger than normal—at least bigger than from my vantage point in the packed-together neighborhoods of Mogadore. The eighty or so acres of land they owned stretched behind their house to the north; once you got past the big garden and adjoining yard that sat next to it (which made for an ideal football and baseball field because of its large size, thick grass and flat grade—and where I could usually be found when I stayed weekends at their house if I wasn't shooting baskets in the driveway) there was nothing but undeveloped land. A small cornfield sat just past the large backyard, but beyond that were about eighty acres of nothing but woods and patches of open land; it was true backcountry.

Growing up, I engaged in two primary activities in the backcountry of Grandma and Grandpa's extensive property: Fish with Gramps and Uncle Jimmy at the "The Pond," and take rides with Uncle Jimmy on his three-wheeler. Uncle Jimmy was the youngest of Grandma and Grandpa's five children and the only boy; due to the fact that he was just nine years my senior, our dynamic was more along the lines of older brother-little brother than uncle-nephew. The three of us spent countless afternoons fishing at The Pond deep within the property, Gramps and Jimmy expertly hauling in their fair share of fish and me just happy if I could bait the hook and cast my line without sending anyone to the emergency room—and that's not an exaggeration. More than once over the years, my haphazard line-casting had Uncle Jimmy shouting, "Tommy, watch where you're swinging that thing!" as he ducked and scrambled for cover while my baited hook whizzed dangerously close to his head. There were many days when I had a better chance of snagging a relative than a bluegill. Let's just say I wasn't—and still am not—much of a fisherman.

The ATV rides were more my speed—figuratively and literally. There was only one seat for the two of us, so I would take my sliver of seat and hang on for dear life as Uncle Jimmy opened it up on the straightaway of the flat, dirt access road that ran toward the back of the property, my hair blowing in the wind as the ATV reached higher and higher speeds. He often would veer off the road at certain junctures and into the brush, the three-wheeler bouncing and jumping through the scrub to the point where I was quite certain that I was either going to lose some teeth or get thrown from the ATV—or both. Somehow, though, I always managed to hang on. Uncle Jimmy would then make his way back to the access road for the exhilarating ride back down the dirt straightaway to the house. Good times.

That access road also marked the western boundary of their property, which actually sat atop the edge of a high plateau. Just past the access road and shallow tree line that bordered it was a steep hill down to more woods and farmland, serving to further insulate their house and property from civilization. In other words, Grandma and Grandpa had a peaceful little corner of the world all to themselves.

We never lived farther than maybe a fifteen-minute drive from their house, but as far as I was concerned growing up, it may as well have been in Nebraska; to me, Grandma and Grandpa lived in the wilds—even if downtown Kent, a college town of about twenty-five thousand people (in the mid-1970s), was only about a seven-minute drive away. My perception of this stark isolation was shaped by the inescapable fact that it was a completely different world where they lived from the one I lived in at home in Mogadore; life at their house was peaceful, slow-paced, relaxed—and quiet. Very, very quiet. The sounds of passing traffic were nothing like I was accustomed to at home; back in the 1970s, traffic on their road usually was light and, while you did hear the occasional vehicle going down the road, they were few and far between—which also added to my sense of isolation (I viewed this isolation as both a positive and a negative, and which way I felt about it was directly related to the time of day—as you will see shortly).

There were sounds out there, though—sounds that I rarely, if ever, heard at home: from all manner of birds that I learned to identify solely by their chirps and tweets, to vocalizations of other animals that sounded anything from rather friendly to quite threatening—the latter particularly at night when it was dark. Very, very dark. I learned at an early age that there is darkness, and then there is country darkness. In the city and suburbs where Mom, Dad and I always lived, there usually was some light still available at night, such as street lights and neighbors' porches; because of this, you could still see enough to get around at night. In the country, though, the dark is much darker; it's oppressive. And when night fell at Grandma and Grandpa's, their house and property took on an entirely different feel to me. As the quiet placidity of day began to give way to night, and the shadows grew longer and longer as the sun sank lower and lower in the sky, things started to get, well, spooky. By the time the last vestiges of twilight faded away and night settled in, an ominous darkness gripped the land. This thick blanket of darkness only served to magnify the house's isolated location; Grandma and Grandpa's old country home felt particularly vulnerable at night to me, when I would look out a window and see nothing but the twisted, ghostly, menacing figures of the large trees that ringed the house in a crescent shape from the front yard around the house to the left, where they formed a wood line that stretched behind the house and bordered the large backyard (the aforementioned "football field"). These big trees—one, a pine, so tall that you could see the top of it from Interstate 76 about a mile to the south—always appeared closer to the house in the dark of night than they did in the light of day. I'm sure it was just my imagination.

Nighttime out in the country seemed to hold so many secrets, so many unknowns, so many ... terrors. I often wondered what snarling, drooling, red-eyed, big-fanged creature was lurking in the blackness, just beyond the glass of the window that my nose was pressed against, that I couldn't see—if some horrid beast was crouched behind a tree or shrub just out of my line of sight, watching me trying to watch it. The front porch lights were usually on at night, illuminating the immediate area in front of the house; a few feet into the front yard, though, this light was swallowed up by the thick darkness, concealing everything within it. When it was time for bed, though, the porch lights were switched off and the house sat alone in the crushing blackness and eerie stillness of the night. I felt safe and secure with Grandma and Grandpa inside the cozy confines of their house—usually, anyway—often with a roaring fire popping and crackling in the living room fireplace, but I wouldn't dare venture outside when the sun went down. My friends and I often played tag, hide and seek, and various sports outside well into the night in the well-lit neighborhoods of Mogadore, but I was quickly chased inside by the setting sun at Grandma and Grandpa's house in the Brimfield countryside. Not that I could do much outside at night there anyway—it was pitch dark and there weren't any other children around—but it wouldn't have mattered if I could. In my young, vivid, overactive imagination, the possibilities of what might be on the other side of the house's walls at night were endless—and none of them good.

The possibilities of what might be sneaking around on *my* side of the walls at night seemed unlimited as well due to the age, size and layout of the house itself. Built in the early 1870s, Grandma and Grandpa's house possessed a charm, personality and mystique all its own. The two-story, white colonial sits back from the road about twenty yards or so and is partially shielded from view by several very large trees in the front and to the sides of the house, giving it a somewhat mysterious look. And while it understandably showed some age (prior to an extensive upgrading project by my aunt and uncle in the last decade), it was not your stereotypical creepy old farmhouse—far from it, in fact.

It was in good condition inside and out, no mean feat considering that it was a century old. The inside was always kept neat, clean and tidy, and the outside was in good shape thanks to Grandma and Grandpa's constant vigilance; with an old house such as theirs, it wouldn't take much for it to start to succumb to the harsh Ohio winters. They were proud of the house, and rightfully so.

The inside layout of the house was unique and fun. An asphalt driveway ended at the east wing of the house, which was comprised of what we called "the back room," which was actually three rooms: The main room, which primarily served as Gramps' work area that housed his work bench, tools, various types of supplies and equipment, and shelving units; and two smaller back rooms behind the main room that once had been bedrooms but were converted to storage areas by Grandma and Grandpa. A small back porch off Gramps' work room led to Grandma's big garden and the backyard.

You could enter the house through Gramps' work room (and thus enter the house proper from there via a door to the kitchen), but the primary entrance was through the dining room, which was accessible via a few steps that connected the driveway to the large cement porch that stretched across most of the front of the house. The main floor consisted of the dining room, complete with chandelier; the kitchen, which was adjacent to the dining room and visible from it through a large cutout in the wall that partitioned the two rooms (there was an eating counter with barstools in front of this partition on the kitchen side, allowing people in both rooms to be able to see and talk to each other); the living room, separated from the dining room by a walled flight of steps to the second level (the front door, which was rarely used, was located in front of this staircase); a bathroom, located along the back hallway that led from the kitchen to the living room; the door to the basement was off this same hallway (more on that in a minute); and a small room at the end of that hallway, next to the entrance to the living room. Just off the living room and separated from it by a pair of French doors was the solarium, which represented the west wing of the house.

I go into this level of detail to give you a picture in your mind's eye of the size and complexity of the main floor; in short, it was large and had a lot going on.

This floor layout was perfect for small children with oodles of energy to burn—like me, for example. Because the dining room and living room connected in two different spots—via the back hallway from the kitchen entrance, and through the small foyer between the front door and the steps to the second level—you could literally circle unimpeded through much of the main floor. I would start by running through the dining room, turn left down the hallway, left again into the living room, race through the living room and turn left into the foyer, and wind up back in the dining room—or vice versa—in a matter of seconds. If I was wearing socks and had built up a good enough head of speed on the carpeted floor of the living room, I could slide on the linoleum tile of the dining room starting from just past the foyer all the way to the side door—a good fifteen feet.

I would go round and round in this manner, changing direction just to switch things up, turning Grandma and Grandpa's house into the Twenty-four Hours of Brimfield. This was especially fun when I was there with my aforementioned Eddy cousins. Since Shelley and I were the same age and a few years older than Jeff and Pam, she and I were partners in crime at Grandma and Grandpa's—and this included the Twenty-four Hours of Brimfield, endlessly chasing each other in that grand circle of the main floor. The fun usually stopped in one of two ways: One of us would get clever and stop and go back the other way, thus catching the other one, who had no way of knowing the trap had been set until they turned a corner and ran blindly into said trap; or Grandma, who could often be found sitting in her rocking chair directly in front of the living room window, would put a stop to the hijinx before somebody got hurt. This would leave Shelley and I giggling and trying to catch our breath—until we began our next escapade.

The second level consisted of a large bedroom and a smaller one on the west side of the house, with another large bedroom and smaller one on the east side, with both sets of bedrooms connected by a hallway at the top of the stairs. A bathroom sat along this hallway nearest the west-wing bedrooms, while the large bedroom on the east wing featured a door to a walk-in attic. Full disclosure: I never cared for the idea that a bedroom was directly connected to an attic, particularly when the attic door is right next to the head of the bed.

Not because of practical purposes. For creepy purposes. Maybe I watch too many paranormal television shows, but nothing good ever seems to happen in—or come out of—attics. Even as an adult, just the sight of the attic door in that bedroom gives me a sense of dread. As a kid, I was downright terrified of it.

Which brings me to the basement. I've always had trouble with basements to begin with—in every horror movie I've ever seen, the basement is where the monster lives and is the absolute last place you want to get trapped (people go in but never seem to come out—alive, anyway)—but the basement at Grandma and Grandpa's house, quite frankly, gave me the willies. In fact, any time I hear someone tell some kind of scary story about ghosts or demons, my mind automatically sets the scene in the basement of Grandma and Grandpa's house. There was just something about it, an unease I always felt down there. I never knew exactly why—nothing ever actually happened to me down there—but I always chalked that up to the fact that whatever I imagined was down there never had a chance to get me because: A. I only went down there if I absolutely had to; B. When I did have to go down there, I only stayed as long as necessary—and not one second longer; and C. When I left the basement, I raced back up the stairs as fast as my legs could carry me, often taking two—and sometimes three—steps at a time, just in case whatever was down there was swiping at my feet as I went. The fear I felt going back up the steps, with my back turned to the basement, could be overwhelming; the sense that I was being watched—or worse, followed—was palpable. When I reached the top of the steps, I would immediately close the door behind me—trying my best not to look back down the steps, although sometimes I just couldn't help myself—and walk as quickly as possible to an area of the house that contained people, getting as far away from the basement door as I could. Sometimes, just walking down the hallway and passing the door was enough to give me goosebumps.

The basement wasn't dark and dingy, it wasn't musty and covered in cobwebs, it wasn't creepy in the classical sense. My fear of that basement was rooted more in the age and rural location of the house, the floor layout of the basement and the fact that I watched too many scary movies. On the surface, it was just an old basement in an old house. It was divided into two equal sections, one on each side of the steps, which were walled all the way down; because of this, when you stood at the top of the steps and looked down, all you could see at the bottom were a few feet of the concrete floor and a tiny portion of the back wall. The two areas of the basement itself were not visible from the steps other than a sliver of their entranceways; in other words, something could be waiting for me just inside the entrance to either side of the basement, and I wouldn't know it until I got down there. At which point, of course, it would be too late.

To the left of the steps was an area that was more like a classic basement, containing a washer, dryer, wash tub, large floor freezer, shelving units and a center work area where Grandma did her indoor gardening, featuring tables and benches full of potted plants, flowers and vegetables that she nurtured until they were hardy enough to go outside. This side of the basement was the darker of the two and contained stone steps that led up to an egress door that opened into the backyard—which always put my imagination into overdrive. It wouldn't take much, I thought, for someone or something lurking around the back of the house to enter the premises through that egress door, and I was always certain that if this was to happen, it surely would be when I was alone in the basement. What's more, the room was often under a dim, eerie lighting for Grandma's gardening endeavor, often giving that side of the basement an unsettling, murky glow.

The other side of the basement was a more finished product—kind of. It had a fireplace, table, chairs, couch, piano and even a large short-wave radio, plus a small bathroom toward the back. Despite this seemingly harmless appearance, I actually felt more uneasy on that side of the basement than I did on the other side—which is saying a lot—because I always felt that something was off about that right side of the basement. I couldn't put a finger on it exactly, I just always had a sense of impending doom whenever I turned right at the bottom of the steps and went into that room. While it did contain all the above-mentioned furnishings, they were down there basically in storage; it was designed originally as a kind of rec room or secondary living room, but when I was growing up it didn't get a whole lot of use compared to the rest of the house.

The room wasn't abandoned or forgotten by any means, it just seemed—again, in my young mind—like the kind of room you see in the scary movies that is fully furnished but everybody is gone and no one knows what happened to them. The room seemed ... lonely.

We cousins would go down there to play at times, but always together. And always during the day. At night, going down to the basement was completely out of the question for me unless Grandma needed me to help her with something like the laundry or tending to her plants—and that usually meant she would be down there with me. But if she wasn't, and I had to be down there alone after dark, I did so with a large lump in my throat. I would stand at the top of the steps and look down into the abyss, my heart about to beat out of my chest, knowing I was tempting fate by descending those steps into the basement. Each time that I went down and made it back up without incident, I considered myself lucky. But if I kept doing it, I figured, it was only a matter of time before I encountered something down there that would make it a one-way trip for me.

I would force my legs to descend the wide, wooden steps. And with each step I took closer to the bottom, the more helpless I felt; I would turn and look back up at the relative safety of the basement door, knowing that the farther away it got, the more dire my position was should I have to scramble back up to freedom. By the time I reached the bottom, I would be so consumed with fear that I could barely function; my hair would be standing on end, all my senses would be heightened, my mouth would be so dry you could light a match inside it. Once at the bottom, I would do what I had to do as quickly as possible— usually in Grandma's work area, and usually counted in seconds—and set land-speed records going back up the steps.

The worst part was turning at the bottom of the steps to go into one of the rooms, which meant my back was momentarily turned to the other room; in the movies, the unfortunate soul in the basement always thinks they're in the clear and breathes a sigh of relief when they turn a corner and nothing is there, only to have the monster come out of nowhere from behind and get them. The second-worst part was realizing that whichever of the two rooms I was in down there, I was completely cut off from the steps—and therefore safety—should something emerge from the other room. Or maybe that was the worst part.

Either way, in both scenarios I was a goner. So my strategy was simple: Avoid the basement. And if I couldn't, then at least avoid it at night. And if I couldn't do that, then run like greased lightning back up the steps. I'm sure my fear was irrational and unfounded, just the product of my impressionable young mind playing tricks on me. I'm sure there was nothing lurking down there—no demons, no ghosts, no evil spirits, nothing. It was just a harmless basement; Grandma and Grandpa never batted an eye when they went down there. So it was all in my head. At least that's what I've always told myself, so I'm going with that.

I'm still not a fan of basements. I can blame at least some of this fear on being a fan of Gothic horror movies, particularly those involving vampires, whose coffins always seemed to be located in the basement or cellar. Always. I loved Dracula movies growing up, particularly the 1931 classic with Bela Lugosi and the Hammer Films series starring Christopher Lee as the Count in the 1950s and '60s. I would sit mesmerized in front of the television, usually late at night with the lights out, as Dracula stalked and claimed one helpless victim after another, the end result being that I would pull the covers all the way up past my neck when I went to bed that night—even in the hot and humid dead of summer. Pouring liters of sweat into the blankets all night long was far preferable to carelessly leaving the covers down around my waist and thus exposing my neck. When it comes to the possibility of vampires hiding in your bedroom, you can't be too careful.

But the movie that really got me, the one that scared me like no other—including *The Exorcist*, which I'm pretty sure shaved years off my life—the one that set me back mentally, emotionally and psychologically, was *Salem's Lot*. It was a life-changer. It was actually a two-part miniseries and was based on the novel by Stephen King. You know how people say they'll never forget where they were and who they were with when a monumental event happened in their life? Well, *Salem's Lot* was that event for me. I was eleven years old when I saw it in October of 1979, sitting on the couch with Dad in the living room of our apartment on Mogadore Road. To this day, I've never been so scared watching anything; I nearly became one with the couch cushions by the time it was over after all my cringing and cowering. The original *Paranormal Activity* comes close, but *Salem's Lot* is still the winner. It was a vampire movie like nothing I had ever seen before; the main vampire, Barlow, was large, gruesome and terrifying, modeled on F.W. Murnau's iconic *Nosferatu* from 1922. Barlow's coffin was inside a big, old, isolated, creepy house on a hill—and, you guessed it, the coffin was in the basement. Which is also where all his victims-turned-vampires were as well.

I was absolutely terrified watching *Salem's Lot*. It scarred my psyche to the point that when we moved into a house in another part of Mogadore a couple months later, I had to switch bedrooms from the second level—which I had all to myself but also meant I was all alone—to a smaller room on the first floor a few feet from my parents' bedroom. I mentally couldn't take it being up there in my bedroom at night by myself; it was just too much. I felt isolated and trapped, and I wasn't getting much sleep because I kept every light on all night, every night, and I was afraid to close my eyes. Needless to say, Dad wasn't exactly thrilled that after hauling all my heavy bedroom furniture upstairs when we moved in, he promptly had to move it all right back downstairs a few weeks later because his son was afraid the vampires were going to get him. It wasn't my fault; his beef should have been with Stephen King and the makers of *Salem's Lot*.

What made *Salem's Lot* especially terrifying to a sixth-grader like me was that it was the first vampire movie that I had seen where young boys were victims. In every other vampire movie I had ever seen, it was the adults who had the misfortune of being bitten and drained of blood by vampires. *In Salem's Lot*, though, boys my age were killed by the vampire, then joined the undead as vampires themselves to attack other victims, including friends and their own parents. No one was safe. And in my mind, that included me.

And this translated directly to my fear of Grandma and Grandpa's basement. I already had serious misgivings about going down into their basement long before I saw *Salem's Lot*, but after I watched it, that fear reached new heights. And it wasn't just limited to the basement: Going to bed at night in the big old farmhouse brought with it a whole new set of issues, namely the stifling darkness that permeated the house when the lights were shut off. I have detailed at length how dark it was outside in the country, but that was easily rivaled by how dark it was inside the house. On moonless nights, I could lie in bed in the smaller of the two bedrooms on the west wing of the house (my customary room when I spent the night there), hold my hand in front of my face, and not see it. I don't mean I could make out a figure of a hand but not see it clearly, I mean I couldn't see my hand a few inches from my face. At all. It was like it wasn't there, like it was just part of the blackness that encased the room. There was no ambient light to allow my eyes to slowly get accustomed to the dark. It was pitch black, and it stayed pitch black all night. If something was in there with me, I'd never know it—an extremely unsettling proposition. I would burrow deep within the pillows and covers and try to force myself to go to sleep, but with every creak and groan of the old house or whistle and moan of the wind as it blew over the eaves and against the windows, my eyes would instantly flip wide open—and see nothing but blackness. Dawn couldn't come soon enough.

However, moonlit nights weren't a whole lot better, casting eerie shadows across the room that resembled ghastly figures creeping along the walls and the folding closet doors—the latter of which were usually closed except for a few unsettling inches where they didn't quite meet in the middle. In my mind, that was just enough space for whatever might be lurking in the closet to watch and wait for me to fall asleep. I did my level best to keep from looking at it, but for some reason my eyes were just naturally drawn to the impenetrable blackness of that ominous vertical crack in the doors, almost as if something was beckoning me to look at it. Sometimes it was all I could do to keep from bolting out of bed, flinging open the door and running into bed with my grandparents. The best I could do, though, was just close my eyes tightly, hope for sleep and pray for morning.

Even today at age fifty, I'm still not crazy about basements, the closet doors either have to be completely closed or completely open when I sleep—small openings are not acceptable—and I still think that house looks like it would be an ideal setting for a scary movie. It's just always had the haunted-house vibe—and even more so after learning, in my adult years, that funerals of family members were held in the living room long ago when it was customary for private homes to host services. If I had known then that bodies had been laid out in caskets in the living room, and that the living room had doubled as a funeral parlor from time to time, my staying the night in the house might well have been out of the question.

I now wonder if my young senses were actually picking up on something all those years ago—something in the basement, something in that bedroom closet, something just outside the house at night. Maybe it wasn't just my imagination, the product of an overzealous young mind. Maybe my fears as a child were well-founded and someone had been in the house, someone who had passed on that I could sense but not see, someone who had received their final goodbyes on this Earth in that living room but returned to check on their family from time to time—or had never left at all.

Maybe, just maybe, my first visitations had actually come decades ago from long-dead family members I had never met, family members who felt compelled to watch over me as a youngster. Maybe they were there with me in the basement and in that bedroom at night, and I was picking up on their presence. Maybe it was even Gramps' own father, who died long before I was born and whose funeral was one of those that was held in the living room, looking out for his little great-grandson. Maybe what I sensed in the house all those years wasn't there to spook me but to protect me.

Maybe I had nothing to be afraid of after all.

Some of my earliest memories in life involve being at Grandma and Grandpa's house. I'm not sure how old I was, probably somewhere between one and two years old, but I had to have been awfully young because I can remember lying in the crib at the foot of Grandma's bed at night. She would hike up the safety rail on the crib, wind up the teddy bear she kept in the crib and set it next to me as it played its soft music. I vividly remember lying on my back, staring up at the darkened ceiling and following its pattern as far as my eyes could see, listening to the sound of Grandma breathing as she fell asleep. The big old house would be deathly silent, and I would begin to feel isolated and vulnerable in the darkness in her room on the second floor of the house, the only person awake. I could hear every creak and groan of its nearly century-old frame, and would close my eyes and curl up in the little blanket and try to force myself to fall asleep. These, in fact, may be the earliest memories of my life.

After outgrowing the crib, I graduated to Aunt Betsy's old room down the hallway (the aforementioned smaller bedroom in the west wing of the house). But I rarely fell asleep there. Instead, I would go up to bed with Gramps and we would lie there in the dark and talk, listen to a game on the radio or watch a game on the television on his dresser. Often, I would ask Gramps to make barnyard noises for me, and he would happily oblige, be it a cow, pig, horse, sheep, whatever. You name it, Gramps made the noise.

One time, though, I threw him a curve. "Gramps, do a zebra," I said. "A zebra?" he asked, puzzled. "Yeah," I said. "What kind of sound does a zebra make?" After several moments of silence, he broke wind. "That's a zebra," he chuckled as I roared with laughter. Of course, from that point on the zebra became my most popular request.

The nightly weekend routine was the same: Grandma would stay downstairs in the living room and watch the late news while Gramps and I went up to bed. Invariably, I would fall asleep and be awakened to the sensation of Grandma scooping me up in her arms and carrying me into Aunt Betsy's old room. She would then set me gently down into bed, tuck me in and walk out of the room as I contentedly drifted back off to sleep.

Total bliss.

Grandma was diagnosed with cancer in September 1984. I was sixteen years old, a junior in high school, and not especially equipped to help my mom deal with watching her mother slowly waste away. I did what I could, but at that point in my life I simply did not possess the emotional maturity necessary to be the rock Mom needed. Grandma's cancer battle took a terrible mental toll on Mom—a toll which I am convinced shortened her own life.

Grandma was a proud woman, and she put up a valiant resistance against the insidious disease. There were times when the family, particularly Gramps, thought she may not live through the night, and there were times she seemed to be holding the disease at bay. This emotional roller-coaster went on for more than a year, our family wondering if she could somehow beat it, or at least hold it off for an appreciable length of time.

But one night in October 1985, Clar Clar paid his first visit to me. And I knew Grandma didn't have long.

By this time I was seventeen, a senior at Mogadore High School and an offensive and defensive lineman on the football team. We were having another great season, undefeated as November neared and eyeing our coveted yet elusive goal of being state champions; Mogadore had won a state title in 1979, and our team was hoping to give the program its second championship after a string of heartbreaking near-misses. The small school on the southeastern outskirts of Akron has a very long and proud football tradition, and we were doing our part to uphold it.

Despite our success, Grandma's health dominated my thoughts. Football was a welcome distraction to the stress and fear of the very real possibility of losing my grandmother, and being on the field with my teammates in practice and during games helped immensely. For a few hours each day, my mind allowed itself to focus on something else: Executing blocks as an offensive guard and carrying out my assignments as a defensive tackle. Games on Friday nights were especially therapeutic with the adrenaline rush of raw competition, the band playing and the crowd cheering. Incredibly, Mom and Gramps somehow managed to attend every single game, home and away, to support me—and each other. No matter how far the drive to a game, both of them were there cheering on the Wildcats. Just knowing that they were in the stands watching our team eased the sense of isolation I sometimes felt on the football field during Grandma's battle, especially games we played away from our home stadium. Mom and Gramps were my lifeline in a sea of emotional distress.

Gramps in particular remained amazingly upbeat during this incredibly difficult time. He was a rock. While Gramps was never fazed by much—it just wasn't his personality—I think he also felt it his duty as the patriarch of the family to be strong for everyone else. I'm sure that on the inside, Gramps was torn up watching Grandma's agonizing battle with cancer; after all, he lived that battle with her every minute of every day. Watching his wife of over forty years and the mother of their five children slowly succumb to the disease must have exacted a terrible mental toll on him, but true to his nature, he kept his emotions in check on the outside. And, as always, he continued to put the needs of others above his own, even during a time when perhaps no one needed emotional support more than he did.

I was in awe at how Gramps was able to soldier on in the face of such overwhelming sadness. He seemed to possess a superhuman inner strength. His personality remained unchanged throughout Grandma's ordeal, and his sense of duty to his family was as strong as ever. The family would have understood if Gramps needed a break, if he needed us to be his rock instead of the other way around, but that just wasn't the way he was wired. He was extremely self-sufficient, he was a practical man and he was a realist, so it wasn't in his nature to feel sorry for himself or become a victim of circumstance. Quite the contrary: Gramps seemed to be made of Teflon, able to withstand anything life threw at him—and he made it look easy. He was, after all, a card-carrying member of The Greatest Generation, which survived the Great Depression, defeated the Germans and Japanese in World War II, kept communism at bay throughout the Cold War and ushered in the Space Age, highlighted by landing a man on the moon, perhaps the single greatest achievement in the history of humankind. His generation didn't cower in fear or shrink from responsibility, it didn't shy away from hard work, it didn't avoid doing what was necessary and what was right just because it might be unpleasant. His generation met problems head-on and conquered them—and so did Gramps. He was the most resilient person I ever met, and that was never demonstrated more clearly than during Grandma's year-long fight against cancer.

Gramps never ceased to amaze me during this time. After our football games on Friday nights my senior year, he would go back to our house in Mogadore and wait for me to come home, which usually wasn't until somewhere around eleven o'clock. Despite the late hour and the fact he still had to drive back home to Brimfield and tend to Grandma, Gramps always made sure he was there to support his grandson. The sense of joy and relief I felt to see his car sitting in our driveway when I pulled in after a game was indescribable. I would walk into the house, my green equipment bag slung over my shoulder, and be greeted with a cheerful, "Hey Tommy, you really played a good game tonight!" from Gramps in the living room. I never felt like I played especially well in any game—there was always room for improvement—but hearing Gramps say those words had a calming effect on me on a variety of levels. Gramps would then detail particular plays I made in the game, basically bragging to me about me. I always focused on the plays I didn't make—I never wanted to get complacent—but it was nice hearing Gramps' kind, sincere words nonetheless. Gramps is on the short list of people in my life that I know were one hundred percent in my corner one hundred percent of the time. He was a special, special man.

The fall of 1985 was also a rite of passage for me in another sense: Just a decade earlier, Grandma and Grandpa would take me to see Uncle Jimmy's football games at Field High School in Brimfield. Those games were a big deal to me. As a youngster, I idolized Uncle Jimmy. He was everything I wanted to be when I grew up: Tough, resilient and well-respected by his peers. Uncle Jimmy played center and linebacker for the Field Falcons, and he was like a raging bull on the field. He wasn't especially big, but he was intense, aggressive and strong as an ox, just a rugged country boy. I've never been as strong or as tough as he is, even though I grew to actually be a little bigger than him. When I was in my early twenties, I worked on a pole-building crew with Uncle Jimmy and saw him easily lift construction materials that I could barely budge—and that's back when I lifted weights and worked out on a regular basis. I was lean and mean, in the prime of my life, and I had not closed the strength gap on Uncle Jimmy one iota; in fact, it somehow had actually widened. He was made from different stuff than I was; when it came to Uncle Jimmy and Gramps, the apple didn't fall far from the tree at all.

I knew from painful experience just how intense and aggressive Uncle Jimmy could be, because he and I often played one-on-one backyard football and basketball against each other. If it sounds like an outstanding high school football player against a little nine-year-old boy wouldn't be much of a match, you would be spectacularly correct. And if you think he took it easy on me because of that size and age disparity, you would be spectacularly wrong. I was the little brother he never had, and he took full advantage of his opportunity. I was often treated to mouthfuls of elbows, knees and forearms as he tucked the football and plowed into me, nearly leaving shoe prints on various parts of my body as I crashed to the ground. The same thing happened when we played basketball in Grandma and Grandpa's driveway. Just like in our football games, he held nothing back. He would drive hard to the basket and barrel into me with shoulders that felt like granite blocks, sending me sprawling to the asphalt as he laid the ball up and in—and then call me for the foul. When I had the ball, I would dribble with my back to him to shield the basketball from his spider-like reach, which of course never worked; he would grab for the ball like he had just found a suitcase full of money, knocking me to the ground—and then call me for traveling. I was surprised I still had any teeth left each time we were done playing. But I always came back for more, because I loved it. I loved sports, and I wanted to be strong and tough like Uncle Jimmy someday, so what better way to get strong and tough like Uncle Jimmy than to experience it up close and personal? And boy did I ever.

CLAR CLAR'S FIRST VISITATION

By the fall of 1985, Gramps had gone from packing his little grandson into the car and driving him to Uncle Jimmy's high school football games at Field, to (a decade later) driving to his then seventeen-year-old grandson's high school football games at Mogadore—which just happens to be Field's archrival. I vividly remember going to Uncle Jimmy's games against Mogadore and vehemently rooting against the team for which I would later play. All five of Grandma and Grandpa's children were Field High School graduates—Mom played basketball, ran track and was a majorette there—so I grew up viewing Mogadore as the great villain. And now, here I was playing for them—since I was eight years old, no less (Yes, I rooted against Mogadore when they played Uncle Jimmy's Field teams, even though I was in the Mogadore Youth Football program by that time. Blood truly is thicker than water). But what should have been a wonderful time for my family was instead one of great sadness because of Grandma's heartbreaking battle with cancer.

That sadness turned into a deep melancholy one morning in October 1985 when I awoke from a disturbing "dream," which I knew was no dream at all: It was a visitation from Clar Clar, who had been dead eight years by this time. In this visitation, I was at Dee Dee and Clar Clar's house in Kenmore, sitting in the living room watching TV when suddenly Clar Clar walked into the room, wearing navy-blue slacks and a button-down green sweater. I was acutely aware that Clar Clar was dead and this shouldn't be happening. We made eye contact; I was too stunned to speak for several moments, trying to rectify in my head how it was that my deceased grandfather could be standing not ten feet away from me in his house. At best, it was too good to be true; more than that, though, it was impossible. But there he was.

Still in shock, I finally managed a few words.

"Clar Clar, what are you doing here? Aren't you dead?" I asked.

He didn't say a word. Instead, he just stood there and looked at me for a few more moments before heading back toward the kitchen (the direction from which he had come), where Dee Dee had prepared one of her family-famous breakfasts of bacon and eggs, toast and orange juice. I immediately got up off the couch and followed Clar Clar out to the kitchen, wondering what was going on; I was still stunned to see him and thought maybe I had imagined his presence in the living room or had dozed off and dreamt it. He couldn't possibly be there in the house with Dee Dee and me when he was, well, dead.

I turned the corner from the living room to the kitchen, and there he was! Clar Clar was sitting in his usual spot at the circular table in the small, cramped kitchen. The table was always pushed against one wall, with Clar Clar's place being the chair on the far side of the table opposite the wall, giving his spot a "head of the table" look. He had already begun eating his breakfast by the time I reached the kitchen. Dee Dee, as usual, scurried about the kitchen while cheerfully humming along to tunes from the 1940s that emanated from a small radio that sat atop the island counter separating the sink area from the table and stove. The whole scene was happy, surreal and perplexing all at the same time. I knew Clar Clar shouldn't be there—it was impossible for him to be there—yet there he was, as real as could be, as if his death eight years before never happened.

I was confused, but I decided to just go with it. I sat at the chair to Clar Clar's right, with the wall to my right. I couldn't take my eyes off him, studying him intently as we silently ate our breakfast while Dee Dee continued to hum along to the radio. He and I didn't make eye contact as we ate, Clar Clar instead concentrating on his plate and staring straight ahead at the wall as he chewed his food. This wasn't unusual; Clar Clar was never very chatty while he ate. To be honest, he wasn't much of a conversationalist, period; he was a quiet, reflective man and somewhat shy, preferring to remain in the shadows (I remember watching an old black-and-white movie with Clar Clar on the living room couch one day and him pointing to a barely visible character sitting way in the back in the scene, his right index finger pressed against the television screen where the guy sat, and saying: "If I was in this movie, I'd rather be this guy than one of the main stars. I'd rather be in the background where no one could see me." Yes, he would). Clar Clar's silence at the breakfast table gave me a good opportunity to size him up and get used to the fact that he was really sitting right next to me.

I noticed that he looked exactly as he did at the end of his life in 1977 (at least, what I had thought was the end of his life), his thinning, graying hair slicked straight back and his eyes and face appearing tired. Unlike his two children—my dad and Uncle Denny—Clar Clar generally looked older than his age (which contributed almost exclusively to my impression as a boy that sixty-three was a ripe old age). Despite his fatigued appearance in the visitation, though, Clar Clar otherwise appeared happy; he was enjoying breakfast with his wife and grandson, and I was enjoying having my grandfather back—even if I couldn't figure out how.

Dee Dee also appeared as she did in 1977, looking young and vibrant at age fifty-six, her platinum blonde hair falling to just above her shoulders. Unlike Dee Dee and Clar Clar, however, I was not the age I would have been in 1977 (nine); instead, I was seventeen, my age at the time of this visitation. This had an interesting effect for me: In life, I only got to experience Clar Clar through the eyes of a young boy, but in this visitation, I got to experience him from the perspective of a teenager who was close to becoming an adult—a very compelling dynamic.

After breakfast, the three of us made our way to the living room and settled down for a peaceful day together. It was just like in the 1970s: Clar Clar watching TV and laughing on the couch (he had a loud, unique HEE-HEE-HEE-HEE laugh when something was particularly funny), playing the piano, Dee Dee smiling and humming her way around the house, and me soaking it all in. I soon relaxed and thought I must have dreamt that Clar Clar had died. A huge sense of relief washed over me upon this realization, and the three of us went about the day as we always did. I rarely was happier and more relaxed than when I was at Dee Dee and Clar Clar's when I was growing up, and this day was no different. All was right with the world—again.

As night fell, Clar Clar momentarily went into their bedroom to change into his customary bedtime clothes: A white T-shirt and gray boxers. Earlier in the day, I had noticed a closed black briefcase sitting on the arm of the couch in the living room, the latched end of the briefcase facing the length of the couch. I had no idea who put it there or what was inside it; all I knew was that the briefcase wasn't there at breakfast time, because I had to walk past that end of the couch to get to the kitchen and it wasn't there then. It just seemed to show up at some point during the day. I couldn't pinpoint when because I didn't actually see someone set it there, but neither Dee Dee nor Clar Clar had paid any attention to it so I didn't ask why it was there. It seemed to me like an odd place to leave a briefcase, but since nobody was sitting at that end of the couch, it wasn't necessarily in anyone's way. The briefcase had sat in that same spot the entire day, and it was still there when Clar Clar came back out to the living room in his night clothes. I was sitting at the other end of the couch watching TV, and Clar Clar, growing tired by this point, decided to lie down at the opposite end, his head resting on the pillow inches below the briefcase. Why doesn't he just move the briefcase out of his way? I wondered.

Instead, he slid his head down rather far on the pillow to avoid it. Odd, but I soon turned my attention back to the television. Clar Clar didn't normally fall asleep on the couch, but I got the sense he was beginning to doze off as we watched TV. He was lying on his back, eyes closed, his hands clasped over his abdomen. It was comforting beyond words to have my beloved grandfather back with me, when I thought I would never see him again. I was completely at peace.

Suddenly, I heard a loud, metallic "click" sound to my left, startling me out of my tranquility. I looked over, and one of the two latches on the front of the briefcase had flung up. I didn't know how this was possible: Clar Clar seemed to be sleeping, so no one could have touched it. Maybe it wasn't fastened all the way and just slipped, I thought. After staring at the briefcase for a few moments, I went back to watching TV.

About a minute later, I heard another sickeningly loud "click"—the other latch had popped up. Both latches couldn't have been loose at the same time, I thought. Something was wrong; briefcase latches don't open by themselves. Plus, the sound they made wasn't normal at all; it was way too loud and sounded like they were made of thick steel, similar to the sound of jail-cell doors latching closed. No way should these small metal latches be loud enough to echo throughout the house when they pop open, I thought. But they were— and they indeed were opening by themselves.

The sound of the second latch opening woke Clar Clar from his sleep. He looked at me, terrified, as the two latches remained ominously flipped up in the "open" position above his head. Clar Clar lay on his back, motionless, his eyes wide in sheer fright. Then, the lid of the briefcase slowly began to open—again, on its own—and Clar Clar turned his head and craned his neck to look up at it, fear still etched across his face. Instinctively, I jumped off the couch and stood a few feet away from it, unsure of what was going to happen next.

The solitude of the evening had abruptly turned into sheer horror as the briefcase continued to slowly open, revealing nothing but a gaping, black void inside—identical to the dark, blank cavity inside the hood of the Grim Reaper as portrayed in illustrations and movies. I was overcome with dread and began to feel physically ill, like I might vomit.

Suddenly, Clar Clar began to wail as the lid of the briefcase opened higher and higher. There was still nothing but seemingly infinite blackness inside the briefcase. And that's when it hit me: This *was* the Grim Reaper, death itself disguised as a harmless, non-descript briefcase throughout the day. And it had come for Clar Clar.

I felt increasingly nauseous as Clar Clar's mournful wails grew louder. Dee Dee rushed into the living room in a panic. "Clarance, what's wrong?! What's happening?!" she asked frantically as she looked down at the disturbing scene on the couch. He didn't answer, instead continuing to wail as the briefcase now yawned wide open. Our glorious day together had turned into a nightmare. The air in the room seemed to thicken and the lighting dimmed, giving the scene a murky feel. I could still see everything in the room, but not nearly as well as before.

Suddenly, his body began to be dragged into the dark void of the open briefcase as Dee Dee shrieked. "NOOOOO! NOOOOOOO!" Clar Clar cried, his arms and legs flailing as he fought against the unseen force. His head disappeared into the briefcase as his body desperately thrashed about on the couch. But resistance was futile; in a matter of moments Clar Clar was gone, swallowed completely by the blackness of the briefcase. Swallowed by death.

I awoke with a start, the emotional intensity of the dream forcing me back into a conscious state. I was perspiring, my body spent. I felt a sense of impending doom as I lay in my bed, because I knew this had been no dream: It was Clar Clar coming to warn me that Grandma's passing was imminent. Clar Clar had been the last family member to die, eight years earlier, and he was preparing me for the next death.

He had come to tell me that Grandma was being called "home." Grandma had been battling cancer for more than a year at that point, going through the usual, terrible ups and downs that come with the disease, but there was nothing to really indicate that her passing would be any time soon.

Nothing, that is, except for Clar Clar's dire warning to me.

Grandma died a couple weeks later.

Grandma passed away on Friday morning, Nov. 1, 1985. Our football team had a game that night at Crestwood High School in Mantua, Ohio, our last regular-season game before the state playoffs started the following week. I wasn't sure of Mogadore High School's policy on players being eligible to play in a game if they did not attend school the same day. Mom drove me down to the high school that morning, well after classes had begun at 8 a.m., and I set about locating our head coach in the building as Mom waited in the car in the school parking lot. I had no intention of attending class that day. I was in no emotional state to do so, and if that meant I couldn't play that night, then so be it. When I found our coach in the school, I explained the situation to him and asked if I could still play in our game that night without attending school that day. "Of course you can, no problem, Tommy," he said. "You do what you need to do with your family and we'll see you tonight." He expressed his condolences for Grandma, and with that I left the building and walked back to the car.

It was going to be a long day. And night.

When Mom, Dad and I arrived at Grandma and Grandpa's house in Brimfield, most of the family was already there. I was a mess. Grandma was such a special woman, she had been like another mother to me, and losing her was a punch to my soul. I sat in the living room sobbing into my hands when Gramps came over to me. He was, as usual, a rock, the patriarch of the family holding it together in this sad time.

"Pick your head up, Tommy. She wouldn't want to see you like this," he said.

"I don't think I'm going to play tonight, Gramps," I said. "They said I could even though I'm not in school today, but I just can't."

Gramps looked at me, his brow slightly furrowed. "You'd better play tonight," he said. "She isn't going to like it if you miss that game because of her. She would want you to play."

I knew he was right. Grandma wouldn't want her grandson to miss his team's football game on account of her. So I decided to play. For her.

First, however, we had to drive to the hospital in Ravenna, where Grandma had passed early that morning. The hospital staff took us up to her room, where Grandma still lay in her bed. This shocked me; I had naturally assumed that her room would have been vacant by this point. While Gramps stood by the bed speaking with hospital personnel, the family one by one said goodbye to Grandma. It was a rough scene, as you would imagine. When my turn came,

I walked over to the bed and stood there for a moment, looking at my poor grandmother's lifeless body.

What God would do this to such a wonderful woman? I thought. It's not fair and it's not right. Where was God when you really needed Him? Apparently not with Grandma. She had suffered horribly. No loving God would allow that to happen, right?

Mom, her voice quaking, said, "Give your Grandma a kiss goodbye, Tommy." I bent down, nearly unable to see because of the tears in my eyes, and gently kissed her on the cheek. "Goodbye, Grandma. I love you," I said softly. Heady stuff for a seventeen-year-old.

Later that day, I went to the Mogadore fieldhouse to begin preparations to board the team bus and head north through Portage County to Crestwood High School in Mantua. When I got to the fieldhouse, I was greeted with condolences by several of my teammates. Our coach had told the team about Grandma's passing, and I was truly touched by their outpouring of support. One of the beautiful things about being a part of the Mogadore football program was the fact that we were a family, and a time like this really illustrated that fact.

I sat alone on the team bus, staring out the window as we made our way to Crestwood, living inside my head and not really paying attention to anything inside the bus or outside the window—until I realized the bus was passing the very hospital where I had said goodbye to Grandma several hours earlier.

I stared at the building as we drove by. And suddenly felt very alone.

I shouldn't have. While on the field for pregame warmups, I glanced into our stands and noticed Mom and Gramps there. Through it all, Mom having just lost her own mother and Gramps his wife of forty-plus years, there they were, in the hinterlands of Portage County, to support me.

Our team was 9-0 and ranked No. 1 in the state. Crestwood was 0-9. But you wouldn't have known it early in the game because we only led the young, gritty Red Devils 12-6 after the first quarter. I just couldn't get my head in the game. All I could think of was Grandma. I missed a couple tackles and couldn't get off blocks. I was just going through the motions.

At one point, my close friend Glenn, who played next to me on the defensive line, walked over to me following a play and said, "What's the matter with you?"

"I can't stop thinking about my grandma," I said.

"Well, you need to get in the game. We need you," he replied.

Glenn's words took me back to that morning, when Gramps had said Grandma wouldn't like it if I missed the game because of her. I knew she also wouldn't like it if I played poorly because of her. I looked up into the night sky and stared for a moment at the nearly full moon that hung over Jack Lambert Stadium. "I love you Grandma," I whispered.

And with that, it was time to play football—the right way. I ended up with a fumble recovery as we eventually found our footing and won 54-12 to finish an undefeated regular season and claim the Associated Press Class A poll state championship.

Grandma would have been pleased.

Check that. I know she was pleased. Because when I had stared up at the moon for those few moments during the game, I could feel her staring back at me from above. She was with me.

And she would be with me again.

Many years after her death, Grandma paid me her first and only visit. One of my favorite things to do when I stayed the weekend at Grandma and Grandpa's house was to shoot baskets in the driveway. I would be out there by myself for hours, playing games like H-O-R-S-E, 21 (Around the World), or just shooting around. Being an only child, doing things alone was never a problem. I had learned to entertain myself at an early age and had come to relish my alone time. So shooting baskets by myself in their driveway was just fine with me.

The biggest challenge, actually, was to try to not miss a shot so badly that the ball went crashing through one of the two tall house windows that were situated several feet behind the backboard. There were many times when, in my youthful exuberance, I would launch a shot a good thirty feet from the hoop; these long-range bombs usually hit nothing but the driveway asphalt short of the basket—and would promptly bounce with enough force that the ball carried right into one of the two windows. I could usually tell when the ball was going to be well short of the rim and would immediately take off after it, knowing it was headed for the windows on one bounce, but I usually arrived too late to do anything but watch—and cringe—as ball hit glass. I would wait for the window to shatter and send glass shards flying into the house and onto the driveway, but miraculously it never happened. The ball would bounce high off the driveway, soar through the air and bang against the window, then drop harmlessly back to the driveway—much to my great relief. The last thing I wanted to do was explain to Grandma that I shattered her window because I stupidly tried to shoot the ball from three-quarters of the way down her driveway. How these windows never broke is beyond me.

GRANDMA'S VISITATION

Shooting baskets in their driveway served as the backdrop for Grandma's visitation, which began with me alone in their driveway on a beautiful summer day. From time to time, I noticed Gramps occasionally stepping outside and puttering around the big cement porch that stretched across the front of the house; I couldn't tell exactly what he was doing, but he never seemed to stay outside long, going back into the house after a few minutes each time. Other than Gramps' occasional appearance on the porch—during which he never acknowledged me (he seemed preoccupied with whatever it was he was doing)—it was just me out there.

It was the height of summer in Northeast Ohio: The grass, shrubbery and trees were green and lush, and puffy white clouds floated lazily through a deep-blue sky as birds chirped merrily in the background. It was a Chamber of Commerce-type day. I became lost in my own little world, dribbling, shooting, rebounding, making moves against nobody, driving to the basket, putting up a variety of shots. I don't know how long I was out there, but it felt like a while. It was a warm day and I was perspiring.

At one point, the ball caromed hard off the rim and went bounding down the long asphalt driveway. I chased after it and managed to catch up to it before it rolled into the road. I scooped it up on the dead run about fifteen feet from the road, stopped and turned back toward the house, my head down as I slowly dribbled the ball back up the driveway. When I looked up after several seconds of dribbling, I was greeted by an amazing—and impossible—sight:

Grandma!

I did a double-take; it startled me to see her just sitting there so casually. She was sitting in a folding lawn chair in the front yard, just a couple feet to the left of the driveway, about fifteen feet or so from the front porch. Her chair was set up in such a manner that she was facing the road, so she was looking right at me when I picked my head up as I dribbled the ball back toward the house. I hadn't noticed her earlier, and I wondered how she could have possibly been there without me seeing her, considering how close she was to the driveway and how long I had been out there shooting baskets. There's no way I could have missed her. But she also couldn't have come out of the house and set up a lawn chair that far into the yard in the few seconds it took me to retrieve the basketball. It just didn't make sense.

Then it struck me: None of this should be happening, because it wasn't possible. Grandma had passed away the better part of twenty years earlier. How she could just casually be sitting there in a lawn chair in her yard, when I knew full well she was deceased, was an absolute mystery. What's more, she looked strong, vibrant and healthy—unlike her appearance during much of her yearlong fight against cancer, when the disease ravaged her body to the point that by the time she died, the family chose to have the casket closed at her services (a common practice for deceased cancer victims). Grandma didn't look like Grandma, and it would not have been dignified to have an open casket.

Here, though, sitting in that lawn chair in the yard, Grandma looked great, appearing as she did when I was a young boy. She was smiling at me, almost as if she was amused that I had just now noticed her sitting there in plain sight.

Grandma was dressed in her customary summer garb: A loose-fitting, buttoned-down short-sleeve top, white with a pattern of blue markings throughout the shirt. The markings were supposed to be something, but I couldn't make out what they were. Birds maybe, or flowers. She was wearing purple shorts, short white socks that came up just past her ankles, and grayish tennis shoes. She was leaning back in the lawn chair, her forearms resting length-wise along each arm rest of the chair, her hands clasping the ends of the arm rests, wearing a big smile on her face as she soaked up the picture-perfect day.

"Grandma, what are you doing here?!" I exclaimed, staring at her incredulously as I cradled the ball in the crook of my arm. I was standing maybe ten feet from her.

"What am I doing here? I live here," she said matter-of-factly, still smiling.

My mind tried to process that revelation: *I live here.* How? I remembered her services that gloomy November morning at the funeral home in Kent, then the chilly, rain-soaked final goodbye at the cemetery in Brimfield; I had stared blankly at my grandmother's coffin that sat on the supports above the freshly dug hole in the ground, trying to stay warm and dry under the awning that stretched over the gravesite as the rain fell around us. *"This is just how funerals are in the movies, cold and rainy,"* I remembered thinking, *"only this is real."* This is the day we had all feared for the better part of a year, and now it was here. Grandma was gone.

Only she wasn't. Now, she was sitting in front of me, full of life. In fact, she looked as good as I had ever seen her.

"But Grandma, you're supposed to be dead," I said, ashamed that I even had to say it. But it was true.

In an instant, her smile changed from a broad grin into the kind of gentle, loving, soul-penetrating smile that a grandmother reserves only for her grandchild. "Oh, I'm not dead, Tommy," she said with conviction. "I'm always here."

Before I could respond, her visit ended. I woke up, my heart pounding. I was drained. This had been no dream; Grandma had come to tell me she was OK. As it turns out, this was (so far) her only visit to me, but it would not be the last time I heard the words "I'm always here" in a visitation.

It also wouldn't be the last time I received a visit from one of my mom's parents.

CHAPTER 4

GRAMPS

I have never met anyone quite like my Uncle Denny, my dad's younger brother and only sibling, or my grandfather Ray Willoughby—"Gramps" as he was known in the family—my mom's dad. These two men were special. Special human beings, and special to me. Both men, now deceased, left an indelible impression on my life that will last to my own dying day.

I have mentioned Gramps in a periphery sense earlier, but I will formally introduce you to him now. I think you're going to like him. A lot.

I will start with this: As with Clar Clar, Gramps also looked "presidential" so to speak, bearing a rather strong resemblance to President Gerald Ford. Again, like with Clar Clar and President Lyndon Johnson, Gramps and President Ford couldn't pass for identical twins, but they could have certainly passed for siblings. And like President Ford, Gramps had a quiet dignity about him, a way of commanding respect and commanding a room almost without saying a word. Gramps did not put on airs.

But he could put on a comedy routine—without realizing it. Plainly put, Gramps was a character who had great character. He had an uncanny knack for being absolutely hilarious when he wasn't even remotely trying to be. Just his mannerisms, his facial expressions and his brutally honest comments were enough to send me into fits of laughter. The sight of Gramps' face buried in his hands as he shook his head, then muttering "Christ" as he pulled his hands away in response to either something someone had said or a situation he could barely tolerate was priceless. Sometimes it was just one hand cupped over his forehead, thus exposing just enough of his face to see the twisted anguish stretched across it—but the message clearly was the same: He would rather be anywhere but there at that very moment. And my reaction would also be the same: laughter. Either out loud or a muffled snicker as I cast a knowing glance at others in the room, who also had spotted Gramps' unwittingly funny histrionics.

Gramps also had an extremely hip sense of humor for an "old codger," a term he often used to describe himself. At one family function, an aunt and uncle of mine were talking about their upcoming vacation and bemoaning the fact that one of their teenage sons was not able to go due to prior commitments. But the good news was their son would be able to take care of the house while they were gone. "He'll be here watching the house for two weeks, just him and his girlfriend," my aunt said cheerfully. "They'll have a ball."

"Yeah," Gramps deadpanned, "a couple of them."

That's the kind of thing I mean.

While Gramps was trying to be funny with that comment—and honest because, let's face it, a teenage boy and his girlfriend having the run of his parents' house for two weeks in the summer has hijinks written all over it—he was at his funniest without intending humor whatsoever. There was a particular Christmas when Gramps was showing my mom some of the presents he had bought for family members, uncertain how these gifts would be received by said family members. Finally, after several minutes of going back and forth on whether he had done well or not with the gift buying, Gramps waved his arms in front of himself dismissively, the way a coach or fan would protest an official's bad call against their team—a trademark Gramps gesture—and said, "If they don't like it, the hell with them."

The quip was an instant family classic, repeated especially often by Mom and me.

At another family function, Gramps was sitting at a table with several other people, enjoying a drink as he quietly took in the scene (he was low-key by nature). At some point, someone remarked how it was a cold night. "I'm going to need a nightcap when I go to bed," the person said, referring to the garment that people wore on their head at night to stay warm in the old days. Without missing a beat, Gramps raised his glass and declared to the entire table, "Here's my nightcap," and promptly took a big swig of his drink.

Gramps even poked fun at death. Grandma and Grandpa's grave plot is at the back of the cemetery in Brimfield, adjacent to a golf course that is separated from the cemetery by a tree line. While visiting Grandma's grave one day, Gramps—an avid golfer—pointed at his name on the headstone, looked over at the flag pin on the green that was just visible through the trees and declared, "Hey, this is the perfect spot. I can jump up and play a few holes whenever I want." Then he proceeded to playfully lie on his back on the grass in front of his side of the headstone, simulating himself in his grave with his eyes closed and arms folded over his chest, and asked one of us to take his picture in that macabre pose.

No one volunteered, but it was vintage Gramps. Always a realist.

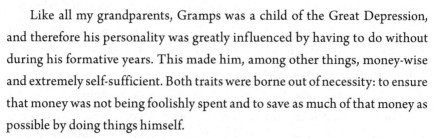

Like all my grandparents, Gramps was a child of the Great Depression, and therefore his personality was greatly influenced by having to do without during his formative years. This made him, among other things, money-wise and extremely self-sufficient. Both traits were borne out of necessity: to ensure that money was not being foolishly spent and to save as much of that money as possible by doing things himself.

And Gramps could do a whole lot of things himself. He was extremely good with his hands, able to build and repair seemingly anything and everything—a gene that skipped right past me. He just knew how to fix things, and if he didn't know how to fix something at first, his mind would immediately go to work figuring out the problem and he would have the object fixed in short order. Gramps wasn't an engineer and he didn't possess a college degree, but he understood angles, measurements and physical properties better than any engineer I've ever met. The man was sharp as a tack.

That included his golden years. Gramps was virtually ageless: The years ticked by and the number of candles on his birthday cake increased every twelve months, but he never really seemed to get older. His appearance stayed remarkably the same. He was rarely, if ever, sick. He had boundless energy. He was always on ladders, painting, cleaning out the eaves, walking around on the roof of his house checking things out, doing strenuous yard work, fixing things around his house and the houses of friends and family. You name it, Gramps was working on it or fixing it with the acumen and stamina of a man half his age or younger.

And he wasn't just physically robust; he was mentally sharp as well. He could recall details from his childhood with amazing clarity, he could recount decades-old events as if they had happened the day before, and he had an otherworldly attentiveness to detail. He kept immaculate weather records, complete with a "weather station" perched just outside the side door of his house that he checked daily. Gramps never spent a day inside a college classroom, but he was without question one of the most intelligent human beings I ever met. Life was Gramps' college. He was a wise man who accumulated knowledge through experience and necessity—which is why his mind worked like that of an engineer's. He had an innate understanding of how things worked, why they didn't work and how to fix them. Only he didn't need advanced mathematical formulas to figure it all out; he could just hold the item in his hands and eyeball it and know what needed to be done.

He and Grandma had five children—my mom was the middle child—and I was the first grandchild on that side of the family by a couple months. Gramps wasn't like another father to me; he *was* another father to me. With only a nine-year age difference between me and Uncle Jimmy, Grandma and Grandpa's youngest child, I often felt like the sixth Willoughby kid. I was certainly treated that way. When I spent weekends at their country home in Brimfield as a young boy, I was raised the same way my mother and her siblings had been raised: with tender love mixed with discipline. That discipline was not heavy-handed, it was more of an understanding—a clear understanding—of what was and what was not tolerated. Grandma and Grandpa were in charge and you knew it, but it wasn't like they ruled their house with an iron fist and meted out discipline when you crossed an inch over the line. The line was laid out well in advance, it was a fair line and you knew exactly where the line was located. If you still felt the need to cross it, then you deserved what you got (usually in the form of reduced privileges). That was your fault. Stupidity has its price.

Gramps was many things to me, and one of those things was my friend. My best friend. He was my buddy. Like I said before, Gramps was one of the very few people in my life who I knew was in my corner one-hundred percent of the time. Always. No matter what. He had his grandson's back. His love for me was unconditional. Gramps was in my corner come hell or high water; he was genuinely proud of me and genuinely believed in me. Without his love, faith and guidance, I would not be where I am today. I may not even be alive today, because he taught me what inner strength and fortitude truly are—not by what he said, but by how he lived his life. He demonstrated to me what it is to be a real man, and if I can come even remotely close to the example he set, then I'm doing all right.

Among Gramps' traits were compassion and ingenuity. Growing up in Northeast Ohio, I was naturally a fan of the Cleveland Indians baseball team. I loved going to Tribe games at old Cleveland Stadium, and especially enjoyed games that featured special promotions. Dad took me to Bat Day a couple times and some other promotional games, but one special game somehow eluded me every year: Helmet Day. I don't know how or why I never managed to attend this game as a youngster, but for some reason I didn't. I longed to own a shiny, dark blue Cleveland Indians batting helmet with the red bill. It became a holy grail of sorts to me. I always thought batting helmets were cool to begin with—I played baseball in Mogadore's Little League system in elementary school and loved how batting helmets looked and how they felt on my head—and owning a Tribe batting helmet (albeit the plastic kind they hand out to fans at the gate) became one of my first bucket list items.

After I missed Helmet Day yet again one year, Gramps took matters into his own hands. He modified a construction hard hat that he had in his back work room, spray-painting it blue and painting a red 'C' on the front. He added some cushioning on the inside and, voila, I finally had my very own Cleveland Indians batting helmet—and a lot sturdier than anything I would have gotten at a Helmet Day game. I proudly wore it whenever I ventured outside to hit baseballs in the expansive backyard at Grandma and Grandpa's house. The feel of that homemade Indians helmet snugly affixed to my head was indescribable. It was a simple gesture by Gramps, but it had an enormous impact on my life to this very day. One of my lifelong bucket list items is to drive to a Major League Baseball game at every existing ballpark in the country—I'm up to forty different stadiums at this point, having to repeat many cities because of old facilities being torn down and replaced by new ones—and my must-have souvenir at every ballpark is the batting helmet of the home team. As soon as Kim and I walk through a stadium gate, we make a beeline for the team store to get my batting helmet. And I'm pleased to say that after swinging and missing on Helmet Day every year as a boy, I am now the proud owner of three different styles of Cleveland Indians batting helmets: the classic crooked C, the standard block C, and Chief Wahoo.

Actually, four different styles. Gramps' homemade Tribe helmet was the first, and my favorite. I don't know whatever happened to that helmet, but it will forever live in my memory. It makes me smile every time I think of it—and so does Gramps. What a special man.

Gramps was rarely sick a day in his life. So it came as a huge surprise when I learned that he had had a medical emergency and was taken to the hospital. He had seemed genuinely indestructible up to that point. It was early November of 2003 and he was eighty-seven years old. Prior to that moment, he was actually in better shape than I was, and I was thirty-five. By that time I had undergone three surgeries on my left knee, been diagnosed with epilepsy when I was eighteen, had suffered a fractured wrist at age nine, a broken leg at age fifteen, and survived a burst appendix and subsequent emergency appendectomy when I was nineteen. The surgeon surmised that my appendix had been burst for up to five days; it was literally in tatters when he removed it. A couple days after the surgery, he told me—while I lay in utter agony in my hospital bed—that my situation could be fatal if the toxins had spread throughout my body. He wouldn't know for sure until he received test results, he said. I honestly thought I was a dead man, and the next couple days were pure mental hell, wondering if I was going to die in that hospital. Thankfully, the test results showed that the surgery had been a complete success and I'm obviously still here, but by age thirty-five my body had been put through the proverbial wringer.

Not Gramps, though. He was the picture of health. It was shocking if he had so much as a sniffle. So when I learned that his medical emergency had been a "mild" heart attack, you could have knocked me over with a feather. A heart attack? Gramps? Nah, that couldn't be right.

But it was. Gramps' body was beginning to show the kind of wear and tear that usually befalls normal human beings much earlier in life. His heart was giving out. He eventually had several of these "minor" heart attacks (of course, it's always minor when it happens to someone else, right?), and these cardiac episodes began to take their toll and wear his body out. He went back and forth between the hospital and nursing home for about two and a half months. The family kept waiting for the doctors to give Gramps the all-clear to go home, but it never came. He just wasn't well enough and strong enough for home care.

But while on the inside his heart was wearing out, on the outside his demeanor didn't change all that much. Yes, he was noticeably thinner, a product of a loss of appetite (which, in turn, was the product of a loss of taste), but other than that, he was vintage Gramps: getting perturbed watching his beloved Cleveland Browns—complete with the trademark exasperated waving of his hands at the TV—and wisecracking to anyone who would listen, up to and including hospital and nursing home staff. Every time I went to visit him, his disposition seemed pretty much unchanged. He was upbeat and cheerful, his eyes always lighting up the instant he saw Kim and me walk into his room and greeting us with his customarily chipper "Hello there!" (pronouncing the word "there" in two syllables as "thayah"). To me, for the most part he seemed to be holding his own, and I even thought there was a chance he could be released to go home any day. Since he had not suffered a singular major cardiac event, I hoped that meant his body was winning the battle.

Death did not seem imminent; if anything, from what I could tell, Gramps could maintain this status quo indefinitely. Years, perhaps.

So when I went to bed in the early morning hours of Friday, January 30, 2004, I did so with the expectation that I would wake up to the same thing I had awoken to since early November: no changes and Gramps continuing to hold his own.

And with that, I drifted off to sleep. But this time, I had company.

GRAMPS' VISITATION

I was shocked to see him looking so good.

It was Gramps, to be sure, but it wasn't the Gramps I had seen the last few months in the nursing home and hospital, his body appearing fragile and vulnerable for the first time in my life. It was a jolt to my senses seeing him in that state, because Gramps always seemed to have atomic energy, constantly on the go. It was as if Gramps had found Ponce de Leon's elusive Fountain of Youth, and it wasn't in the Bahamas or Florida, it was in Brimfield. Even in his eighties, Gramps had no intention whatsoever of just puttering around the house and slowly withering away. There was life to be lived, and Gramps was going to live it to the fullest—just as Grandma had. Following the onset of his heart issues in November 2003, however, Gramps finally started to look his age.

Now, though, he looked strong, vibrant and happy. He was even sporting a broad smile.

I'm not sure where we were, or if we were even there together. We may have been, or it may have just been Gramps there alone and I was able to see him through some window or portal connecting my dimension to his; it was hard to tell one way or the other. Either way, I didn't recognize the place; it was jet-black dark, and the only thing in it was Gramps (or me with him; again, it's hard to say). It was just somewhere in space and time. In fact, it looked a lot like space— minus anything in it. Despite this impenetrable darkness, Gramps was fully illuminated—by what, I couldn't tell; there was no light anywhere. It was as if Gramps himself was the light, and his entire body was clearly visible. He was wearing the red pajamas Kim and I had bought him while he was in the nursing home, and he seemed to be floating in place looking at me; I say floating because wherever he was—wherever we were—appeared to be infinite. There were no discernible edges or boundaries, no walls, no ceiling, no floor, just unending darkness. So I assumed he was floating because there was nothing for him to actually stand on, although he was in a standing position, facing me. His entire body was moving, but only slightly, adding to my feeling that he was floating.

I instinctively knew this was a visitation.

"Hi, Tommy!" Gramps exclaimed, a wide smile stretched across his face. The cheerful greeting and his facial expression were identical to how he would receive me when my parents dropped me off at his and Grandma's house for the weekend when I was a boy. Gramps would wait on the front porch as our car pulled into the driveway, and as I walked toward the front porch, Gramps—usually wearing a T-shirt and slacks—would smile and exclaim, "Hi, Tommy!" as I approached him. This was that, only he wasn't in Brimfield, Ohio. He wasn't even on Earth. He was just … somewhere. Somewhere I could see and hear him, somewhere I may even have been with him.

"Hi, Gramps," I answered, unsure of what was happening. He looked robust, like he had before his series of heart attacks. I knew this shouldn't be the case, considering his condition the last few months. He couldn't possibly have improved to this point so quickly. His color was great, his eyes sparkled, his voice was strong. It was refreshing to see him looking like his old self again, even if I didn't know how it was possible.

After what I guessed were several seconds of Gramps looking at me, he finally spoke.

"I've come to say goodbye, Tommy," he said in his trademark Gramps drawl, still smiling. This caught me off guard. Goodbyes were usually melancholy events, not happy ones.

"Gramps, you can't go anywhere. Your heart is in bad shape," I told him, surprised that he would even entertain the thought.

He gazed at me for a few moments, then, with a twinkle in his eye, Gramps said confidently, "Where I'm going, my heart will be all better."

He continued to smile at me for a few seconds, then he was gone. I was alone, either in this dark, empty void to infinity or gazing into it somehow. Gramps had vanished right in front of my eyes. I didn't actually see him go anywhere, he was just there in front of me and then he wasn't. No 'poof,' no slowly melting away, nothing. Just … gone.

His poignant message forced me to wake with a start. I was no longer in, or viewing, that dark emptiness; I was in our bed and the room was bathed in daylight. I lay there for a few moments, contemplating what I had just experienced.

And I knew.

"He's gone," I thought to myself. "He just told me goodbye. He's gone." I knew in my soul that Gramps had passed away.

I got out of bed and went downstairs to make my customary coffee. I checked the telephone in the kitchen and could see that there were several voice mails. They were all from my mom, calling from the nursing home. As I listened to them, each was more urgent than the last.

"Tommy, it's Mom. You need to get to the nursing home right now. Please hurry," she said.

Then the second voice mail. "Tommy, where are you? If you're sleeping you need to get up and come down here." She was beginning to sound angry that I wasn't responding, but I was sleeping and I couldn't hear the voice mail anyway. "Gramps isn't doing well. Please get down here." The nursing home was located just ten minutes away in the same town we lived in, Stow.

The third voice mail: "TOMMY, GET DOWN HERE RIGHT NOW. EVERYONE IS HERE EXCEPT YOU. WAKE UP AND GET DOWN HERE." Mom was downright angry now.

The fourth voice mail: "Tommy, please get down here. Hurry. Please." She sounded frightened.

The fifth voice mail: "He's gone, Tommy. Gramps passed away a few minutes ago. Please come down here as soon as you wake up." Mom was crying and her voice was faint, as if it took every ounce of energy to utter those words. Which I'm sure it did.

I looked at the time of that last voice mail. Mom had left it a few minutes before I had awoken—at precisely the same time that Gramps had come to tell me goodbye. I replayed his final words in my mind: "Where I'm going, my heart will be all better."

I knew, beyond any doubt, that Gramps had come to see me on his way to Heaven. It had not been a dream. The focus was too sharp, the interaction too logical, the information too contemporary to be the jumbled workings of the subconscious mind. I was the only member of the family that had been asleep at that time, in the dream state and therefore able to communicate astrally, so I was the one who received his visit.

"Goodbye, Gramps," I said out loud in the kitchen. "Thanks for that. I love you."

I went upstairs to get dressed and head down to the nursing home to be with Mom and the family, who were mourning Gramps' death at his bedside. It was going to be a long, sad day, but I was buoyed by Gramps' goodbye. For a few days, at least, it would be our little secret. It was my first and only "real time" visit, when my loved one came to me as they died and passed over to the other side, on the way to Heaven.

I wondered if, just for those few short moments with Gramps, I had been on the other side, too. I wondered if I had been close to Heaven during that brief visit. I wondered if, had Gramps' visitation lasted longer, I might actually have gotten to see Heaven, if the blackness in which we had been immersed would have given way to the magnificence of God's Kingdom.

And I wondered what that looked like.

Little did I know that I would find out soon enough.

Before concluding this chapter, it must be noted that Gramps did not believe in any kind of an afterlife. I guess that made him an atheist, although he mostly kept his views to himself rather than force them upon everyone else.

But when the topic came up, you knew where he stood on the issue of death.

For instance, I recall one time during such a conversation when Gramps said, "Go stand in the middle of the freeway and see who's looking out for you then. You'll be dead as a doornail."

I chewed on that for a little bit and couldn't deny the fact that he was absolutely right. If I were to go out and stand in the middle of Interstate 76 in

Akron, I would be in a morgue that same day. So, who *was* looking out for me? This is where the idea of free will comes in, of course, but Gramps' logic did seem to make some sense at the time.

In another instance, someone brought up the idea of Heaven and Gramps wasn't buying it. "I don't believe in any of that. I believe when you die, you're right there in the ground," he said, pointing downward at the floor as he made his point.

Gramps only made his views known when the topic came up. He was always respectful of how others felt and was careful not to gratuitously impose his viewpoint. But if others began doing that to him, he would cut them off at the pass.

"Anyone tells me to go to church," he'd say, "I'll tell them to go to Hell."

Of course, Gramps said all this with his customary unwitting humor. He was serious about what he said and how he felt, but the way he said it and his accompanying mannerisms were just plain funny and would cause those within earshot to smile and laugh.

Gramps just didn't like being preached to or made to feel guilty about the way he felt and what he believed. Despite some of his strong words on the subject, I always felt that Gramps was more agnostic than atheist. I think he absolutely believed what he said, but I also think that deep down, he wasn't entirely sure what came after death. He *believed* there was nothing afterward, but he wasn't *sure*.

I bring this up only because here was someone who was not what you would call a true believer in any sense, yet he went to Heaven and essentially told me so on his way there. This cements in my mind that his visitation was a real occurrence. Had he been someone of deep religious faith, it would have been easy for me to define him as such and for my subconscious mind to see him as such. But he wasn't, so the fact that he said what he said to me in the dream state is more evidence that the visitation was real. It's nothing that I would have expected to hear—or would have ever heard—come out of his mouth while he was alive.

Following his death, I was told that toward the end when he was bouncing back and forth between the nursing home and the hospital, Gramps had accepted

Jesus into his heart (I did not know this prior to his visitation). In fact, I did notice something of a change in his personality at that time, and one episode in particular had caught my attention. Gramps had served as a volunteer fireman with the Brimfield Fire Department, and growing up I remember several times when his dispatch radio would go off in the middle of the night with orders that there was an emergency somewhere and all personnel had to report to the fire station at once. A groggy Gramps, awoken out of a sound sleep, would climb out of bed and scurry about the house, collecting his boots, helmet, etc. and racing out the door in a matter of minutes. I was always fascinated with his boots and fire helmet and often proudly wore them around their house, my legs swimming in the big rubber boots and the red helmet swallowing up my entire head to the point that I could barely see out from under it. I thought his firefighting equipment was neat, and it made me feel like I had a little piece of Gramps every time I donned his boots and helmet and went stomping around the house. It was literally the uniform of a hero, the equipment Gramps wore to risk his life to save others.

Well, one night in December 2003, Kim and I presented him with his Christmas gift as he lay in his hospital bed in Ravenna: a small, red metallic fire truck with a little clock on one side of it. The truck was a collectible, maybe four inches long and a little over half that tall, and its finely detailed workmanship was impressive, highlighted by a silver ladder that ran the length of the top of the truck. We handed Gramps his present, and his eyes lit up the moment he unwrapped the package and saw the truck. He studied it intently as he held it gently in his fingers, spinning the little truck around to view it from all angles. Kim and I glanced at each other knowingly and smiled; it was obvious that the truck held sentimental value for him. We had done well.

He appeared to be deep in thought as he stared quizzically at the little truck in his hands. Physically, Gramps was in his hospital bed just a few feet away from us, but I sensed that his mind was miles—and decades—away from where he lay. I'm sure that fire truck represented many things to Gramps: his youth, his health, happier times before death had begun its grim attrition on the family, how much time had gone by since those happier days, and even the fact that his own time in this life was slipping away. Gramps had always been strong and vibrant, but he was at his peak during his days as a fireman. As a first responder, he had to be physically fit, mentally sharp, dedicated, brave and focused, able to perform tasks that the average person can't do. He had to make split-second decisions and put himself in harm's way without giving it a second thought in an effort to save life and property.

I wondered what he was thinking as he continued to twirl the little truck in his fingers. Gramps never talked much about what he saw and did on those emergency dispatch calls; at least I never heard of anything specifically. I hadn't given it much thought when I was younger, but as I grew older I often wondered about the things Gramps must have experienced on those calls: house fires where families lost everything, their lives shattered. Grisly fatal car accidents. People in hysterics, sobbing at the loss of their home as flames engulfed their house and lit up the night sky, or over the loss of a loved one whose body had just been pulled from the mangled wreckage of an automobile accident. To this day, I have never heard of any of Gramps' experiences on those calls, but I can only imagine how unpleasant they must have been and how he had to steel himself for what he knew he was about to encounter as he backed out of his driveway and headed to the fire station in those wee hours. There must have been a witches' brew of emotions churning within him: dread for what awaited him and his fellow firemen in the darkness; excitement as adrenaline coursed through his body, knowing he might soon be rushing into harm's way; sadness with the realization that someone's life was about to change forever, if it hadn't already. All while he was fatigued from not getting enough sleep yet still required to perform at his physical and mental best; after all, lives depended on it. But it's what he signed up for because Gramps loved to help people; it's just who he was. Whether painting a house, doing odds-and-ends repair work, serving as a volunteer fireman or crafting a homemade Cleveland Indians batting helmet for his grandson, Gramps enjoyed giving of himself to others. He was as selfless an individual as I have ever met.

While Gramps exhibited no outward emotion as he examined that little red fire truck, I could tell by his stoic reaction that internally he was deeply affected. Maybe he was thinking about certain instances, perhaps a particular fire or accident or victim or survivor that stood out above the others. Maybe that little red truck jarred his memory and it all came rushing back to him, or maybe it was already seared into his memory but he had compartmentalized the visuals in his mind over the years, and now the sight of the little red truck brought those memories out of the dark recesses of his mind. Maybe he was thinking of the people he had helped, scenes that he couldn't forget for better or for worse, some of the fire department's greatest successes or most bitter disappointments. And maybe that little red truck made him realize that he had done everything he could to make the world a better place, and that he was leaving it in better shape than he had found it.

As Gramps marveled at his gift, I couldn't help but think of a few things, too. I remembered all those joyous times of Christmases past, the big family dinners every year at Grandma and Grandpa's house on Christmas afternoon after we had opened our presents at home in the morning. The family get-togethers at their house on Christmas Day were a tradition; I couldn't remember a year when we didn't do it prior to Grandma's passing. They had presents for us to open, too, which extended the coveted gift-opening for just a while longer. After dinner in the dining room, everyone would retire to the living room to exchange presents, talk, watch television and even nap (you could almost set your watch to Dad falling asleep on the floor in front of the television within fifteen minutes). Gramps would take his customary spot by the hearth and alternate between passing out gifts and stoking the crackling fire next to him that served as a cozy backdrop for those cold, snowy Christmas nights in Northeast Ohio.

Back then, I thought those magical moments would last forever. But now I stood with my wife in a stark hospital room, gazing down upon my grandfather in what turned out to be his final days. This is what Christmas had become: an unspoken farewell, a goodbye to a man who was a true hero, who was my hero. For that very reason, though, Christmas 2003 was more poignant than all the others. Even though Gramps was in a hospital bed and the only sound in the room came from the television mounted on the wall, it was special nonetheless because it was just the three of us in that little room sharing what would be our final Christmas together. And watching him react to the little red fire truck with quiet introspection made it even more enduring.

"Thank you very much. What a nice gift," Gramps said without looking up, still holding the truck and inspecting it closely.

"You're welcome, Gramps," I said. "We thought you would like it."

Then, as he studied it for a few more moments, he said something I'll never forget:

"I'll have this forever."

Gramps died about a month later. Looking back, I realize now that Gramps knew he didn't have long at that point. His use of the word "forever" was telling, and the tone of his voice when he said that sentence chilled me even then. It sounded a bit off, like something wasn't quite right. He normally didn't talk in those terms, and as time went by I came to understand what he had really meant when he said "I'll have this forever": that he knew he was dying, and he would have that little red fire truck in his heart forever.

Following his death, Kim and I asked the family if we could have that little fire truck as a keepsake. And to this day, it is prominently displayed on a shelf on the entertainment center in our family room where I can see it every day.

My little piece of Gramps.

CHAPTER 5

UNCLE BILLY

D ee Dee and her two older brothers, my great uncles Bill and Gomer, were saints, members of the Greatest Generation who were raised to be kind, generous and respectful, traits that are sorely lacking in our society today. Dee Dee, Uncle Billy and Uncle Gomer were goodness personified. I never heard any of them utter a bad word about anybody, even those who would have richly deserved it. They saw the best in people, even cretins who didn't have a best. I never heard any of them even so much as raise their voice in anger. They were what all of us should strive to be.

They were special. Uncle Gomer had survived polio as a young boy, at a time when polio was as dreaded a disease as any on the planet. After retiring he was diagnosed with cancer, which eventually took his life in 1988. Not long before his death, I saw Uncle Gomer at the funeral service of a relative, and the following episode illustrates the kind of man he was. Uncle Gomer was battling cancer and relying heavily on a cane to get around, but all he wanted to talk about with me at the service was how my knee was doing following the surgery I had on it. When I tried to steer the conversation back to his own health, Uncle Gomer said, "Don't worry about me, Tommy, you take care of that knee," and proceeded to pepper me with questions about my prognosis. I eventually had three surgeries on the knee, an irrelevant happenstance considering that cancer took Uncle Gomer's life not long after our conversation at the funeral home. But that was Uncle Gomer, always putting others' needs and concerns above his own.

Dee Dee, the youngest of the three, was the last to die, passing away in September 2008. In between was Uncle Billy, the oldest, who died in 1995. Uncle Billy was a ray of light in this world, a man of unimpeachable scruples and a heart of gold. He once suffered a heart attack at a carnival—as a teenager—when he paid for an item and the carny took the money, then accused Uncle Billy of not giving him any money at all. Uncle Billy got neither the item nor his money back, and as he began to protest he was stricken with a heart attack. The episode at such a young age weakened his heart, which eventually contributed to his death. Even so, Uncle Billy managed to live to a ripe old age. But the fact that he reacted so strongly to a dishonest carny that it almost killed him only illustrates what the man was made of: pure goodness.

He even looked the part: He had a slight build, always wore a smile on his face and sported an almost-handlebar mustache that served as his trademark. He had a naturally disarming demeanor, always pleasant and courteous, and possessed great insight and intellect. His integrity and dignity commanded respect, traits that led to him becoming an employee of high regard in the United States Postal Service.

Among other qualities, Uncle Billy was a talented writer and possessed a beautiful singing voice (he was once a member of a barbershop quartet); I inherited one of those abilities—and trust me, it wasn't singing. He was a gifted writer, and upon being informed of his writing exploits when I was a youngster, a seed was planted in the back of my mind: Writing professionally sounded interesting and fun, and I filed it away as something I might want to try my hand at someday. When I decided to become a writer in college, I went to Uncle Billy for advice. He told me to develop my own style and to write honestly, from the heart. Words of wisdom, indeed.

My dad initially balked at my decision to major in Mass Communications at the University of Akron and pursue a career as a sportswriter, citing the notoriously low pay in that profession and the dearth of opportunities that might make relocating a necessity. I later learned from experience that Dad had been spot-on with that assessment, but at the time I was dismayed at his lack of support for my decision. Uncle Billy, on the other hand, was extremely encouraging and supportive of my career choice, which helped to buoy my resolve at making a go at being a sportswriter. Uncle Billy assured me that I would be a success—he enjoyed reading my articles whenever he had the chance—and said he had a good feeling about my career.

It wasn't the last time he gave me an indication of what the future held in store.

—————

UNCLE BILLY'S VISITATION

Clar Clar's warning in the fall of 1985 that Grandma's passing was imminent was the first visitation I received that foreshadowed death.

Uncle Billy's was the second.

Uncle Billy died in 1995, and if any soul was destined for Heaven without passing Go, it was his. His was not a restless spirit. But six years after his passing, he paid me his first and only visit one night in October 2001. Kim's friend Becky had been diagnosed with breast cancer several years earlier, and her resulting battle with the disease included periods of remission and recurrence. During remission, Becky seemed fine, a warm, loving person living a normal, wholesome life. But by the fall of 2001, her cancer had returned, and her friends and family hoped and prayed it would again go into remission.

Uncle Billy visited me one night that fall. And when I woke up, I knew there would be no remission this time for Becky.

I believe that in a visitation, the deceased can create the vehicle for the message they are trying to convey—in other words, shape the reality. In Uncle Billy's visitation, I was seated at a large, oval-shaped oak table with several other people in an elegant dining room. It was a room I had never been in before, and I was never shown the rest of the house. Judging by the richness of the room we were in, however, I guessed the house to be something along the lines of a French chateau. The room, while fairly small, was adorned in Gothic architecture with dark wooden walls, with the wood planks offset by panels of red velvet between them. The chairs we sat in were also made of heavy dark wood, featuring exaggerated raised backs, with red velvet seat and back cushioning. The carpet, too, was red, and the room was illuminated by dim lighting that gave the entire scene a somewhat murky feel.

I noticed that every chair at the large table was occupied, but nobody was speaking. Nor was there any food or drink being served. It was just people sitting at a table. I sat at one end of the oval, and Becky was at the other end, facing me. I couldn't make out who the other people were at the table. At the time I thought maybe that was because the lighting was poor, but I had no trouble at all seeing Becky and she was the farthest person from me at the table. Following the visitation, the reason for this became evident: who sat at the table, aside from Becky, was irrelevant.

Uncle Billy suddenly appeared in the room. I never saw him actually enter the room from a doorway, he just showed up. I wasn't sure if he had been there the whole time and I just now noticed him, or if he had not been there until that moment. Either way, he was the second person I could actually discern in the gloomy lighting. Since all the chairs at the table were occupied, I wondered where he was going to sit. And I still had no idea why we were there.

Uncle Billy proceeded to slowly walk around the table. He was wearing a gray suit with a white shirt and red tie. He looked sharp, but his face was expressionless. He walked behind each chair as he circled the table. I followed his every movement and thought of saying hello, but he seemed unusually sullen so I stayed silent. It was then I noticed that no one else at the table was paying any attention to him, and it dawned on me that I was the only one who could see him. Everyone else was oblivious to his presence.

Another thought hit me: Uncle Billy is dead. How can he be here, and why is he here?

Uncle Billy proceeded around the table. When he got to Becky's chair, he stopped. He stood behind her chair and grasped each side of the back of it with his hands, holding the chair tightly in his grasp. He then looked directly at me from across the table—the first time he and I made eye contact since I had noticed him in the room. Becky, like the others at the table, was oblivious to Uncle Billy's presence. After several seconds of fixing his gaze toward me, Uncle Billy solemnly looked down at Becky, his eyes sad and sunken, his lips nearly drawn into a grimace. He continued to stare downward at Becky, then after a minute or two lifted his head back up and looked at me again, the forlorn expression still etched on his face. The reason for this visit then hit me like a punch in the gut.

I woke up, and I instinctively knew: Becky was about to leave this Earth. There would be no remission this time. God was calling her home. And a short time later she was gone, her gentle soul finally freed from her cancer-ravaged body—as Uncle Billy had warned.

I'm not sure why Uncle Billy was the one who visited me with this information. He and Becky never met each other. Maybe it's not for us mere mortals to understand. If I had to proffer a guess, I would surmise that his honesty, integrity and compassion in life would capture my attention that what I was experiencing was real and that his message was genuine.

I never said a word to anybody about Uncle Billy's visit, just as I had never told anyone of Clar Clar's visit prior to Grandma's passing in 1985. I didn't want to alarm people, even though I knew beyond any shadow of a doubt what was about to occur. I kept that information to myself. I assumed that the visitations happened to me, and not others, for a reason. What that reason was, I don't know. Visitations gave me some of the answers, but not all the answers.

Check that: One visitation did give me all the answers—the big answers, anyway. And another came to me in a most unlikely manner from a most unlikely messenger.

CHAPTER 6

SYLVIA

K im never liked cats.

Until she met Sylvia.

My wife had always been a dog person, primarily because when she was growing up her family only owned dogs—primarily because her father did not like cats. So Kim grew up believing that cats were unaffectionate and unintelligent.

Sylvia blew those notions—those lies—out of the water.

Kim and I had been together a couple years, and married nearly one year, when we began debating whether or not to get a pet. A dog was problematic: We liked to travel, and obviously dogs are high maintenance when it comes to care. With a dog, we just couldn't up and leave for a weekend getaway, which we often liked to do. I suggested a cat, which Kim wanted no part of. So, a pet in the Hardesty household seemed like a dead issue.

Until Kim called me one day from work. A co-worker's daughter was moving and had to get rid of her seven-year-old female cat, Sylvia, who was a purebred, long-haired, seal-point Himalayan. The woman was in a bind, and her dad asked Kim if we might be interested in taking his daughter's cat.

"But you don't like cats," I said to my wife. "Now you want to own one?"

"I don't know," she replied. "We could try it, but if I don't like her we're getting rid of her."

I said, "Well, you have to give her a chance to adjust to her new home. You can't have her a couple days and decide you don't like her and we have to get rid of her. That's not fair to the cat."

"OK," Kim said. "She has three weeks. If I don't like her after three weeks, she's gone."

Sylvia stayed in our home—and melted Kim's heart—for nearly seven years.

I had never actually owned a cat either, but many of my friends and relatives did, and I adored those unique creatures. Contrary to what Kim had been told, cats are extremely intelligent animals, very affectionate—in their own way and on their own terms, of course—and are wonderful company. They are also very amusing animals—cheap entertainment, I call them.

There was only one problem when we brought Sylvia into the house: We couldn't find her. Kim brought her home one day, set her down on our living room floor, and she promptly disappeared. And, as far as we knew, vanished.

Kim had brought Sylvia to the condo while I was at work. I had been anxiously counting the minutes until I got home to see the furry new addition to our family. Upon my arrival, I opened the front door and happily asked, "So where's the cat?"

"I don't know," Kim said. "I put her down and she ran off. I haven't seen her since."

"Is she even in the house?" I asked, only half-joking.

"Yeah, but I don't know where she went," Kim said.

We scoured our three-level condo for a while, and eventually Sylvia turned up underneath the living room couch. We had lifted up the skirt of the couch and there she was, this dark brown little doll face with big blue eyes peering straight ahead, making no eye contact with us whatsoever, chin flat on the carpet, obviously frightened. We gently tried to coax her out of her hiding spot, to no avail. So we dropped the couch skirt and left her alone, thinking she would come out shortly once she became comfortable with the fact that she was safe in her new home.

Wrong.

A while later we lifted up the couch skirt again to check on her, and she was gone! How she had slipped past us was anyone's guess, but clearly she had skittered off to another hiding place. We decided not to force the issue and instead simply let her acclimate herself at her own pace, certain she would eventually show herself on her own terms. The more we pressed the issue the more she was going to hide and avoid us, we figured, so we simply went about our business in the condo as if she wasn't there—until we reached a point where we realized she might never come out if we *don't* force the issue. Like it or not, we were going to have to drag her out from wherever she was hiding, because clearly she was too traumatized and terrified to come out on her own—at least when we were in the house. Her litter box was being used and her food and water dishes were being emptied, so we knew she was sneaking out when we weren't around. Knowing that she was at least eating and drinking was a relief all by itself. Wherever she was, she was obviously paying close attention to where we were and what we were doing at all times: She was waiting to see when the coast was clear, doing her business at her bowls and litter box, then ducking back into her hiding place when she was finished. But damned if we knew where that was.

Prior to getting Sylvia, one of my selling points to Kim was that cats keep to themselves and don't really bother you for anything. In fact, I had said, "You may not even see much of her."

I had thought that if Kim didn't see much of Sylvia, it actually would help the cat's chances of staying. And I knew from experience that many cats just do their own thing—you almost don't know if they're even in the house—but Sylvia was taking that notion to extremes. "You said we may not see her much," Kim said, "but it would be nice to see her sometimes. It's like she's not even here. This is ridiculous."

So we put on the full-court press in search of Sylvia. She was obviously scared to death, and it was no way for her to live.

After a couple more days of searching the condo—which was an average-sized unit, with only so many hiding places—we finally located her. Once again, she had taken up residence under the couch (which we had looked under countless times). This time, I lifted the back of the couch up and Kim pried her off the carpet. Sylvia's eyes were as big as saucers and she was trembling with fear. Kim clutched Sylvia in her hands and cradled her against her chest as I stroked her fur. Sylvia made no move to escape as we softly talked to her, trying to calm her down and reassure her that she was safe.

"Ohhh, it's all right Sylvia," Kim cooed to the little light-brown ball of fur in her arms. "You can come out and see us. No one's going to hurt you." We continued to hold and soothe her in an effort to put her at ease. We then put her back down on the floor—and this time she didn't run.

In those few short minutes, Kim's life had changed forever.

And so had mine.

Kim instantly fell in love with Sylvia, and who couldn't? She was smart, sweet, playful, affectionate and fun. She was a tiny little peanut of a cat, and she was beautiful—just absolutely gorgeous. She added so much to our lives, bringing a joy and energy to our house that made me wonder how we ever lived without her.

And when I say she was smart, I mean brilliant. I know, everyone thinks their dog or cat is the smartest ever, but Sylvia was genuinely a cut above all the dogs I ever had, and I had some smart ones. She was cunning, always a step or two ahead of me when we were playing or "stalking" each other. She had an extensive vocabulary, and she was an extremely quick learner. I found her level of intelligence to actually be somewhat eerie; it's an odd feeling to get outwitted and outsmarted by another creature, especially when it happens a lot. She was like having another person in the house.

I quickly learned that Sylvia just knew things. You couldn't explain how she knew them, but she did, like the time we were going to take her to the vet to get her fixed. We had toyed with the idea of having it done for a while— particularly because when she went into heat (which seemed often), she would wail at the top of her lungs for hours. There was nothing you could do to stop her or distract her. It would wake you up out of a sound sleep, and you could forget about going back to sleep because her wailing would just go on and on. When she was in heat, if Sylvia was up, everyone was up.

We figured as she got older, she would stop going into heat as often and may even stop. And while the frequency did become less, the intensity of the episodes did not. When we moved from the condo to a house a few blocks away, by which time Sylvia was nine, we teetered on the edge of whether or not to get her spayed. Her age was a concern: We weren't wild about putting a cat her age through such a procedure, worried that it might be dangerous for her. So we decided against it.

A year later, with Sylvia now ten years old, she had a particularly intense episode of heat, which was dismaying because it had actually seemed to be lessening. This one was like the old days back in the condo, so we decided we had to take the chance and get her fixed. It was becoming intrusive to our sleep patterns, and we thought it really couldn't be good for her either to have this occurring at age ten. So we reluctantly made the appointment.

You had to be quick when you nabbed her to take her to the vet, because she knew in an instant what you were up to when you came her way. You couldn't wear a jacket, jingle your car keys or do anything that even remotely indicated you were taking her out of the house, or she was gone. You had to be as subtle as possible, and even then catching her before she caught on was fifty-fifty.

Using all the stealth at my disposal, I caught her. And she wasn't happy about it. Kim was already in the car in the driveway, with the car started. The plan was for me to nab Sylvia, whisk her out to the car and off we would go. Everything was going according to plan. I caught Silly (one of our nicknames for her, along with Sillypuss), jumped in the car, handed her to Kim and prepared to back out of the driveway.

"You think we're doing the right thing?" Kim asked.

I thought for a moment; deep down, I had never stopped having reservations about putting Silly through surgery. "I don't know," I said. "It seems like we don't really have a choice. This heat thing isn't stopping, and it seems to be getting worse."

"But I feel terrible about taking her in for surgery," Kim said. "She's ten years old. What if something goes wrong? We'll never forgive ourselves."

I knew Kim was right. We were taking a chance. Was it really worth it just to keep her from going into heat? No, it wasn't. Nothing was actually wrong with her, so why take the chance?

It just seemed too risky.

"OK," I said, "let's cancel the appointment."

Kim, holding Sylvia in her lap in the passenger seat, looked at her and said, "You got lucky, Silly, you're not going to the vet today. But if you keep doing this, we're going to have to take you."

So we climbed out of the car, took Sylvia back inside the house and cancelled the appointment.

She never went into heat again.

Sylvia warmed up to us quickly. After her several-days-long game of hide-and-seek when we first got her, she was a terrific companion. She always hung out with us, and especially liked to lounge with us on the living room couch or in our bed. Her favorite thing was to sleep right in between us at night. She would park it between our pillows and proceed to preen and clean for an extended period of time before finally curling up and going to sleep. I found it comforting to have her right next to my head, falling asleep to the sound of Sylvia licking her fur before she settled in to sleep between us. She even would carve out a place that was partially on my pillows and partially on Kim's, in order to get as close to us as possible. And every time I turned over during my sleep to face the other direction, I would crack an eye to see Sylvia sound asleep inches from my head. It was a feeling of extreme contentment. There was nowhere on Earth I would rather be. For variety, Sylvia would move down to the foot of the bed on Kim's side and sleep right against a stuffed animal we kept there, a white seal we nicknamed "Seal Friend" because Sylvia enjoyed sleeping next to it so much. (Seal Friend is still a staple of the bed, with our cat Boo serving as its current nighttime companion).

Sylvia did this at the condo, and it carried over when we moved a few blocks away. Then suddenly, after about a year at the new house, Sylvia stopped coming to bed with us at night. Just like that. I knew cats went through phases, but this came out of the blue. She went from sleeping with us every night for a couple years, to being nowhere to be found when we went to bed. I figured it was a phase and she would be back soon enough. But she wasn't. When we went to bed, Sylvia went somewhere else in the house.

I kept waiting for her to switch again and start coming to bed with us, but it didn't happen. For months, Sylvia went her own way at night. I missed her. It didn't feel right, falling asleep without her right next to us. I figured her new phase was permanent and she would never come to sleep with us again. One night, as we lay in bed, I could see Silly sitting in the hallway just outside our bedroom door. She was looking into the room.

"Silly's just sitting there in the hallway, Hon," I said to Kim. "I wonder why she doesn't come to bed with us anymore. I wish she would, I really miss that."

A few moments later, I felt the familiar thump of Sylvia jumping onto the foot of the bed. She dutifully trudged to the head of the bed, plunked it down right in between us and promptly began to clean herself.

I looked at Kim. "You heard what I just said, right?"

"Yep. She understood you. She speaks English," Kim said. "She heard you say you felt bad that she didn't come to bed with us anymore, so here she is."

And from that moment on, Sylvia came to bed with us every night again. It was as if she had never stopped. All was right with the world.

Like I said, Silly just knew things.

When we moved to our current house in winter of the year 2000, I thought maybe Sylvia wasn't coming with us.

Because on the final day of our move, I couldn't find her.

We had been moving from the old house to the new house in piecemeal fashion, with the old house slowly emptying out and the new house slowly filling up. After a couple weeks, the old house was beginning to lay bare, with only a few big-ticket items remaining. Sylvia and our other cat, Halen, a big, rough-and-tumble Siamese we had gotten in 1998 (much to Sylvia's chagrin— she was perfectly happy being an only cat), had noticed that something major was going on as the house became a jumbled mess of boxes and furniture moving around then disappearing. Silly and Halen began to act a bit out of sorts, lying in places they normally didn't. And on the final day of our move, after we had packed up the car with the last of the items that the big furniture truck wasn't going to haul, we only needed to grab Sylvia and Halen and head to the new house.

Kim and I searched the house up and down looking for Sylvia and couldn't find her anywhere. The house was mostly empty, so her hiding places were extremely limited. The house itself was small, a Cape Cod that was less than one thousand square feet, so the fact that we couldn't find her began to concern me. Every cat we have ever owned—including our current cats—are strictly indoor cats. They never, ever go outside for any reason, nor do they want to. Silly was no different. She never even made an attempt to get out. But I began to worry that with the topsy-turvy nature of the move and with items constantly leaving the house and the front door often being left open, if only for brief periods of time, it was possible that she had become traumatized by the goings-on and decided to slip out. I began to feel nauseous thinking of that possibility as I raced through the house looking in every nook and cranny.

My stomach was in knots and my blood ran cold. She's gone, I thought.

"I can't find her," I said to Kim, exasperated. "I'm not even sure she's still in the house. We've looked everywhere."

"She has to be in here," Kim said. "She wouldn't run out. Keep looking."

I retraced my steps for the umpteenth time. I knew for certain that she wasn't in the basement or on the main floor. I had scoured the finished attic a couple times, but that was the only place she could possibly be. So upstairs I went for another sweep of the attic. She definitely wasn't in the main area of the attic, but there were cubbyholes that ran the length of the house on each side of the attic. Both cubbyholes were about three feet deep and twenty feet long. I had checked these already, but they were fairly dark and had some blind spots, so I began to crawl around and look around corners in the tight space, continuing to call out to Silly as I had been during the entire search.

I really felt that she was gone. I honestly thought I was going to vomit. Just when I was about to prepare to live life without Sylvia and forever wonder what happened to her and where she went, I saw something that looked like a beige sweater pressed against the inside of the cubbyhole I was searching. The item could easily have been missed: It lay in a small dark area between two openings in the cubbyhole where light couldn't hit it. I reached for the sweater, put my hand on it—and felt long, soft fur.

Sylvia!!

She had blended in with the wood flooring and interior wall of the cubbyhole. In fact, there was a good chance I had already seen her once or twice and just didn't notice her in there. Waves of relief rushed over me as I picked up my beloved cat and clutched her tightly against my chest. She absolutely did not want to leave her home, and almost didn't.

With Silly in my clutches, I made my way out of the house and to the car. I handed Silly to Kim, who put her on her lap, and I went back into the house to fetch Halen, who thankfully had not been hiding.

However, Halen was problematic. He was young, strong, lean and mean—to the point that even reaching out a hand to pet him could draw his ire. He was suspicious of every move you made toward him, and we had never actually picked him up in the year and a half we had had him. Shoot, we had barely laid a hand on him, period. He was unpredictable, and there was a good chance he would lash out at you like a coiled-up snake, or whack you with a paw, if you even dared try to pet him. Now I had to pick him up, and I didn't know what to expect, whether he would go along with it or claw me to ribbons. I gently grabbed him, talking to him in a soothing voice, his eyes wide as he wondered why he was being spirited out of the house. I expected to feel razor-sharp claws digging bloody canals into my back and shoulders at any moment as I whisked him out the front door, down the porch steps and to the car in the driveway. I reached the driver's side door and, to my surprise, still had not spilled any blood. I got into the car and quickly handed Halen to Kim in the passenger seat. Success! We had Halen in the vehicle, something I wasn't sure would be possible, and off we went for the twenty-minute drive to our new house in Stow. Halen disappeared into the back of the car, but Sylvia lay in Kim's lap the entire drive over, rarely even picking her head up, clearly traumatized by the ordeal. Kim stroked her fur and talked to her as I steered the car toward our new home.

We got off the highway, drove down a couple main drags and then entered our new neighborhood. As soon as we turned onto our street, Sylvia suddenly stood up and put her paws on the dashboard, peering intently through the windshield, her eyes wide with excitement. She stood and looked out the windshield the entire drive down our street to the new house.

Somehow—and I have no idea how—she was acutely aware that she was about to arrive at her new home.

Sylvia just knew things.

———

I was convinced that Sylvia, like many—if not most—cats, had the ability to communicate telepathically (this will come into play shortly). I knew exactly what she wanted and what she was thinking just by looking into her big, beautiful blue eyes. No meow was necessary. All she had to do was give me "the look," and I instantly knew what she was telling me. This, combined with her posture and where she was in the house, told me everything I needed to know. And her eyes could also make me do her bidding, a kind of feline Jedi mind trick. She was daddy's girl, she knew it, and she played it for all it was worth.

Silly began to experience health problems in the fall of 2002. She had just turned fourteen, and of course all bets are off for dogs and cats at that age. We noticed that she had begun losing weight, which was alarming because she didn't weigh much to begin with. The veterinarian diagnosed her with hyperthyroidism and immediately put her on a treatment program of pills to reverse the weight loss. This proved to be another testament to her intelligence.

The vet said all we had to do was pop a pill in her mouth two or three times a day. Nothing to it, right? Just hold her in a vise grip, pry her mouth open and drop a foreign object into her mouth. What could go wrong?

This is a tough call of duty for anyone who has ever owned a cat. On the long list of things our feline friends hate, having something shoved down their throat is right near the top. But with Sylvia, it was damn near impossible. Oh, she was cooperative enough when we put the pill in her mouth—most of the time, anyway. But *getting* the pill into her mouth wasn't the problem. *Keeping* the pill in her mouth was.

I would stand in the kitchen holding Sylvia in my arms, Kim would force her mouth open and drop the pill into her mouth, then close her mouth shut. We would lavish praise on her while Kim massaged Sylvia's throat to help the pill go down. I wouldn't put Silly back down onto the floor until we saw her swallow for proof that she got the pill. Once we saw her swallow, I would place her on the floor and she would skitter away. Mission accomplished.

Or so we thought.

Sometime later, we would notice a tiny, white object on the kitchen floor— almost always tucked away in a corner where it was difficult to see. We would walk over, pick it up … and it would be the pill that we had given Silly earlier! That cat had the presence of mind to not only fake like she was swallowing a pill, but also to wait for us to leave the kitchen before spitting the pill back out—in a place where it had a good chance of never being found, no less.

This happened many times—and those were just the times we actually found pills "hidden" in kitchen corners. There is no doubt in my mind that Sylvia often succeeded in spitting out pills that went undiscovered.

It got the point that we gave up on the "shove it down her throat" method, which was failing miserably, and decided to trick her: We would bury the tiny pill in a generous helping of tuna fish on a saucer. This would be foolproof, I thought. Silly loved her tuna, and she no doubt would wolf it down—none the wiser that the pill was hidden deep within the tasty treat. So as to not draw suspicion, we gave our other two cats, Halen and Nookie, their tuna on a saucer in the kitchen at the same time that Sylvia got hers. The first time I gave it to her, I watched intently as the food disappeared on the saucer as she ate. Considering that I had carefully snuck the pill into the middle of the food, and that the food was rapidly vanishing, I surmised that she had to have eaten the pill by now.

Sylvia finally finished the tuna, licked her lips and walked out of the kitchen with a full belly.

I picked up the saucer—and there, sitting all alone in the middle of the ceramic plate, was the pill! Sylvia had somehow managed to eat all around the tiny object, leaving it as the only remaining morsel on the saucer. Even more startling was the fact that the pill itself was still in near-perfect condition, meaning she hadn't even had it in her mouth. She simply ate around it as if she knew the pill was there. I only could shake my head and smile at having been outwitted by my cat—again.

This back-and-forth with the pills continued for several months. Sometimes the humans won, sometimes the cat won. We had to get creative in our trickery, breaking the pill in two—no easy feat considering its small size to begin with— and hiding the separate little pill parts throughout the tuna, or holding Silly in my arms for as long as a couple minutes after Kim had put the pill in her mouth to make sure she swallowed it (and even that wasn't entirely foolproof). We tried everything. The cat was smart—and she knew things.

However, Silly got enough pills down to begin to put weight back on. She had gotten down to around six pounds, and then bounced back up to about nine pounds. We were encouraged that we were winning the battle. We had had her since the spring of 1996 and it was now March 2003, and it was beginning to look like she would live to a ripe old age—riper than she already had at age fourteen.

~

SYLVIA'S VISITATION

Things seemed to be going well with Sylvia. She was putting weight back on and beginning to look like her old self again. She was active, eating well and seemed well on the road to recovery—until late one night when she suffered a seizure in the kitchen. She had another a few days later, and a few minor ones where she seemed to be out of it a little bit before coming to. The vet said Sylvia might be dehydrated and gave her a shot of fluids and still more pills. She said that should stabilize her. The seizures stopped, but I was worried. Something wasn't right. But at least another fire seemed to have been put out.

Then one night in early March 2003, I had one of the most amazing experiences of my life: Sylvia communicated with me telepathically in the dream state. Yes, technically it was a dream, but upon waking up I instantly knew it had been much more than that. I have never experienced anything like it. To this day, it's the one and only time a living being has reached out to me in the dream state.

In this "dream," I saw Sylvia sitting by herself on a floor. I couldn't tell exactly where she was because all that was visible was a close-up of her sitting on a cream-colored carpeted floor. It could have been our house, it could have been any house. She was sitting in profile, facing to the left. I then noticed a small, dark object lying on the floor about a foot from the side of her body. I couldn't tell exactly what it was, but it had the size and shape of a mouse—elongated, maybe oval-shaped like a football. I couldn't tell if the mouse was alive or dead. It wasn't moving, and Silly paid no attention to it. I wasn't sure if she even knew the mouse was lying there next to her.

After maybe a minute, she glanced down to her left and looked at the object for several seconds, then looked up at me. Her eyes were trying to tell me something, but in the dream state I wasn't getting the message. I sensed sadness in the look she gave me and had the sensation that it was a melancholy scene. I felt I needed to do something, but I didn't know what.

The heaviness and frustrating nature of the dream forced me awake. As I slowly came to, the visual of Sylvia sitting by herself on the carpet with the small, dark object that was ostensibly a mouse lying next to her was fresh in my mind's eye. I was disturbed by the dream but didn't know what it meant. I got up and went downstairs to check on her, and everything seemed status quo. I breathed a sigh of relief and began my day.

Several days later, Sylvia stopped eating and drinking and she was lethargic, barely moving at all. We took her to the vet, where she was diagnosed with kidney failure. The vet said it could be chronic, which would give her a chance to live with the disease for a while, or it could be acute, which would quickly be fatal.

We took her home, and there was no improvement. One day, two days, three days, her condition remained unchanged. She wouldn't eat, wouldn't drink and only got up to dutifully use the litter box—which was an ordeal in itself because she was weak and could barely make it to her box. It became clear her condition was acute. She was dying.

Suddenly, the dream of Sylvia sitting by herself next to the small, dark object came rushing back to me. As I replayed the image in my head, I realized that the object lying next to Silly in the dream was not a mouse at all. It was a kidney. It was all so clear now. She had telepathically communicated to me that her kidneys were failing. The sadness in her eyes as she looked at me in the dream—and again, I use that term very loosely, because I don't believe for a second that it was an actual dream—was Sylvia telling me that she was dying and she didn't have long.

I know beyond any shadow of a doubt that Sylvia was conveying this information to me. Prior to the dream, the possibility of kidney failure had not come up and had not crossed my mind, so there was no seed of it planted in my brain to even conjure up that scenario in a dream. And the timing of the dream, the kidney lying next to her, the look in her eyes ... Sylvia had shown me what was wrong with her and to prepare me for what was about to happen. There is just no doubt in my mind.

She and I had a special connection, and as stated earlier, she had communicated with me telepathically often over the years. Not telepathically in the sense that I could hear a little cat voice in my head, the stuff of tinfoil hat fodder; rather, a non-verbal communication consisting of a deep, mutual understanding between two living beings who are in complete mental, psychological and emotional synchronicity with each other—on the same "mind frequency," if you will. This episode was no different, except she did it while I was in the dream state. She may have been in the dream state as well. Dreams were mysterious thousands of years ago and they're mysterious now. They still aren't fully understood and may never be. The brain itself is largely a mystery, let alone the mind. So I don't fully understand the ethereal nature of what happened, I just know it happened. The information in the dream mirrored precisely the heartbreaking situation that played out. That's not a coincidence.

I don't question what the dream was—that became obvious following Sylvia's diagnosis of kidney disease—I only question the nature of the dream. Was it telepathic between just Sylvia and myself, or was it telepathic on a spiritual level? In other words, had she already begun to pass over to the other side, therefore making it easier to communicate with me in that realm?

I'll never know, but it doesn't matter. It happened. She told me goodbye.

And we said goodbye to her on March 17, 2003, St. Patrick's Day. We had to end her suffering and have her put down. I have never truly gotten over it. It left a hole in my soul that I am sure will be there until I cross over to the other side myself. It was the first time that I had to be involved in the excruciating decision to end the life of someone I loved so dearly, and my heart still aches. We never really get over the death of a loved one because they are irreplaceable. Their absence leaves a permanent void in our lives. And that most certainly goes for our pets as well. After all, we see them every day, we share our lives with them, they love us unconditionally, they are our constant companions. We play with them, care for them, fall asleep with them, laugh with them, cry with them, live life with them. They are omnipresent in our lives. And when they're gone, it's unbearably traumatic. The house suddenly has a different feel to it. Something seems off. Your trusty partner isn't in their usual spot, they're not sleeping where they always sleep, they're not hanging out with you, they're not at your side begging for food. You think you see them out of the corner of your eye, sitting there or walking toward you, then you turn to look and it's just a blanket or a rug, and it hits you: They're gone. You dream about them, happy times when they're in the prime of their lives and you're together again playing with them and holding them close to you, then you wake up and the realization that it was only a dream is like a cruel prank.

Losing a pet is like losing a part of ourselves. It's been nearly sixteen years since that awful day when we said goodbye to Silly, and to this day tears well up in my eyes when I think about her—due to the overwhelming sadness of losing her and the overwhelming love I felt for her. Ending her life was one of the most gut-wrenching things I've ever gone through, but we knew it had to be done.

She wasn't getting better, and she wasn't going to get better. She was suffering needlessly. The end result was going to be the same, only she was going to suffer longer if we didn't have her put to sleep. God was taking her into His kingdom. She had been ours for nearly seven years. Now she was His forever.

I did a lot of soul-searching after Sylvia's death. We had two other cats at the time, Halen and Nookie, and I was hit with the stark realization that someday Kim and I might well have to make the same decision with them that we did with Sylvia. And I began to wonder: Is it even worth it to have pets? Is it worth having your heart ripped out when they die? Is it worth watching them go downhill, begin to suffer, then have to decide when it's time to say goodbye to them? It's a horrible sequence to endure—for them and for us. Halen and Nookie were much younger than Sylvia in 2003—Halen was seven, Nookie four—but even then I began to dread the terrible day when we would have to bid farewell to them, even though that day was far off in the future. I would go to bed at night with Halen and Nookie at my side, their soft, warm bodies pressed against me, Nookie purring loudly until he fell asleep (Halen rarely purred; he was a little rough around the edges), content in the knowledge that there was a good chance they could be with me for another decade or more as I coped with the loss of Sylvia. And they were: Halen lived to be seventeen, Nookie eighteen.

But you never get used to hearing the veterinarian's terrible words that there is nothing more they can do for your friend and their life is measured in days, hours or even minutes. The awful finality of it hits you like a sledgehammer. I get the same feeling of helplessness, the same pit in my stomach, the same waves of nausea, the same lightheadedness, the same feeling that this can't be real, every time I'm in the vet's office and hear the words, "I'm sorry." They are about to leave this Earth, and I am about to live the rest of my life without them. It is absolutely unbearable. It's not that we think our pets are going to live forever, it's that we're never ready to say goodbye. We always hope for that one miracle, that one Hail Mary pass that will improve our pet's condition and keep them with us. But in our hearts, we know it's over. Their time has come, the way our time will come someday, too.

Those who see pets as little more than household accessories do not understand this level of love and attachment with an animal. Those who see their pets as beloved members of the family know exactly what I'm talking about. I can look into my cats' eyes and see their soul in there, the same way I can when I look into a person's eyes. At one time or another we've had seven cats, and they have all had very distinct personalities. They have likes, dislikes, favorite foods, favorite toys and favorite spots in the house. They get happy, sad, angry, jealous and affectionate; without a doubt, they experience the same range of emotions that we do. We often are closer to them than most other human beings, if not all other human beings. In a very real sense, they are our best friends. And losing them is devastating.

I was so emotionally wounded after Sylvia's passing that I told myself no more pets, that losing them is just too hard and once Halen and Nookie were gone, that was it. Done. Finis. And for almost four years, it remained just Halen and Nookie. They were best friends—an odd match, because Halen was a high-strung, fairly aggressive Siamese and Nookie a laid-back, watch-the-world-go-by Persian—and Kim and I were content to let them happily live out their lives together.

Then in the first week of January 2007, Kim came home from work late one afternoon holding a cat carrier in her hand. She set the carrier on the kitchen table, and I leaned down and peered into it; two gold eyes were peering back at me. It was a little black cat! I didn't know we were getting a cat; he had been a stray living in the immediate area around the large industrial building where Kim worked, and had somehow managed to keep from getting squished by the steady stream of eighteen-wheelers that were constantly going back and forth through the parking lot. She took him sight unseen, and now he was ours: A small, scrawny, malnourished, grease-and oil-slickened, six-month-old ragamuffin of a cat. We named him Boo, and as excited as I was to have him, I could hardly sleep that night in the fear that he would be dead when I woke up the next day. He looked that bad.

Boo has now been with us for twelve years.

And we got Boo, in a large sense, because of Sylvia and her impact on us. The way Sylvia enriched our lives, and the happy, loving home we provided for her, far outweighed the pain of losing her. Being blinded by grief, this was not evident at the time; over time, however, it was obvious that our lives had been far better for having Sylvia in them. To not get another cat would be to say that Sylvia wasn't worth it, and she most certainly was. Boo is her legacy—as are Roxy, Morrie and Ashton, our other rescue cats, and Noel, our rescue dog, all of whom are following in Silly's paw steps. Every day with them, like every day was with Sylvia, is a gift from God. Rather than focus on having to say goodbye to them someday, I cherish every moment I get to spend with them. The fear of death cannot be allowed to snuff out the joy of living.

I miss Sylvia terribly. I will never be over losing her. Never. It hurts as much today as it did then, and not a day goes by that I don't think about her in some capacity. She was truly an angel and the most beautiful cat I have ever seen. She impacted me deeply in ways that I can't accurately convey or even fully understand. She changed me, and I couldn't imagine my life without having had her in it. In my mind, Sylvia was proof of God's existence: Something so pure of heart, so precious of spirit, so perfect of soul, could only have been created by a divine being.

Because of that, I hoped I would see her again someday in Heaven. One thing bothered me, though: I wasn't sure if animals even went to Heaven. I had certainly hoped so, of course, and was convinced they have souls like we have souls, and if that was the case then, yes, it made sense that animals go to Heaven. But, still, I just wasn't sure.

Several years later, that uncertainty was erased forever.

CHAPTER 7

UNCLE DENNY

Uncle Denny was the funniest, wittiest, most cheerful person I've ever met. My dad's younger brother and only sibling, Uncle Denny seemed perpetually happy. He was always in a good mood, and I do mean always. I never saw him angry in the forty-three years I was lucky enough to have him in my life. If he did happen to be in a bad mood or upset about something, you almost never knew it. Along with Gramps, Uncle Denny was the most remarkable man I've ever been around. He just had a charm about him, a gleam in his eye and a wry smile that just made you feel good about, well, everything.

You wanted to be around Uncle Denny; just being in his presence was a natural stress reliever. When you were with him, the grass looked greener, the sky seemed bluer, the air smelled cleaner. He was cut from the same cloth as his mom, Dee Dee, and his uncles, Gomer and Billy; they don't make them like Dee Dee, Gomer, Billy, and Denny anymore. I'm certainly not made that way, and I wish I was. I have their DNA, but not their spirit. All four of them were at another level of virtue and righteousness than most of the rest of humanity; that's a big statement, but it's the truth. If the rest of our species was like those four, all our problems on this planet would be over. I try to emulate them, but

I can't; they set the bar astonishingly high, and I can't hope to reach it. But if I am somehow able to even get close, then that's good, too.

And that's how I always viewed Uncle Denny: I may never be the man he was—in fact, I'm sure I won't (few are)—but if I at least try, then I'll be all right in this life. He was so much more than an uncle to me. He was a friend, a mentor, a father figure, someone who's smiling face and easy laugh could brighten the worst of days. I miss him every day. What a huge loss it was when he unexpectedly left us. The void in my life—and the lives of everyone he touched—cannot possibly be filled. That void is palpable; I literally can feel his absence. His death was the kind that remains fresh in your heart and soul no matter how many years go by; time does not heal that wound. When I think of him, which is often, tears fill my eyes just as easily now, more than seven years after his passing, as they did the day Aunt Kay called to tell me he was gone. I was in shock then, and that shock has yet to wear off all these years later. He was that exceptional. The best I can do is close my eyes and shake my head in disbelief that he's gone, because in my mind it just can't be possible. But it is.

Just being around him made me feel secure and at ease, like all was right with the world. When I was growing up, I spent a lot of time at Uncle Denny and Aunt Kay's house with my cousins Shelly, Dennis (Brub to those of us in the family) and Doug, and when I stayed weekends there—and often longer—I was never treated like a nephew and a cousin, I was treated like a son and a brother. For all intents and purposes I was Denny and Kay's fourth child, and there was just nothing like being at their house with them and my cousins; I had the time of my life there. Being an only child, I saw Shelly as the sister I never had, and Brub and Doug as the brothers I never had. I still do. And Denny and Kay were like a second set of parents to me. I will never forget those wonderful times at their house, going out to eat, going to the movies, staying up late into the wee hours eating chips and dip, drinking pop and watching TV and playing board games—often with Uncle Denny right in the middle of it all enjoying it as much as we did.

As heartbreaking as his loss has been, I also smile when I think of him because I know he got to live the life he wanted to live, the way he wanted to live it. And also because of his incomparable sense of humor. Uncle Denny wasn't just funny, he was hilarious. He had a dry wit and deadpan delivery in the mold of Bob Newhart and, as he aged, he even began to resemble Newhart to a degree. He just had that look. He wasn't a spitting image of Newhart, but Uncle Denny bore a resemblance to the legendary comic actor in build and particularly his mannerisms. Like Newhart, Uncle Denny was relatively short, standing about 5-foot-6 or 5-foot-7 (Newhart is listed as being 5-8) and had a slight frame, and his hair was similar to Newhart's: brown and beginning to thin and recede. His sense of humor and his delivery, however, were a dead ringer for Newhart. And like Newhart, Uncle Denny laughed with his eyes, both men possessing a twinkle and a gleam that gave their eyes a humor all their own. He just had that Newhart vibe.

Uncle Denny could bring tears streaming down my cheeks—in laughter. Sometimes he didn't even need to say anything; just casting a knowing look in my direction was all it took to send me into fits of guffaws and belly laughs. His quick wit and sense of humor were second to none, and he often had me laughing at things he said days and weeks after he had said them. I still laugh at many of them now, decades later.

One instance came on Jan. 31, 1988, the day of Super Bowl XXII between the Washington Redskins and Denver Broncos at Jack Murphy Stadium in San Diego. First, some background: Two weeks earlier, our beloved Cleveland Browns had lost to hated John Elway and the hated Denver Broncos (did I mention they were hated?), 38-33, in the AFC Championship Game at Mile High Stadium in Denver. It was the second straight year that Elway and the Broncos had ripped our hearts out of our chests and did the can-can on them. The year before, our Browns had lost to the Broncos 23-20 in overtime in the AFC Championship in Cleveland, a game forever known as "The Drive" after Elway drove Denver 98 yards in the final 5:32 of regulation to force overtime with a TD pass with thirty-seven seconds left. I remember watching that game and thinking the Browns had it won, leading 20-13 in the fourth quarter and having the Broncos backed up on their own 2-yard line. I watched that game with my parents and a bunch of their friends and friends' kids—and a few people I didn't know—wearing a pair of big, floppy dog ears on my head and holding a box of Milk Bones in honor of the team's iconic Dawg Pound section of Cleveland Stadium. When quarterback Bernie Kosar hit wide receiver Brian Brennan with a 48-yard touchdown pass to put the Browns ahead 20-13 with 5:43 left in the fourth quarter, I began dancing around the room shouting, "We're going to the Super Bowl! We're going to the Super Bowl!" In my euphoria, I actually ate a couple of the dog biscuits—and liked it. I received a few nervous glances from a couple of the people that I didn't know in the group, but I didn't care. The Browns were going to the Super Bowl.

So when the Broncos kicked a field goal in overtime to win and end the Browns' quest to play in their first Super Bowl, the wound was deep. Bone deep. It was a crushing loss for Browns fans everywhere; defeat had been snatched from the jaws of victory. The Broncos had rallied with an improbable drive for an improbable victory on enemy turf, our Browns would not be going to the Super Bowl, and I had eaten Milk Bones. It was a dark day, indeed.

Now, on Jan. 17, 1988, Elway and the Broncos had done it again to our Browns in the AFC Championship. In a game infamously known as "The Fumble," the Browns were driving for the tying touchdown late in the fourth quarter to potentially force overtime when, to every Cleveland fan's horror, running back Earnest Byner fumbled at the Denver 3-yard line with 1:12 left in the game and the Broncos recovered. It was another gut-wrenching loss to the Broncos and forever cemented Elway (along with Michael Jordan of the NBA's Chicago Bulls) in Cleveland sports lore as Public Enemy No. 1. Byner's fumble was an especially hard punch to the gut because, from the television angle, it initially appeared that he had scored on the play; Byner ended up in the end zone, and it wasn't immediately obvious that the ball had come loose before he reached the goal line. I thought he was in and began jumping around and shouting in celebration with others in the group (yes, it was basically the same group of people that had watched the game together the year before, in almost the same place), when I heard someone behind me utter the six most devastating words I had ever heard in my life up to that point: "It's not a touchdown. He fumbled." I peered at the television screen and, sure enough, the Broncos were celebrating near a dejected Byner. Denver ball. Game over. It was like reliving a nightmare.

It was against this backdrop of monumental disappointment, then, that Uncle Denny came through with a true gem that demonstrated perfectly his blend of wit, whimsy and humor. Two weeks after beating the Browns in the AFC Championship for the second straight year, the Broncos jumped all over the Redskins early in Super Bowl XXII, leading 10-0 in the first quarter; Elway seemed well on his way to getting his first Super Bowl ring after being denied by the New York Giants the year before. To long-suffering Browns fans—like Uncle Denny and me, for instance—Elway seemed to be blessed; everything the then-future Hall of Fame quarterback touched seemed to turn to gold for him and his team. And on this particular day, that gold no doubt would come in the form of the sterling-silver Vince Lombardi Trophy, awarded each year to the winning team in the Super Bowl.

But then the improbable, the unthinkable, the miraculous happened: The Redskins caught fire and the Broncos fell apart. Washington erupted for 35 points in the second quarter—a Super Bowl record—to take a commanding 35-10 lead at halftime. The Broncos were finished. I watched this unfold with unbridled glee from our living room in Mogadore (Browns fans, of course, instantly became Redskins fans the moment that the Super Bowl combatants were finalized—you know, the enemy of my enemy is my friend), while Uncle Denny was watching the game from his favorite football easy chair in his living room in Kenmore. I knew that he must have been enjoying this as much as I was; after watching Elway and the Broncos torture our Browns in the last two AFC Championship games, it was extremely satisfying to witness this dramatic turn of events on the West Coast.

So I decided to call his house to talk with him, Brub and Doug about the Broncos losing by 25 points at halftime. I dialed the phone; it rang a couple times on the other end, then someone picked up.

"Redskins headquarters," they answered. For a split second, I thought I had the wrong number.

Then I realized it was Uncle Denny.

No "Hello?" first, just "Redskins headquarters" in a formal, professional tone—but with just the slightest yet unmistakable hint of cheer—as if I had somehow reached the switchboard operator at the Washington Redskins' front office in Washington, D.C. It caught me completely off guard for a moment, then I broke down in laughter. It was vintage Uncle Denny, and it was proof positive that he was enjoying the goings-on in San Diego every bit as much as I was. The Redskins eventually won the game 42-10, denying Elway his Super Bowl ring for the time being.

Uncle Denny and I were certainly California dreamin' on that winter's day.

Some of the things I still laugh about today when I think of them—and always will—are amusing phrases that I call "Denny-isms," droll sayings of his that are well-known around the family:

1. "Boo-hookers" when things don't work out as planned.
2. "Yikers!" when something unexpected—usually bad—happens.
3. "Patience is a flower that doesn't grow in everyone's garden" when talking about someone growing impatient.
4. "Curses" when something was upsetting but in a non-serious way.
5. "That's the scoopies" when catching you up on what was going on in his life.
6. And my favorite, on potential girl troubles: "Early to bed, early to rise, while your girl goes out with the other guys."

He always said these things with a gleam in his eye and a knowing smirk, giving you a look that just made you laugh. He was the funniest person I ever met. Most of these Denny-isms he said on a regular basis, but some he saved for just the right moment to be infused into the conversation for greatest effect—usually greatest humor effect. For example, Uncle Denny would wheel out "boo-hookers" if someone wanted to do something fun but couldn't due to other obligations, to which he would look at them and deadpan, "Boo-hookers," and chuckle. Even when it was directed at you, you couldn't help but laugh because it kind of put the moment in perspective: While you were disappointed that you couldn't do what you wanted to do (in this hypothetical discussion), it wasn't the end of the world.

Same with "yikers!" If, say, you were having car trouble and were bemoaning the high cost of repairs, you were sure to get a "Yikers!" in response. Or if we were watching a Cleveland Browns game on TV and Uncle Denny had left the room for a few minutes then came back in and asked if he had missed anything, and we would tell him that the opponent had scored another touchdown, it would be met with a resounding "Yikers!" That sort of thing.

The Denny-ism "curses" was actually interchangeable with "boo-hookers" and "yikers!" It basically just depended on the severity of the situation—and even then, he said it with humor. If I were to complain, in an off-handed way, about, say, how bad traffic had been while running errands because other motorists were rubber-necking an abandoned car on the side of the road, he no doubt would utter "Curses." Again, said in a tone that, while acknowledging your situation, also let you know that it wasn't worth dwelling on for any length of time—something Uncle Denny excelled at and another trait of his that I always admired. Nothing seemed to get him down, or at least keep him down. He was always upbeat and chipper, somehow able to slough off any negativity that came his way. He never let his emotions get the better of him; he was always in control of himself in a way that I can only dream of.

And his patience was a prime example of that. Uncle Denny possessed a level of patience that I found almost otherworldly. Situations that would have had the average person climbing the walls in fits of anger, situations that undoubtedly would have left me stewing and annoyed, would barely move the needle on Uncle Denny's patience meter. His outward warmth and cheerfulness belied an inner strength that gave him amazing staying power in the face of potential emotional triggers. He had a cast-iron, almost unnatural, patience, which made him a natural leader and achiever. Those who knew Uncle Denny looked to him for guidance and hope; they saw him as a port in the storm, largely because of his patience. They knew that, unlike many people, he didn't rush to judgement and he was measured in his analysis of, and response to, a situation. You knew you could trust him to do the right thing, make the right decision, and do right by you. Every time.

Of course, he had fun with those who let their impatience grab hold of them, which is where his Denny-ism, "Patience is a flower that doesn't grow in everyone's garden," was born. He was amused by this lack of patience in others but understood its place in the human condition. So if, hypothetically, we were waiting in line somewhere and he heard someone complain about the wait time, he would look at us and say quietly—with that trademark gleam in his eye—"Patience is a flower that doesn't grow in everyone's garden." Or if we were sitting in Denny and Kay's house on Sutherland Avenue in the Kenmore section of southwest Akron and someone was bemoaning how long it was taking to receive something in the mail or for an anticipated phone call to come in, something of that nature, he would look at them and say, in a sing-song voice, "Patience is a flower that doesn't grow in everyone's garden," and finish it with a hearty chuckle.

"That's the scoopies" was a Denny-ism you would commonly hear on the phone, often when he would deliver information regarding what a certain family member had been up to recently. This often involved his three children—my Hardesty cousins—who lived out of the area. I would ask him how they were doing and he would bring me up to speed on what was new with them, finishing with "That's the scoopies" at the end. I often find myself saying these Denny-isms—and others—almost automatically now; they have become ingrained into my psyche and are a permanent part of my lexicon.

Without question, though, my favorite Denny-ism was, "Early to bed, early to rise, while your girl goes out with the other guys." This phrase epitomized his witty playfulness. Uncle Denny had an uncanny ability to make you see the humor in your own situation, often unexpectedly and often with your own unexpected reaction to it. One instance of this stands out in particular. Uncle Denny, my cousin Doug and I were sitting at the kitchen table in the house on Sutherland. It was a weekend night, and Doug and I were complaining about having to go to bed early because we had to get up in the morning for some reason or other, and therefore would miss out on being with our significant others that night.

Uncle Denny asked us what our significant others would then be doing in our absence. We actually weren't sure. "Probably going out with some friends," I told him. Doug, too, didn't know exactly what his girlfriend had planned for that evening, but it was probably something similar. Bottom line: While Doug and I were chained to the house, our significant others would have the run of the city.

It was an opportunity that Uncle Denny just couldn't pass up, and he pounced immediately; he eyed us from across the table, raised his eyebrows and stated in a mock matter-of-fact tone: "Early to bed, early to rise, while your girl goes out with the other guys." We laughed almost before he did. He had brightened our day with his own special brand of humor—and the fact that it had come at our expense somehow made it even funnier. He was playing on our greatest fear of what the night might hold with us in absentia; it was very well-played by him, and I smile to this day when I think about it.

It was quintessential Uncle Denny: He had a way of boosting your spirits just by being, well, him. He really cared about people, and he tirelessly gave of himself to help others. He treated people with dignity and respect, and he handled himself with class and humility. The example he set for those around him has shaped countless lives and will continue to do so far into the future. He truly was one of a kind.

Uncle Denny was also a world-class prankster (no doubt passed down genetically from Clar Clar), and the unsuspecting victim of many of his pranks was my father. I often watched those two revert to their teenage years at family gatherings, playing practical jokes on one another in an hours-long game of one-upmanship. My personal favorite was "the dirty sock." Dad could fall asleep anytime, anywhere, regardless of noise level. I was convinced that Dad could fall asleep next to an airport runway as a 747 roared past him on takeoff. Inevitably at family get-togethers, Dad would fall asleep on the floor in front of the television, out like a light within seconds. Once he started snoring, Uncle Denny would pull off one of the sweaty socks he had been wearing all day, quietly creep over to where Dad was sleeping and carefully place the sock right under his nose. The look on Dad's face when he woke up and realized he had unwittingly been breathing in the unholy aroma from his brother's dirty sock was priceless. Of course, Dad would get his revenge at some point at another family gathering, which would result in laughter from

Uncle Denny when he awoke and realized that he was the latest victim of the dreaded dirty sock.

Uncle Denny was a constant in my life; I knew I could always count on him. When Dad passed away unexpectedly in 2005, Uncle Denny was there for me, and I for him, as we coped with the sudden loss of a father and brother. I couldn't have made it through that somber time without Uncle Denny. I leaned on him hard for love and support, and he was there to help his nephew through it. He was my rock. We would talk for hours on the phone, and Kim and I would go to Uncle Denny and Aunt Kay's house to visit. Uncle Denny and I attended a Cleveland Indians baseball game with great seats behind the plate, and he and I even bit the bullet and went to a Cleveland Browns football game in December (if you attend a football game in our climate at that time of year, you are taking a serious roll of the dice with the weather). We huddled together in high winds and a cold, driving rain that drenched the shores of Lake Erie as we watched the Browns defeat the Tennessee Titans, and there was Uncle Denny—soaking wet and chilled to the bone—laughing and smiling through it all. We had a ball that afternoon.

But that was Uncle Denny: He was a good Christian man who loved life and got the absolute most out of every single day. His outlook on life should be a lesson for us all. He was the most optimistic person I ever met, and his optimism was contagious. There are many times when I feel down or a bad mood coming on and I will think to myself: "Uncle Denny wouldn't react this way to this situation. You need to handle it better than this, Tom." He was the perfect role model. And that is the true measure of a man's life: It's not what you've accomplished, it's not what you have, and it's not the wealth you've accumulated. It's the legacy you leave, and Uncle Denny left an indelible legacy of love, caring, humor and friendship. He was a special man.

As it turned out, the last time I saw Uncle Denny was on my birthday in April 2011, the year he died. Kim arranged for a surprise birthday dinner with Denny and Kay. When I walked into the restaurant and saw them sitting there, smiling, knowing the surprise had been achieved, it made my night. The last image I have of Uncle Denny is a fitting one: sitting next to me at dinner that night, talking, laughing and enjoying a pleasant evening—just like so many others before. That image is forever burned into my memory.

Uncle Denny passed away unexpectedly at age sixty-eight three months later.

It's been more than seven years since he died, and it's still hard to believe that I can't pick up the phone and hear his cheerful voice, get his advice, tell him what's going on in my life and hear what's going on in his. Talking to Uncle Denny made me feel closer to my dad, and I believe it made him feel closer to his brother. I wish I had called him more often and visited him more often. But I will always cherish the memories I have, like Uncle Denny going to my high school football games on Friday nights in the fall to watch me play, or him driving through a snowstorm from Kenmore to Mogadore for my fourteenth birthday party (even though we implored him not to do so due to the extremely hazardous driving conditions. He made the trip anyway).

And the best (and unlikeliest) memory of all: Uncle Denny and Aunt Kay actually vacationing on the same floor of the same hotel at the same time as Kim and I during our honeymoon on Maui in July 1995—by total coincidence. It went like this:

We were at a restaurant for a family dinner and the topic of our honeymoon came up. We told Uncle Denny we would be honeymooning in Hawaii. He looked at us from across the table and said, "When are you going? Kay and I are going to Hawaii."

"The first of week of July, for our honeymoon," I said. "We're leaving the morning after our wedding."

"We'll be there the first week of July, too," he said. "Which island are you going to?"

"Maui," I replied.

"So are we," he said. "Where are you staying on Maui?"

"The Kaanapali Beach Hotel," I said, thinking that ought to end the eerie similarities.

"Well that's where we're staying!" he exclaimed.

No way is he being serious, I thought. He's putting me on, in typical Uncle Denny fashion. I wondered how far he was going to take it.

"What floor are you staying on?" he asked. Now I know he's full of it, I thought.

"The fourth floor," I told him ... and waited for it.

"Well so are we!" he exclaimed again.

I couldn't take it anymore.

"Come on, there's no way you guys are going to Hawaii at the same time we are, staying on Maui at the same place we are, on the *same floor* we're staying," I said.

"Yes we are," he deadpanned with that twinkle in his eyes.

"We couldn't have planned it that good if we tried," I said. "Are you being serious? I mean, we're going all the way to Hawaii."

He looked at Kim and me, a broad smile stretched across his face. "That's not far enough," he said in a sing-song voice, clearly reveling in his just-discovered role as honeymoon crasher.

I thought he had been kidding, but it was obvious now that he wasn't. Everything he said was true—against every odd known to man, but true. They arrived at the hotel a few days after we did, and Kim and I ended up spending quality time with them on our honeymoon. We had breakfast together at the hotel, ate dinner on the beach literally just yards away from the Pacific Ocean and enjoyed a drink to some Hawaiian music and dancing in the hotel courtyard.

I can't lie: It was bizarre to see Uncle Denny and Aunt Kay there with us in such an impromptu manner, so far from home, like we were in some sort of time warp or another dimension. It was surreal. I kept expecting to wake up one morning having dreamt it all, but no, it was real. And I can also say that having them there for our honeymoon made the most special week of my life even more special. That unplanned, unexpected, unlikely time with them half a world away in paradise was truly a gift from God.

The examples of Uncle Denny's humor, graciousness and love are countless. The moment his soul left this Earth, our world became a less hospitable place to live. But my life has been immeasurably enriched for having him in it.

UNCLE DENNY'S VISITATION

As you've read in this book, the visitations I have received have been for a specific purpose, usually to deliver a message of some kind. All of these messages, even those prophetic in nature, involved events that have since come to pass.

Except one.

That was Uncle Denny's visit, and I'm still waiting for his message's outcome. It's not much of a mystery, though. I know full well what that outcome ultimately will be.

Some of the warmest memories from my childhood involve the old Hardesty family gatherings at Dee Dee and Clar Clar's house, especially over the holidays. They were filled with mirth, Clar Clar playing Christmas songs on the piano and Dee Dee busily preparing dinner while the three members of my immediate family and the five members of Denny and Kay's family crammed into the tiny house for a wonderful evening of fun, food and fellowship. I wished those nights could last forever. For me, life didn't get much better than playing with my Hardesty cousins, hearing Uncle Denny's laughter and enjoying Clar Clar's virtuoso Christmas performance at the piano. It was a Norman Rockwell and Thomas Kinkade collaboration come to life.

It didn't have to be a holiday celebration, of course. Any Hardesty get-together would do. Any time I got to hang out with my Hardesty cousins at Dee Dee and Clar Clar's, life was good. Regardless of how much time I got to spend with them, it just never seemed like it was enough.

As I said earlier, I believe the deceased can create their own reality in the dream state for their visit, like an artist sweeping his brush across the canvas. As the artist paints a picture with the brush strokes, the deceased does the same with ethereal imagery. And they do this in such a way that the living subject of their visit can best understand and recognize the message.

And so it makes sense that Uncle Denny's lone visit to me involved a Hardesty family gathering.

Uncle Denny had been gone several years before he paid me his one and only visit. Each time I have to say goodbye to a loved one, it makes me acutely aware of my own mortality, aware that someday it's going to be me laid out in that casket. It's not that this ever really slips our minds; we know that all of this is temporary, that life is fleeting and our Earthly existence is barely a blip on the cosmic radar. We are, as the rock group Kansas so poignantly wrote, just dust in the wind. Every time we bury another loved one, we know we are that much closer to joining them.

And with that comes the great question that humanity has been asking itself since, well, humanity began: What comes after death? Are we simply that motionless, lifeless shell of a human being in that coffin, to be lowered into the ground and never to see the light of day again, mortal beings whose time on Earth is over? Or are we immortal, beings of energy and light whose souls live for eternity after physical death?

Uncle Denny may have answered that question for me—and for all of us.

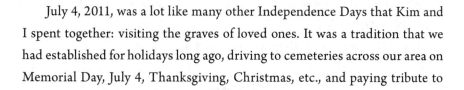

July 4, 2011, was a lot like many other Independence Days that Kim and I spent together: visiting the graves of loved ones. It was a tradition that we had established for holidays long ago, driving to cemeteries across our area on Memorial Day, July 4, Thanksgiving, Christmas, etc., and paying tribute to those we had lost.

On this day, we were making our way to Greenlawn Cemetery in southwest Akron, not far from Kenmore, to visit Dee Dee and Clar Clar's grave in the mausoleum, amongst other of my family members. As we neared the cemetery, Kim noticed a snazzy-looking sports car in a dealership parking lot and wanted to take a look at it (she comes from a car family and has always had an intense interest in cars—unlike myself). We pulled into the parking lot, parked and walked toward the car. Since it was July 4, the dealership was closed, but Kim still wanted to look at it; she had been toying with the idea of buying a Corvette or Camaro, and this particular car had caught her eye.

I've never been a fan of car shopping, and my impatience wasn't lost on Kim. "I know, you're bored," she said. "I'll be done in a minute."

"You know what you should do?" I told her. "You should call Uncle Denny tomorrow and see if he wants to come out here and look at the car with you. He only lives about ten-fifteen minutes away. He loves cars; I'm sure he would like that."

Kim thought for a moment, then said, "Isn't there a family get-together at his house today? Maybe we could just stop by and say hi and I could ask him there."

Yes, Denny and Kay were having relatives over to their house for a big July 4 cookout. I considered it as we looked over the car, and the more I thought about it, the more I talked myself out of it. It was getting late in the day; although there was a good hour or two of daylight left, by the time we went to the cemetery and drove to their house, it would be getting late. We wouldn't have much time to spend with Denny and Kay.

"We'd better not go over there today. It would be kind of rushed at this point," I told Kim. "Let's just go over there another day. We can see them any time."

Kim agreed, and we finished at the car dealership, paid our respects at the cemetery and drove home.

Uncle Denny died less than twenty-four hours later.

Death had wiped out much of my family by the time of Uncle Denny's visitation—in a very short period of time. Gramps died in 2004, Dad in 2005, Dee Dee in 2008, Uncle Denny in 2011, my mother-in-law Joan in 2013 and Mom in 2014, along with our cats Sylvia in 2003 and Halen in 2013. Each loss was devastating, and it was beginning to exact a mental toll on Kim and me. Nearly everyone closest to me in my life was gone. My entire support system was crumbling underneath me. I was starting to feel like a man trapped alone on a deserted island, with no hope of rescue. And worse yet, no one left *to* rescue me. I became consumed with my own mortality. How could I not? I was surrounded by death, and it seemed to be closing in on me. Yes, I had received several visitations that had strengthened my faith that we continue after death, but no one had ever said, "Yes, Tom, we continue after death. Rest easy, life is forever." Faith I had, concrete evidence I did not.

Uncle Denny's visitation didn't offer that concrete evidence, but it came awfully close.

It began with a classic Hardesty family get-together. The usual suspects were there: Mom, Dad, Uncle Denny, Aunt Kay, Brub, Doug, Shelly and Dee Dee. I couldn't discern what the gathering was for exactly, but it was obviously celebratory. There was a lot of laughter and the mood was light. We were in a house I didn't recognize, but I got the sense that wasn't important. All I saw of the inside was the main floor of the house, but from the outside I could see that it was fairly large and modern, painted a dull yellow, not more than twenty or thirty years old, at least two levels and maybe three, with a fir tree and evergreen shrub on either side of the front stoop along the front of the house, giving the home a rather cozy look. The house was situated in a typical suburban neighborhood where the homes were somewhat close together but not right on top of each other. You entered the house via the front stoop, comprised of three or four steps with a thin, black, iron railing on either side; the front door opened directly into a large living room that featured white walls, beige or light tan carpeting and cream-colored furniture. There was a large TV in the front corner of the living room, where Mom, Dad, Uncle Denny, Aunt Kay and Dee Dee spent most of their time. My cousins and I were in a bedroom down the hallway off the living room, playing around on a desktop computer and talking.

It occurred to me that everyone in the living room, with the exception of Aunt Kay, was deceased and should not be there. However, not only were they there, they looked great. All of them appeared as they did in the prime of their lives. And my cousins and I were adults, looking in the visit as we appeared physically in real life at that time. I found this interesting because the majority of the old Hardesty gatherings occurred when we cousins were youths or very young adults, so the fact that the cousins' appearance was contemporary while that of the older generation was a snapshot of their prime indicated to me that I had to be an adult in the visit to understand the message. A child would not grasp its meaning. Uncle Denny had painted the perfect scene.

Nothing of real substance was said throughout most of the visit. It was just chatter, typical family-gathering fare. Our parents and Dee Dee talked and watched television in the living room, while my cousins and I visited in the bedroom down the hallway. There wasn't a whole lot of interaction between the two groups except when one of us cousins walked through the living room on our way to the kitchen to grab something to eat or drink. It was good to see my cousins, because it had been a while since we had all gotten together—not since Uncle Denny's funeral, in fact. It seemed like old times.

After a while, the night began to wrap up. Each family member slowly exited the house one after the other, walking out the front door in the living room. I held the door open and bid goodbye to each one as they filed out, realizing for the first time that the house must be mine because I was the only one who wasn't leaving. This was, after all, Uncle Denny's canvas, not mine. It was his brush, his palette, his imagery.

Everyone was cheerful as they left, smiling and turning to wave goodbye as they headed to their cars in the darkened driveway. Dad and Uncle Denny were the last to leave. Dad walked out the door first, Uncle Denny right behind him. As Dad continued out the door and disappeared into the darkness, Uncle Denny suddenly stopped in the doorway and looked over his shoulder at me. With his trademark Cheshire cat grin and twinkle in his eye, he said, "We'll see you soon, Tom." Then, still sporting that grin, he walked out into the night and was gone.

I slowly closed the door behind him, and the visitation ended.

"We'll see you soon, Tom." Uncle Denny's parting words echoed in my head as I awoke, and they haunt me to this day. The way he said it, with that knowing smile and gleam in his eye, like he knew something I didn't … The meaning was unmistakable. He hadn't said goodbye, he had said everyone was waiting to see me again. He had issued a declaration of future contact—and the affirmation of eternity I had long been seeking.

"We'll see you soon, Tom."

I have no doubt that is true. Mom, Dad, Uncle Denny, Dee Dee and all my other deceased loved ones—pets included—will see me again. And I have no doubt where that will take place. Uncle Denny's visitation confirmed in my mind that my loved ones are waiting for me, like your loved ones are waiting for you. Our soul does survive physical death.

"We'll see you soon, Tom."

Indeed. I know I will see them again.

But even with Uncle Denny's comforting words, two questions continued to gnaw at me: What is the nature of Heaven, and, in my case, how soon is soon?

I didn't know it then, but I wouldn't have to wait long for the answer to the first question.

As for the answer to question No. 2, well, I guess I'll find out soon enough. Like everyone else.

———

CHAPTER 8

DAD

D ad was a child of the 1950s. He graduated from Akron's Kenmore High School in 1959 and could have served as the poster child for that era: He loved fast cars and rock 'n' roll, and in his senior portrait he looked so much like a young Elvis Presley that you almost had to do a double-take to make sure it wasn't. He was a sharp-looking guy and always looked young for his age, his jet-black hair and piercing brown eyes giving him a striking appearance. Dad wasn't very big—only about 5-foot-6—but he always looked fit, going out of his way to keep himself in reasonably good shape to avoid what we in our family call "The Hardesty Curse," which is the untimely death of Hardesty males in their sixties or younger due primarily to genetically bad hearts. Clar Clar died at age sixty-three, and Clar Clar's dad and grandfather also died in their early sixties. Clar Clar's two older brothers, Ralph and Wayne, died young as well, one at age forty-seven and another at fifty-four. Clar Clar's younger brother Frank lived to be eighty, something of a miracle for a Hardesty man.

Dad had only recently graduated from the University of Akron and was busy enjoying young adulthood to the fullest when I came along in 1968. Let's just say I was something of a surprise. Mom and Dad had already set a wedding date when she discovered she was pregnant with me. The running joke—years later, after I had done the math that the length of time between October (their wedding) and April (my birth) was sixth months—was that I got to attend their wedding and tag along on their honeymoon to Niagara Falls. Looking back, I don't think Dad, at age twenty-seven, was anywhere near ready to be a father and was forced to learn his new role on the fly—which actually made him very much like a lot of new fathers. I think Dad was a bit frightened to have such a monstrous responsibility placed on him so quickly and never felt entirely comfortable in his dad role, at least not until I was old enough to be somewhat self-sustaining.

But he was a wonderful provider—I never went without, and when the time came he followed through on his long-held promise to pay my way through college—and the man never, ever laid a hand on me. Not once. He didn't believe in hitting a child, a form of discipline he learned from his own mom, Dee Dee, who steadfastly refused to strike a child (this, during an era when spanking was a common and widely accepted form of punishment in the United States). Instead, Dad would either simply get angry with me or, worse, express great disappointment in my behavior—in other words, he would shame me, which was an extremely effective form of punishment because the last thing a little boy wants to do is let his dad down. That cuts deep. Mom, on the other hand, was not afraid to spank me if my transgression rose to that level—which also was very effective because spanking, well, hurt.

Dad often stayed out of the discipline business altogether, except for my grades in school; he took education extremely seriously, and I never saw him madder than the times—thankfully rare—when I brought home a rough report card. I once got a 'D' in art class for a grading period in elementary school, and Dad's face literally turned red when he saw it. I thought, "If he's ever going to hit me, this is going to be the time." But he didn't. Instead, he took away some privileges—an excruciating punishment for a kid—and explained to me the importance of getting good grades, even in classes I disliked. I said, "But Dad, I'm no good at art. I'm not going to be an artist. What does it matter if I don't get good grades in art?" To which he said, "I'm not mad that you're not good at art. I'm very disappointed that you're not trying your best. No matter what you do in life, you always have to try your best."

I was in fourth grade, and Dad's message has stuck with me ever since. Thanks to his wisdom, I learned more from that 'D' in art class than any 'A' that I ever received.

⁓

If Dad was a child of the 1950s, he was a product of the 1960s, culturally and politically. He leaned left in the political spectrum and was heavily into the music of that era. I grew up listening to Led Zeppelin, Pink Floyd, Black Sabbath, etc. with Dad, sitting together in the darkened finished basement of our apartment in Mogadore, the soft red glow of his lava lamp and the spicy aroma of burning incense emanating from a ceramic Buddha statue sitting atop one of Dad's large floor speakers setting the mood for the music. A large Oriental rug hung on the wall behind Dad's elaborate stereo system; it was hippie heaven, and I loved it. I found the loud music in that setting to be incredibly relaxing, and I could easily fall asleep—and often did—on the floor in front of the speakers as the music blared.

It's where I learned the importance of "me time," of mentally decompressing after a stressful day. I can vividly recall, at four and five years old, literally counting the minutes until Dad got home from work, then accosting him the moment he set foot in the door to play Led Zeppelin's legendary song "Stairway to Heaven" on the record player (it was my favorite song then, and it's my favorite song now). This became an almost daily occurrence. Dad would come home exhausted from a long day at the office, and I would beg him to play Stairway to Heaven until he broke down and did it—before even getting the chance to change out of his work clothes. I would watch with excitement as Dad carefully pulled the *Led Zeppelin IV* album from its protective dust sleeve, delicately placed it on the turntable, pulled the arm over the record and set the needle onto the vinyl. After a couple pops and hisses as the needle traced the grooves, Jimmy Page's iconic guitar intro would begin and my day would be made. It got to the point that Dad found it easier to just teach me how to work the turntable by myself, entrusting a young boy to not ruin his expensive equipment. Which, I'm happy to say, I did not. And once I learned to operate the turntable, I hungrily delved into Dad's extensive record collection and quickly developed a love and appreciation for the rich chords and harmonies of guitar rock that I possess to this day. Music was Dad's respite from the rigors of everyday life, and it's mine as well.

Music, among other things, also served as the centerpiece of my parents' inclusion in a tight-knit circle of friends known as "The Group," which amounted to several married couples and their children. The Group got together for parties nearly every Saturday night, rotating among the houses of the members of The Group, and it was not uncommon for the children to be present at these legendary bashes. It would be frowned upon now, but this was the 1970s, and the kids playing downstairs while the adults partied hard and blasted music upstairs was the norm, not the exception, as I was growing up. We kids of The Group thought nothing of it. And these gatherings weren't always on weekends, either. More than once, I had to step over passed-out bodies on the living room floor as I got ready for school in the morning, and I never batted an eye. These people were like family to me, I loved them like family, and closing the door behind me as I headed to the bus stop while they lay on the floor like fallen timber was just business as usual. They were fun people and they never endangered us kids in any way. If any party was expected to be particularly raucous—and some certainly were on the wild side (to put it mildly)—then the kids would be safely shipped off to relatives' houses.

I often wondered what exactly must be going on at some of these parties to warrant the quarantining of the children. As a youngster I was perplexed, but by the time I was in high school it didn't take much imagination to figure it out. Mom and Dad were very careful not to expose me to anything even remotely harmful. But in most cases, the kids were present at these parties; they were events unto themselves, taking on a life of their own. Like I said, it was the 1970s, and the rules were different in the '70s. I can say this: The Group and their parties certainly broadened my horizons.

I mention The Group and these parties as an illustration of Dad being a better father than I think he sometimes gave himself credit for. He had excellent instincts; he always preferred to let me see and experience things for myself rather than have him or someone else preach them to me. He figured (rightly) that exposing me to life in small doses as a youngster would prepare me better for adulthood than someone else doing it for them in large doses later on. At least this way, Dad could control what and how much I experienced. In this respect, I felt that I received a crucial head start over many kids my age; whereas too many of them became embroiled in drug or alcohol problems as they got older, I was well aware of those dangers and knew how to avoid them.

Dad always told me knowledge was power.

Like a lot of fathers and sons, Dad and I had a complicated relationship—partly because we were nothing alike, and partly because we were entirely too much alike. Dad could be high-strung, moody, unpredictable and quick to anger, but he could also be warm, funny, compassionate, laid back and introspective. In my younger years, particularly as a young adult, I wasn't much different. I wasn't high-strung or unpredictable in my personality like Dad, but moody and quick to anger were apt descriptions of my younger self. It's fair to say I could be a hothead. And Dad's moodiness and quick temper, combined with my stubbornness and immaturity, was a recipe for some rather heated verbal sparring between us. Unfortunately, some of our arguments got rather nasty, and looking back I blame myself for much of it. Dad could be insulting and hurtful, but some of the comments I fired back at him were completely unacceptable to say to a parent, and to this day I regret them and am ashamed of myself for saying them. Dad said things to me out of frustration, and I responded without thinking. Cooler heads did not prevail.

These clashes seemed to increase as the years went on, and the single biggest regret of my life was the inescapable feeling that Dad died thinking I didn't love him. That haunted and tormented me for nearly a decade following his death, and it took the most incredible experience of my life to put those fears to rest (more on that later).

I loved my dad dearly. I couldn't even begin to measure his positive impact on my life—his love, his support, his guidance, his wisdom, the things he taught me. His influence can be found everywhere in my life: My likes, my dislikes, my interests, my passions. As I mentioned earlier, things like Ohio State football, the Ohio high school boys state basketball tournament, rock music, history (particularly military history), geography, space and astronomy, and the late Art Bell, who created and hosted the late-night paranormal-themed radio show Coast to Coast AM, are gifts that Dad passed down to me. He spurred my interest in all of them, and they dominate my life to this day. They're not just hobbies of mine, they help to define me. And in many ways, Dad lives on through those interests and passions that he instilled in me. I can't engage in any of them, whether I'm watching the Buckeyes on TV or sitting in the arena at the state basketball tournament or listening to old Art Bell shows on my laptop, without feeling Dad's presence. It's tangible.

And his greatest gift: my wife Kim. On a cold, snowy January night, Dad called and asked me to come down to the little bar he was at; he said he was there with Kim and some other friends and that she had expressed interest in seeing me again (Kim and I had met briefly once before a few months earlier). Dad had a couple longtime friends that worked with Kim, and they and others would all get together at this bar on Friday nights to wind down from the long workweek. Through these almost-weekly gatherings, Dad got to know Kim fairly well and was impressed with her character; as time went on, he became convinced that she and I would be a good match. I didn't know any of this until Dad called me to come down to the bar on that cold night in early January; I balked at first due to having plans with friends, but relented at his persistence and headed to the bar.

A year and a half later, Kim and I got married—with Dad as my best man.

Some of my fondest memories of Dad actually involve his misadventures. I recall them fondly not just because of the misadventures themselves, but also because of his unwittingly hilarious reactions to them. Quite often the unfortunate situations which he created or found himself, and his responses to them, were downright funny. As he became angry, the words he wanted to say weren't always the words that came out of his mouth. The words somehow got out of order as he spoke them and made no sense whatsoever; sometimes he even said words that I swore he made up. His tongue-twisted sentences didn't match his rising anger, and that farcical contrast often left me trying mightily to suppress my laughter. And the madder Dad got, the funnier it was. His emotions overrode his thought process, his enraged brain unable to formulate words as quickly as his mouth could say them. The end result was Dad nearly speaking in tongues—and giving an impromptu stand-up routine that rivaled that of the best comedians.

And an inordinate number of these comical blunders occurred during our annual family vacations, with several taking place in one unforgettable two-week driving sojourn to Florida in the summer of 1982—a family expedition that Dad had coined our "Busman's Holiday" trip because of the intense sightseeing nature of it and the large amount of territory we were going to cover. And by "intense sightseeing nature of it," I mean we spent almost the entire two weeks trapped inside our two-door Honda Accord literally watching the country go by. It was a real-life *National Lampoon's Vacation*: I was an awkward fourteen-year-old, in between eighth and ninth grade, so I filled the Rusty Griswold role quite nicely, while Mom and Dad did a bang-up Ellen and Clark Griswold bit (it's fair to say that Anthony Michael Hall, Beverly D'Angelo and Chevy Chase could have learned a few things from our trip). The Hardestys' vacation of 1982 and the Griswolds' Hollywood version that was released in 1983 were frighteningly similar in their unrelenting misfortune.

I spent most of those two weeks to Florida and back sharing the back seat with blankets, pillows, grocery bags full of food and drink, and any items of luggage that didn't fit in the hatchback—which, from my perspective, seemed like most of them. And the more ground we covered and more places we visited, the more souvenirs we accumulated—and the more cramped my back seat quarters became. America's Magnificent Seven astronauts of the early 1960s were less confined in their rudimentary Mercury capsules than I was in the back seat of that car. To pass the time—and there was plenty of it to pass—I read, slept or served as Dad's navigator with my trusty road atlas (it was the pre-GPS era, after all). This was long before cell phones, iPods, iPads, portable DVD players and in-car video systems, so my entertainment options were extremely limited. Plotting our course with our AAA TripTik ended up being my primary activity of choice; I had never been to most of the places on this trip and found myself enthralled with the TripTik's detailed description of the landscape on each page and the corresponding view outside the car windows.

As I pored over the maps and assorted travel information in the back seat, however, I had no way of knowing the run of bad luck that lay in store for my dad. I'll detail a few of those instances here:

—The first real hint of "trouble" on the Busman's Holiday came on the first day of driving. Dad had grown road weary not long after we got past Cincinnati and into Kentucky on I-75. He had been driving for the better part of four hours and wanted a break; Mom, who rarely engaged in freeway driving back home (the high speeds and traffic volume of expressways made her a nervous wreck almost to the point of completely shutting down), was especially not interested in freeway driving hundreds of miles away from home on unfamiliar highways. Dad insisted, saying his eyes were tired from watching the road; Mom flatly said she wasn't driving. At an impasse, Dad pulled into a rest stop and said we would sit there until he was ready to drive again, which could be hours.

The ploy worked. Mom caved and reluctantly slid into the driver's seat. I moved up to the passenger seat, and a tired but relieved Dad crawled into the back. He assured Mom that she was in good hands with me as navigator (which she was; Dad had taught me how to read maps when I was very young, and by this time it was second nature to me) and said he was going to take a nap for a little while. Mom pulled out of the rest area, and within minutes Dad was out cold behind us.

Mom was jittery behind the wheel as we headed south on the interstate through Kentucky, but between our conversation and the radio, her fears slowly began to ease. The tranquil setting of the Bluegrass State relaxed her, and it was a smooth drive through the countryside. I surveyed the pastoral scene outside my car window as dusk began to fall, knowing that each mile we covered brought us a little closer to the fun and excitement that awaited us in the Sunshine State.

Little did I know that the excitement was about to start early ... in Kentucky.

Not wanting to drive at night, Mom decided to pull off at the next rest area after about an hour to change drivers. Dad was sound asleep in the back seat as Mom got off the interstate, drove into the rest stop, pulled into a parking space ... and promptly slammed the front of the car into the curb. The car lurched upward and forward, almost going completely over the curb, before bouncing back down to the asphalt of the parking lot. The forceful jolt sent a sleeping Dad careening into the back of the front seats with a resounding thud. Unceremoniously startled out of his slumber, a groggy, confused—and angry—Dad wanted answers.

"What the hell was that?! What happened, Laura?" he inquired.

"It's starting to get dark and I didn't see the curb," Mom snapped back. "You need to get up here and drive now. I'm done." I thought Mom's answer to be somewhat odd, considering that although it was dusk, there was still plenty of light left to see the curb; I figured (at the time) that she had simply misjudged the distance from the front of the car to the curb. Lighting had nothing to do with it.

Dad, still annoyed, got out and inspected the front of the car to ensure there had been no damage caused by the impact. Satisfied that there wasn't (and I was amazed that there wasn't, because that car hit the curb with some serious force), he promptly got back in the driver's seat—and remained there the rest of the trip.

I have since become convinced that Mom hit the curb on purpose so that Dad wouldn't ask her to drive again—which he didn't.

Well played, Mom. Well played.

—The next major incident of the trip—not counting the dinner faux pas in Tennessee when Mom and Dad couldn't agree on where to eat and therefore passed up exit after exit littered with all manner of restaurants, then were forced to settle for fast food (much to Dad's great chagrin) because nearly everything else had closed for the night (it was a Sunday, and back then most establishments shut down early on Sundays)—was when Dad shaved in our hotel room one night in Fort Lauderdale, Florida, only to realize after finishing that he had forgotten to pack his aftershave lotion.

Our first stop in Florida had been to visit Mom's older sister in the Orlando area. After a few days there, which included the obligatory trip to Disney World, we continued on to south Florida. Ultimate destination: Miami. What Dad didn't know was that his much-needed aftershave lotion stayed back in Orlando, which was very unfortunate for his face. Dad had extremely sensitive skin, so shaving without using aftershave lotion or balm was bad. Very bad. Very, *very*, bad.

In this particular instance, it nearly ruined the entire vacation. Dad absolutely had to have his favorite aftershave lotion; not just any moisturizer would do. Without it, his face would nearly fossilize. After money and gasoline, Dad's aftershave lotion was the single most important item on the trip.

It all started out harmlessly enough. After checking into the hotel in Fort Lauderdale, the three of us settled in for the night; after making the drive from Orlando, which included stops at several quiet beaches as we made our way south down Florida's Atlantic coast, it was time to unwind. Mom and I went about the business of getting things set up and organized for our brief stay while Dad made his way to the bathroom to shave, filling the entire hotel room with his customary loud, cheerful humming as he did so. Upon finishing his shave, a refreshed Dad exited the bathroom and started digging through his luggage in search of his aftershave lotion—and couldn't find it.

"Have you guys seen my aftershave?" Dad asked. "I thought I had it in my suitcase, but I can't find it."

I knew it wasn't in my luggage.

"I don't have it, Doug," Mom answered. "Did you pack it back up after you shaved at my sister's?"

"I don't know, I thought so," Dad said, each word dripping with worry. "Maybe one of you guys grabbed it and put it in your suitcase by mistake."

It was obvious where this was headed. This is going to be an all-timer, I thought.

The three of us immediately set about feverishly tearing through our luggage looking for the elusive aftershave lotion, on the off chance that it had gotten mixed up with other items when we left Orlando. Nothing.

Things got worse when, a few minutes into this desperate search, Dad's face started to turn red. Not a hot pink. Not a deep orange. Red.

Dad grew increasingly frantic as we searched in vain for the obviously absent aftershave. His face grew tighter and tighter, making it harder and harder for him to talk. Frantic then gave way to full-blown panic when it became clear that his aftershave lotion was, indeed, in Orlando. At this point he didn't know what to do with himself; he was in pain, he could barely move his mouth, and it was getting worse by the minute.

"Uuuuhhhhhhh, uuuuhhhhhh," he moaned as he stomped around the room, his mouth barely able to formulate words as the skin on his lotion-less face completely lost its elasticity. He did manage to mumble that we needed to take him to the hospital because his face was on fire and he couldn't move it at all. Those words certainly didn't come out of his mouth smoothly, but he somehow slurred and jumbled enough of them together that we got the gist of his message.

"Uuuuhhhhhh, uuuhhhhhh, uhhhhhhuuhh." Dad continued to stagger around the room, his eyes wide with fear and his mouth barely open—a credit card may not have fit between his lips. The anger he had demonstrated when this fiasco started had since transitioned to helplessness and fear. Quite often, it was hard to tell if Dad actually had some sort of malady or if he was being theatrical; when it came to illness and such, he had, shall I say, a flair for the dramatic. But not this time. The man was genuinely scared.

Within a few minutes, Dad's face was fire-engine red. To this day, I've never seen anything like it. I've seen people who fell asleep on the beach for hours whose faces were less red, and in far better working order, than Dad's face was in Fort Lauderdale that night following his shave.

Of course, Mom and I found the whole thing to be nothing short of absolutely hilarious. His pain wasn't funny—I felt badly for him in that regard—but his theatrics certainly were. We tried not to make our laughing obvious, but all it took was for Mom and me to make quick eye contact with one another and we would scurry in opposite directions trying to suppress our laughter—which, of course, only made it funnier. That's just human nature.

"Uuuuuhhhhhhh, uuuuhhhhhhh, uuuhhhhhhhh."

Dad's histrionics during this saga were priceless; he was known to be overly dramatic when it came to pain and illness, but that night he took it to an entirely new level—except this time, his pain and fear appeared to be legitimate. Even so, the louder he moaned, the more animated he became, and the redder his face got, the funnier it was until I thought I might explode. Even now, the image in my mind's eye of a panicked Dad tramping aimlessly around that hotel room in his robe and moaning loudly—a poor man's Frankenstein's monster—as his face turned deeper and deeper shades of red, makes me laugh out loud. It was, as they say, an instant classic.

As it was, Mom and I went to a nearby store (it was getting rather late, so we weren't sure any would be open) and bought Dad his coveted aftershave lotion, eventually ending his misery. But not before she and I nearly split our sides open laughing going to the store and back.

I have often wondered what would have happened if Mom and I had been unable to find an open store that night. I really don't think that Dad could have gone all night and into the next morning before getting aftershave lotion on his face, and it was very doubtful that aspirin—or anything else, for that matter—would have had much impact on his condition. We might well have had to take him to the hospital; it would have been the only way he could have gotten any relief. The rest of the vacation would have been in jeopardy.

Dad told me many times over the years that he thought he was in trouble that night. He figured he was headed for the emergency room. I took it as a lesson learned: To this day, I will not shave without first making sure there is aftershave lotion at the ready. I would rather look like Grizzly Adams before enduring what my father did all those decades ago in South Florida.

It was truly a night to remember—for a lot of reasons.

—If there was one thing you could count on with our family vacations, it was that Dad would have them meticulously planned.

For weeks and even months before we left, Dad could often be found lying on his bed with maps and travel brochures strewn all around him. He would lie there in his robe and hum to himself while he pored over these atlases and booklets into the wee hours of the night, jotting down list after list of routes, sights, lodging and restaurants to consider on the trip. He took this task very seriously, as evidenced by the countless scribbles, symbols, notations and other assorted markings he made throughout his small library of vacation publications. Words would be underlined, sentences would be highlighted, symbols such as stars, question marks and exclamation points would be set off in the margins, entire paragraphs would be circled. When it came to our annual summer vacations, Dad left no stone unturned.

Dad's intense trip-planning didn't stop once the car was packed and the wheels had left the driveway; he often would only have his choices narrowed down, with final decisions to be made at some point during the vacation itself. Sometimes, these final decisions weren't made until hours before we were to engage in a particular activity. Dad would torture himself on which routes to take, what city or town we should overnight in, what restaurant we should eat at, etc. This combination of indecision and procrastination left us in some rather precarious positions, including one night in Daytona Beach, Florida, during our 1982 summer vacation.

Most of our family trips involved excursions to the East Coast; living in Northeast Ohio, it just made geographic sense that, if we wanted a beach vacation, then our destination would be the East Coast. We didn't take our first vacation until the summer of 1976, when I was eight years old, when we went with "The Group" to Wrightsville Beach, North Carolina. We repeated that trip the following two years, went to the Outer Banks of North Carolina by ourselves in 1979, then switched to Ocean Isle, North Carolina with "The Group" in 1981. By '82, Dad was ready for a change of scenery and chose Florida as our new destination. I would have loved a big driving trip out West to the Pacific (something which I have since done many times in my adult life— thanks in part to never getting to do it as a youth), but our trips had been limited to one week to keep costs down. The 1982 trip was our first two-week junket, and thus, it required unusually intricate planning on Dad's part.

And of all the planning Dad did for any vacation, potential places to eat took up the lion's share of his time. Dad loved seafood, so on these annual excursions to the ocean, eating anywhere but a seafood restaurant was absolutely out of the question—which was fine with me, because I was a seafood lover as well and still am. Our trips to Wrightsville Beach and Ocean Isle were filled with nightly drives to the famous seafood meccas of Calabash, North Carolina and Murrells Inlet, South Carolina. The '82 Florida trip was a different animal, however; we were covering new ground, which meant Dad was out of his comfort zone when it came to picking seafood restaurants.

Finding one in Daytona Beach was particularly daunting for Dad, simply because there were so many. The possibilities were endless, which Dad saw as a golden opportunity for some top-shelf seafood dining—and as such, he didn't want to be hasty in making his final decision. Therefore, he scrutinized his trusty AAA Florida travel guide for hours in our Daytona hotel room, thumbing through the pages and reading many of the choices aloud for Mom and me, rattling off every last detail of a restaurant then asking us what we thought. It finally reached a point that Mom and I didn't care where we ate, we just wanted to eat; it became paralysis by analysis.

"This place has an upper deck that looks out over the ocean. What do you think of that one?" Dad would say.

"We don't care, Doug. Just pick one," Mom would answer.

This dance continued for a couple hours, Dad lying on the bed intently studying the AAA travel guide like he was preparing for a college exam, with Mom and I growing restless being cooped up in a hotel room while so many tantalizing dining choices were out there waiting for us. Dad furiously marked up the travel guide with his customary notes and symbols as he narrowed the list of restaurants, which only made us hungrier.

Dad would say something like, "This one place specializes in crab dinners, but this other place is known for lobster. Triple-A has them both rated with five stars. This is a tough decision," as my stomach growled at the mere mention of these delicious morsels. All I could think of was sitting at a table in some rustic restaurant by the ocean with a heaping, steaming seafood platter in front of me, its contents likely fresh off the boat that very morning. I couldn't take much more of Dad's culinary descriptions.

Mercifully, he finally settled on his choice: a five-star seafood restaurant that had somehow gained an edge over the other five-star seafood restaurants in the travel guide. Something about this particular restaurant had caught Dad's attention, though, so after what seemed like an eternity of tedious deliberation, we finally jumped in the car and headed off to what I figured had to be a seafood restaurant like no other.

And boy was it ever.

By now it was dark as Dad navigated the streets of Daytona Beach in search of this magical restaurant with its mouth-watering menu. Considering how long it had taken Dad to choose this particular establishment, and the stiff competition it had defeated to become Dad's coveted top choice, this place had to be something special. I stared anxiously out my car window hoping that, at any moment, Dad would pull the car into the parking lot of this restaurant and a night of scrumptious dining would begin.

Instead, we drove. And drove. And drove. Up one street, down another. Everything started to look the same: gas stations, hotels, souvenir shops, convenience stores, restaurants. I swore we passed some of them multiple times. We seemed to drive past every structure in Daytona Beach except the one we were looking for. Turn onto this street, turn onto that street, go back down the main drag, turn onto a street we had already been on. Our dinner night out was turning into the 24 Hours of Daytona.

By this time, we were all frustrated, hungry and ready to give up the hunt and just go to one of the countless other restaurants that Daytona had to offer. At this point, anything was better than this.

Dad then turned onto yet another street which looked like it would not be home to a five-star seafood restaurant. Suddenly, he slowed the car to a crawl. I looked around but didn't see anything that would pass for a high-end restaurant.

Dad brought the car to a stop in the middle of the road and looked off to his right. "Hmph," he chuckled. "There it is."

There's what? I thought. Where's this killer five-star seafood restaurant he had promised us? We were at a dead stop in the middle of the street, and the only thing I saw to our right was something that could only be described as a glorified double-wide trailer with a bunch of rough-looking bikers and their motorcycles out front.

"That's it," Dad said matter-of-factly. I was horrified. Then he let out a loud, sarcastic laugh, incredulous that after all his painstaking restaurant research, after our frustrating forty-five minute drive around Daytona, after hoping that this maddening search would end with a succulent seafood dinner, our big prize was a seedy biker bar.

I had no idea how this place got a five-star rating as a seafood restaurant, because all I saw were a bunch of burly, leather-clad bikers milling around outside the bar. Some of them had chains hanging off their pants and jackets—not jewelry mind you, but actual chains—and were wearing those police-style hats that bikers customarily wear. I had never seen an actual biker bar before except in movies, and this place and its clientele could have been right out of Hollywood central casting. (Looking back, in fact, these bikers—particularly their attire—bore a striking resemblance to those in the *Police Academy* movie franchise; the costume designers nailed it in those films. That said, this is not meant to cast aspersions on the motorcycle culture; I relate this story through the eyes of a sheltered fourteen-year-old boy from the Midwestern suburbs.)

On one level, this was all so funny: Dad had poured his heart and soul into picking a nice restaurant for us, and this was the end result. On another level, it wasn't funny at all: The bikers looked like they meant business. If Dad was still planning on eating at this place, I thought, he was going to dine in there alone. And maybe die in there alone.

It never came to that. After several seconds of looking the place over, Dad tilted his head back and repeated his sarcastic laugh, hit the accelerator, and off we went into the Daytona night.

This story had a happy ending—sort of.

We eventually found a rather high-end looking restaurant on the Daytona main drag. It looked fancy from the outside, at least, so that was a step in the right direction. It was also in a well-lit area in the main section of Daytona

Beach, so that was another step in the right direction. Our only concern was that we might not be admitted into this particular establishment because of our attire; we were casually dressed, and this place looked pretty formal. Other than that, things were finally looking up for us.

And then we got out of the car.

A carload of (presumably drunk) young rowdies roared past on the main drag as we walked across the restaurant parking lot. Hearing the loud rev of the engine, I glanced toward the car just in time to see one of the guys lean out a window and shout "GANG BANG!" at us as they raced down the street. At least the bikers had been quiet, I thought.

Undaunted, we entered the restaurant and, after Dad had been assured that our casual attire was acceptable, we were led into the large dining room. Upon entering, it was obvious that my initial hunch had been correct: This place was formal. And by formal I mean stuffy. I instantly felt like we didn't belong there. This was a fancy restaurant in every sense: Nearly everyone was wearing a suit or dress, the décor was such that I felt I was soiling the place just by walking through it, and there was even a pianist playing some soft mood music near the center of the room, sitting at an elegant piano with a surface that literally gleamed. There was one small table located just in front of this piano, and to my great shock, that's where we were seated.

After receiving our menus, we began to look around and noticed that people were staring at us. Sitting where we were—the only table adjacent to the piano—we were kind of hanging out in the open by ourselves, on full display to the rest of the diners. At first I thought maybe everyone was just watching the pianist, but no, they were looking at us.

I started to feel self-conscious, and I wasn't the only one.

"This is uncomfortable," Dad said. I couldn't agree more.

After several minutes, though, we started to adjust to the uptight ambiance, and the feeling of being on display began to wear off; we actually started to embrace our catbird seat in the restaurant. The pianist smiled at us as he played, making us feel like we were kind of a big deal. This is pretty cool, I thought; those people staring at us are just jealous. Our luck had finally turned.

Then the maître d' arrived at our table.

"I'm sorry, but we're going to have to move you from this location," he said, and with that we were promptly whisked away to a table in a back corner. We weren't given an explanation for our sudden removal, but it became painfully obvious when we saw a suit and dress get seated at our previous table: Restaurant management had decided that we were riff-raff and must be made to dine in the shadows.

It was a microcosm of Dad's luck on the Hardesty Busman's Holiday tour of 1982: Even when he won, he lost.

Clark Griswold would have been proud.

I thoroughly enjoyed that trip to Florida in the summer of '82. It was quintessential Dad, and not just because of the aforementioned misadventures; it was also a wonderful learning experience. It broadened my horizons, both literally and figuratively. Since our previous four vacations had been one-week stays at the beach in North Carolina (and as such representing the farthest south I had traveled prior to the Florida trip), Dad had intended the Busman's Holiday to be as much an education as it was a vacation—and I must say mission accomplished. We saw a lot and did a lot in those action-packed two weeks on the road; highlights for me included a walk along Miami Beach, a bus tour of the Kennedy Space Center and an unexpected glimpse of the Orange Bowl stadium from a distance as we drove on the Miami expressway. I had watched so many games on TV that were played in the Orange Bowl that it almost felt like an old friend, so to actually get to lay my eyes on it in person was a pleasant surprise—but also very frustrating because we didn't pull off the highway to see it up close. I studied the famous structure as best I could from afar as we drove by on the freeway, noting its unique neighborhood location in Little Havana—a stark departure from the downtown lakefront placement of Municipal Stadium, which at the time was the home of my favorite NFL team, the Cleveland Browns.

As I forlornly watched the Orange Bowl fade from view through my rear-seat window, craning my neck until I could no longer distinguish it from its surroundings, I vowed right then and there in the back of that car that when I got older and started taking my own vacations, I was going to visit—and photograph—every college and professional stadium and arena on my route. All of them. And I have held true to that promise: In the nearly twenty-five years that Kim and I have been together, we have driven to (yes, driven; flying to stadiums is prohibited per my own self-imposed policy) hundreds of stadiums and arenas in our extensive travels across the United States and Canada; I have thousands of photographs of stadiums and arenas in all fifty states stretching back a quarter of a century. While we incorporate these stadium visits into the larger scope of our trips, many of our vacation destinations are actually chosen based on which stadiums we plan to see—a passion whose fire was lit in the back seat of my parents' car as we zipped past the Orange Bowl that day in July 1982. (I finally did get to visit that iconic stadium when Kim and I drove to Florida in 2001—I still have grass clippings from the Orange Bowl's field that I sealed in a plastic bag—before it was demolished seven years later.) I never blamed Dad for not stopping by to see the Orange Bowl that day; it wasn't on the itinerary, and I don't think he had any idea that we would be driving anywhere near it in the first place. But by not exiting the highway to see it, Dad unwittingly instilled in me a lifelong zeal that I have coined "The Great Stadium Hunt."

Dad did, however, directly influence my fervor for seeking answers to the big questions. Whereas the high-energy Busman's Holiday trip represented Dad's love of geography, history and education, our laid-back vacations to Wrightsville Beach and Ocean Isle reflected Dad's love of the ocean—and brought out his spiritual nature. Dad was a thinker, and he could sit by the ocean and contemplate the larger things in life for hours while watching the surf roll in and out in front of him. But that was during the sun-splashed heat of the day. At night, it got even deeper: Dad and I would stand alone on the beach together and stargaze, the roar of the waves crashing in the darkness serving as an eerie soundtrack while we stared up at the breathtaking blanket of stars that hung over the Atlantic Ocean. With very little light pollution at Wrightsville and Ocean Isle, the constellations lined up magnificently across the velvet blackness above us. The possibilities seemed endless as I literally peered into infinity.

"It makes you realize how small and insignificant we really are," Dad would solemnly say as he gazed into the vastness of the Milky Way. "Our time on Earth goes by in the blink of an eye. Those stars up there were here long before we were, and they'll be here long after we're gone."

As a young boy with most of my life still ahead of me, I understood but didn't fully appreciate Dad's statement. Time is relative, and to an elementary school-aged kid like I was back in the mid- to late 1970s, living for another sixty, seventy, eighty years was a length of time on a par with the stars and planets. It seemed like forever, so far into the future so as to be rendered irrelevant in my young mind. But I got his point: We're not here long, so make it count. In fact, Dad used to tell me all the time: "Life is not a dress rehearsal. We only get once chance at it." Not a day goes by that I don't hear Dad's voice in my head saying those wise words. I live my life by that credo, and the older I get the more poignant those words become. I'm fifty years old now, and I can feel the sand slipping through the hour glass of my life the way I know Dad did as he gazed at the panoply of stars above him during those nights on the beach in North Carolina.

Dad usually was silent as he stared into the heavens, no doubt contemplating where he was in his life, where he was going, where he wanted to go, how much time he had left in this existence. The cool sand always felt good around my feet, and if the breeze was just right, the ocean spray would continually moisten our skin as if we were standing in a cloud. Every now and then I would see a flashlight in the distance as someone made their way toward us along the beach, eventually reach our position and then disappear into the night, and it would just be Dad, me, the waves and the stars again. In the thirteen-plus years since his death, I've learned to focus more on wondrous times like those together rather than our regrettable moments in later years. I can't go back and change things that happened between us, but I can leave them where they belong: in the past.

I am now older than Dad was then by at least a decade, and when I go out on our back deck at night and stare up into the night sky, I feel what I know he felt all those years ago on the darkened beaches of North Carolina. I feel the awe and curiosity and wonder like he did, I feel the hands of time inexorably moving forward like he did, I feel an increasing sense of urgency like he did. There are no streetlights in our neighborhood in Stow, so it gets very dark and quiet here at night; you'd never know you were in a large suburb in the middle of the sprawling Akron-Canton-Cleveland metropolis. If there is no cloud cover and the Moon is at a quarter phase at most, the sky is so clear that the constellations seem to be hanging just above our backyard. It's as if I can just reach up and touch the stars of Cassiopeia, the Big Dipper, Orion and the Pleiades. In summer, I'll lie down in a lounge chair and get lost in the heavens, surrounded by a chorus of crickets and the occasional bullfrog as the stifling Northeast Ohio humidity wraps around me like a wool blanket. In winter, I'll bundle up and head out to the deck, the hard-packed snow crunching under my shoes as I walk across the wooden boards to an optimal point for night-sky viewing, my frozen breath forming tiny clouds around my face with each exhale into the icy air. There is no sound in the dead of night in the dead of winter; it's like I'm the only inhabitant of a snow-bound planet. And I think that if I peer upward long enough, my eyes penetrating deeper and deeper into the black abyss of space above me, that I'll be looking at my deceased loved ones. Up there, somewhere. Not actually seeing them, mind you, but looking toward where they are, out of sight but not out of contact. Looking toward ... Heaven.

I'll quietly call out to each of them by name, pets included. I'll tell them I love them and I miss them and I'll see them again. And when I get to Dad, I'll add an "I'm sorry."

Because I truly am.

Even so, it wasn't like Dad and I were constantly at each other's throats. In between, he was my pal. We attended numerous sporting events together over the years, particularly high school basketball games. Our annual weekend trip to the boys state basketball tournament at Ohio State's St. John Arena in Columbus every March retains a special place in my heart and always will. Those excursions were wonderful father-son bonding moments, and every March when I'm at the state tournament, Dad is never far from my mind. And he's never far from me when I'm sitting in my seat in the arena; I can feel his presence there with me, enjoying the games like we did all those years ago.

But even when he was happy, a deep-rooted sadness lay just under the surface of his cheerful veneer. Dad was never satisfied with his lot in life—he felt he deserved more and often fixated on what others had and he didn't have—which often caused him to be negative and moody. The way he saw it, he worked just as hard as everyone else he knew, so he should have a big house, expensive cars and take big vacations like they did. Because of this, I learned at an early age never to compare myself to others. I saw firsthand how counterproductive and damaging that mindset could be, because it ultimately helped destroy my dad's sense of self-worth.

I know that deep down he viewed himself as a failure, and that because he didn't have what others had or accomplish what he had set out to accomplish, he had come up woefully short in life. This created a perpetually pessimistic and defeatist attitude that prevented Dad from truly enjoying life. He trapped himself in this mental quicksand, and there was no escape. Dad's negative outlook on life became a vicious cycle: The more bitter he got about where he was in life, the more negative he became, and the more negative he became, the more bitter he got about where he was in life. Because of his low self-esteem, he didn't have the mental or emotional wherewithal to flip the script and take charge of his destiny. Instead, he sat back and let the tides of life sweep him out to sea, leaving him hopelessly adrift in an ocean of dejection and bitterness.

But it didn't have to be that way. Dad was the smartest person I ever met. He knew a lot about a lot. He was extremely well-read and had an intense interest in history—something he got from his dad, Clar Clar, and passed on to me—and had planned to be a history teacher after college. But with his degree almost in hand, Dad decided teaching wasn't for him—he wasn't comfortable standing in front of a classroom full of students—and ditched it as a career. He eventually landed a good job at a large tire company in Akron, but he despised selling his soul to corporate America. He lasted over thirty years there before retiring, but working in the corporate environment contributed largely to his near-permanent malaise. Even though he made decent money—decent enough to support his family and send his only kid to college—it made him miserable. By the time he retired, he was just a shell of a man.

It saddened me to see what the corporate environment did to him. It sapped his soul and destroyed his sense of worth. It devalued him as a human being. Dad didn't belong in the corporate setting and he knew it, but he felt tied to his desk financially—another factor that weighed heavily in his deep-seated bitterness toward his lot in life.

He lived in constant fear that he would lose his job—a fear that he unfortunately passed along to Mom and me. Even when I was in elementary school, I was often treated to hearing Dad announce, "If I get fired, we'll lose everything. We'll be out on the street." That's a hell of a way for a young child to live—or anyone to live, for that matter. A kid has no control over what their parents do for a living and what that living entails, and to lay that burden and stress on them is grossly unfair. Nobody's perfect and we all have said and done things we regret and wish we could take back, and I forgive Dad for most of the things he said and did and I hope he can forgive me as well, but constantly putting that albatross on my back is something I just haven't been able to forgive. Maybe someday, I will. The times I lay in bed at night crying, thinking we were going to lose our house and all our things and have nowhere to live, well, that fear is a living hell. The fact that Dad didn't like his job had nothing to do with me; he chose it, and he chose to stay there. The person he had a beef with was staring back at him in the mirror. And if losing his job was a true fear of his, then that was for the adults in the house to discuss; the kid had nothing to do with it. Being on the hook for something that is totally out of your control is an absolutely terrible feeling.

Dad also brought some of that fear on himself. Yes, people lose their jobs at a moment's notice every day. One minute you're sitting at your desk doing your job, and the next minute the boss comes over and says he wants to see you. And the next minute after that you're unemployed, wondering what just happened. I'm sure Dad felt the constant stress of being the breadwinner in the family and that it was on him to keep us afloat, but I always got the feeling that Dad's sense of impending job doom was more imagined than real. Mom worked as well, but Dad made significantly more money and, therefore, shouldered the lion's share of the mental burden of making sure we could make ends meet. But again, as a kid, that wasn't my rodeo, and putting me in the arena with the bull was inexcusable.

This isn't meant to trash my father; it's only an illustration of where his mind was at and why it was there. I am not bitter toward him about it, I am heartbroken that he let outside forces in his life dictate his relationships with his immediate family; those forces broke him down mentally. Dad was such a smart man, such a good man, such a well-intentioned man, and for him to allow his very existence to be defined by others and by material things he didn't have is nothing short of tragic.

I watched all this very closely as a youngster. I watched, and I learned what to do and what not to do. It often seemed to me that Dad victimized himself and made the mistake of living life on everyone else's terms but his own. I vowed early on that wasn't going to happen when I grew up. I was going to be master and commander of my life. I was going to live it on my terms, the way I liked it, the way I wanted it, the way that was comfortable and worked for me, and if someone had a problem with that, that was their problem, not mine. Life is too short to bend to the will of others who don't have your best interests at heart in the first place.

In the case of my dad, I saw what it looked like to not live life on your own terms, and it wasn't pretty. I firmly believe that contributed to his early passing at the age of sixty-three. It caused undue stress that would not have been there otherwise had he taken the bull by the horns and lived life on his terms. But Dad was a people-pleaser; it was important to him that people liked him and he went out of his way to make them happy, even those who, in my estimation, didn't deserve his graciousness in any way, shape or form. Others often took advantage of Dad's kindness and generosity, furthering eroding his already-fragile self-esteem. I was bitter about it then, and I'm bitter about it now. They knew what they were doing and how it was affecting him, and they didn't care. They saw his altruism as a weakness to be exploited, his mental state be damned.

My takeaway from Dad serving as a doormat, to be walked on at will, was to always be wary of people, particularly upon first meeting them or only knowing them from afar. Because, as I saw firsthand, those grins and guffaws can often hide sinister motives, something Dad could not or would not see. After watching what happened to Dad, I just don't trust people until they prove that they can be trusted. Some might think this is unfortunate, but it's a defense mechanism I put into place after watching too many cretins disrespect my dad for too many years, going back to when I was a young boy. He treated people very well, and to get treated poorly in return left an indelible impression on my young mind. The early, unmistakable lesson for me was simple: If you're too nice to someone, they will take advantage of you. It made me leery of people. I didn't want to be that way, but I didn't want what happened to Dad to happen to me. It was a lesson learned, and a tough way to learn it. Being nice is one thing, getting trampled underfoot is another. Why Dad didn't stand up for himself more often, why he was so timid in the face of such inconsiderate behavior, is beyond my comprehension. Maybe he didn't believe in himself, maybe he didn't have the will to give back what he got, maybe he just didn't think it was a big deal. But I did, and still do. Dad deserved better from some people, even if he didn't think so. He was a good man with a big heart.

To that end, Dad always taught me the importance of treating people with kindness and respect, and I certainly do—for those who deserve it. Dad wasn't nearly as judicious as he should have been, and it cost him a big piece of himself. He always tried to give people the benefit of the doubt, where I'm more apt to hold their feet to the fire. I guess you could say I don't suffer fools. Dad, on the other hand, often turned the other cheek—a Biblical phrase that took on new meaning one night when he taught me another lesson.

Years after he died.

I dealt with guilt issues for years after Dad died. I largely blamed myself for our rocky relationship, that if I had shown a little more understanding and maturity, many of our issues could have been overcome. I recognize now that it was a two-way street and we were both to blame; however, we did make a good-faith effort to let bygones be bygones and take steps to reestablish our relationship shortly before he died. I had been semi-estranged from my parents for years for a variety of reasons; my contact with them was intermittent at best. But by June 2005, I felt that the time had come to repair the damage that had been done. Mom and Dad had moved into their brand-new home just a few months earlier, and Dad and I had had some very nice phone conversations where we caught each other up on things going on in our lives.

One of those conversations took place on the afternoon of June 28, 2005, which I have mentioned earlier in this book. I had not seen Mom and Dad's new home, so Dad invited me over for a house tour and to show him pictures from the vacation Kim and I had taken to Alaska a couple weeks earlier. Since Kim and I were also about to take a long weekend trip to New York City within the next week, I suggested that I wait to visit their house until after we got back from New York so that he could see pictures from both vacations. Dad agreed, saying that it made sense to do it that way. It had been well over a year since I had seen my parents, and I was very much looking forward to visiting with them in their new home. It was nice to see that after all their tribulations they could finally start to enjoy their retirement.

After nailing down those plans, our phone conversation continued with Dad spending several minutes bringing me up to speed on family and friends. As he spoke, I glanced out a front window in our family room and marveled at the glorious summer day. The scenery on the other side of the window just popped in the bright sunlight: The grass and trees were a deep green, the sky a magnificent blue, the flowers a kaleidoscope of color. It actually crossed my mind that all the colors seemed richer than usual, as if they had been enhanced through high definition.

I was mesmerized by the beautiful scene outside as Dad continued to catch me up on family affairs.

Finally, he said: "There was something else I was going to tell you, but I can't remember what it was now. Oh well, I'll just tell you the next time we talk."

It was the last time I heard my father's voice. Two days later, he was dead.

There Dad and I were, on the verge of rehabilitating our relationship, just days away from my visit to their house, and he was gone. Just like that. No warning whatsoever. It seemed cruel then, and it seems cruel now. All those things I was planning on saying to him that he never got to hear. I tortured myself for the longest time thinking I should have just gone to their house in between our Alaska and New York trips rather than wait until we got back from New York, but how was I to know that his time on this Earth was measured in hours at that point? I have taken solace in the fact that we at least had those pleasant phone conversations just prior to his passing, and he knew I was planning on going to their house, so he must have known that I did not harbor a grudge against him and, more importantly, that I loved him.

He must have known, but did he know for sure? That's the question I asked myself almost from the moment Mom told me he died. It haunted me. For weeks after his death, after Kim would go to bed, I would sit on the couch in our family room late at night and sob into my hands in anguish, telling him I was sorry and that I did love him and always would. I would thank him for being a great father and provider and tell him that I never would have had such success in life if it hadn't been for his love, support and influence. I would talk out loud to him because that somehow made me feel closer to him, my words quivering as tears streamed down my face. It felt like the bottom had fallen out of my existence. I was so unprepared for his passing, yet had prepared so hard to get our relationship back on track, that I felt like I was free-falling into a black void and there was nothing to catch me. I didn't know how to rectify the unfinished business of repairing our relationship. He was dead, and that was that. He wasn't coming back.

At least I thought he wasn't.

DAD'S SECOND VISITATION

While the nightly sobbing fits on the couch gradually subsided over time, my guilt and anguish did not. Months went by, then years, and there was no end in sight to my overwhelming sense of remorse and regret. I learned to internalize it, though I know it affected my personality to some degree—maybe a large degree. I didn't laugh or smile as often, I became less and less tolerant of people and their actions and comments, I became more cynical, I got less and less enjoyment and satisfaction out of life, my faith in God began to be shaken. Sure, there were also many wonderful moments in my life that certainly made me happy, but always lying just underneath the surface was my unreconciled guilt and the vexation of not knowing if Dad died believing I didn't love him. And as more and more of my closest loved ones passed away, I felt more and more isolated, my lifelong emotional support system eroding around me, the noose tightening with each death. There was nowhere to turn. I was overcome by a crushing sense of abandonment and left to fend for myself.

I was suffocating emotionally, psychologically and spiritually. I needed a lifeline, and I needed one fast.

And Dad threw me one.

———

A few years after his death, while mired in the depths of my inner despair which I had tried mightily to conceal, I went to bed one night and woke up the next day a changed man.

In between, Dad showed himself to me for the first time since his death. Yes, he had visited me once before with that powerful aroma of cologne in our bathroom to say goodbye shortly after he died, but this was different. This time I actually saw him, and his visitation couldn't have come at a better time, because it felt like my very soul was drowning.

In what turned out to be Dad's first "visual" visitation, I was sitting in our family room watching television. I was alone and sitting on our wraparound couch, the side closest to the television. It was our family room, but the setting was slightly different: The walls were painted white (we actually had beige wallpaper at the time), the couch was cream colored (it's actually brown), and some of the items in the room were missing. I believe these changes were to give the effect of a cleaner vision, to remove distractions and enable me to focus my attention on the purpose of the visit.

Since I was on the side of the wraparound that angled toward the television, my field of vision for the rest of the room was limited, particularly anything to my left. I do know I was alone in the room. I don't know how long I had been sitting there watching television, but it had been a while. At some point, I casually turned to my left and I gasped: There, sitting at the end of the other side of the wraparound near the lamp and end table, was Dad. He was watching TV, too. I just stared at him for several seconds, unable to make sense of what was happening. He did not acknowledge me, instead staring straight ahead at the television.

I started to study his appearance: His hair was jet black, not the salt-and-pepper hair he had later in life. His skin had great color, he looked vibrant, he looked sharp, he looked … young. He looked like he did in his mid-thirties, when he was in the prime of his life. He looked great.

Still, he didn't seem to notice me, instead continuing to watch TV. Finally, I couldn't take it anymore.

"Dad!" I exclaimed.

This got his attention and, at last, he looked at me and smiled softly.

"What are you doing here, Dad?" I asked incredulously. "You're dead. How are you able to be here?"

It was a common-sense question, because this just didn't make sense to me at all.

His smile grew, and he looked at me reassuringly, his piercing brown eyes boring through me. Then he said matter-of-factly: "I'm always here, Bear. You just can't see me."

I didn't know what to say to that; it caught me completely off guard. His assuaging tone, however, brought an instant calm over me. I glanced at the TV for a few moments, digesting Dad's soothing words. I had so many questions to ask him, I didn't know where to start. I was taken aback by the whole thing. I then turned my head to look at him again, prepared to finally say something.

He was gone. The couch was empty, and once more I was alone in the room. I hadn't heard or seen him leave, and he would have had to walk right past me to leave the room, which I know he did not. I glanced around, but there was no sign of him. He had vanished.

But the inescapable feeling of being alone that had tormented me for so long evaporated the instant I awoke from his brief visitation. Never again have I felt alone, because I know I'm not. Dad is always here with me, and he has been all along. The fact that I can't see him doesn't mean he's not there, because he is. He told me so himself. His pacifying words changed my outlook on life.

His next visitation changed my outlook on death.

With each passing visit from a deceased loved one, the nature of the "other side"—of death—became clearer and clearer to me. There obviously was more to life, more to the end of life, than just this Earthly existence. My belief in an afterlife, that our soul survives the body's physical death, had become a conviction. I knew this to be true, because I had experienced it. I had seen my dead loved ones, I had interacted with them, they had given me contemporary information, and they had warned me of impending events.

I no longer took the idea of life after death on faith. As far as I was concerned, it was fact. I had seen enough and experienced enough to be convinced beyond any shadow of a doubt.

But what I had not seen or experienced was Heaven.

That changed with Dad's third visitation—an encounter that transformed my life.

Losing so many close family members in such a short period of time had rattled me and shaken me to the core. It greatly affected my mental state, forcing me to circle the psychological wagons and steel myself against future sorrow. While I was convinced by this time that there was an afterlife, I was not sure about the nature of this afterlife. I had hints of that nature through the visitations, but nothing that resolved it once and for all in my mind.

And I certainly wasn't sure about Heaven beyond my own personal faith and beliefs. I figured I would find out someday, the hard way: by dying. But Heaven is also a sort of hope. We hope it exists. The idea of eternal life in

God's Kingdom is a wonderful prize to receive upon your Earthly life being extinguished. We want it to be true. It's better than any of the alternatives, be they Hell or nothing at all. The concept of Heaven is one of the few things— perhaps the only thing—that enables our minds to handle the fact that each day brings us one step closer to death. If Heaven is real, and eternal life is waiting for us, then death doesn't sound so bad. If it's not real, then death is the end, it's all over for us. We either rot in our coffins or our ashes are interred or scattered somewhere. Our light is forever snuffed out.

So we want Heaven to be real. That way, our life continues forever in divine glory with our loved ones.

But is it real? And if it is, is it the magical place that we want to believe it is?

The overwhelming loss I had endured in such a short period of time had begun to shake my faith just a little. I strongly believed in Heaven, but I was not comforted by the fact that in all the visitations I had received from my deceased loved ones, there had not been a single specific reference to it. The closest was when Gramps had said that where he was going, his heart would be all better. I knew he had meant Heaven, but he didn't say it. There was no doubt in my mind that he was referring to Heaven, but I wanted more. I needed more. I needed ... truth.

And as one close loved one after another died, I continued to wrestle with my emotions surrounding my father. I was still wracked with guilt, anger, shame and frustration. I assumed if those feelings hadn't gone away years after his death, they never would. They would forever be part of my psyche. Closure would not be possible.

But then I got a glimpse of Heaven.

CHAPTER 9

DAD'S THIRD VISITATION: A WALK IN ETERNITY

Since the day my dad died in July 2005, hardly a night went by without me softly talking to him when I went to sleep. It almost always went the same way: "Goodnight, Dad. I love you. I miss you. Thank you for everything you did for me. I'm sorry."

The last part was an apology for not showing him enough appreciation for all the things he did to ensure that his only child could make it in life, an apology for needlessly giving him a hard time about far too many things, and an apology for him going to his grave thinking I didn't love him.

Sometimes I whispered these words with a tear running down my cheek and onto my pillow, moments before I drifted off to sleep.

One night, however, I drifted into another world. A world that I entered as my physical body lay asleep in Stow, Ohio.

Where and what this world was, I didn't know—at least not right away. I found myself walking down a wide, flat, straight sidewalk that bordered a beautifully landscaped park area. This sidewalk was about fifteen feet wide, much wider than an average sidewalk along a street (it was more like a concourse, but I'll stick to calling it a sidewalk), and I noticed that it had no markings of wear and tear on it at all. The smooth, cream-colored concrete was immaculate; it seemed brand new, as if it had just been finished yesterday and nobody had yet set foot on it. It seemed ... perfect.

I looked all around me, but I couldn't identify where I was. To my left was what appeared to be the interior of the park, which consisted mainly of large trees with leaves so green and perfectly textured that they almost looked fake. The trees were tall, ranging between fifty and one hundred feet high or more, with thick trunks and long, sturdy branches whose leafy foliage covered the majority of the park in shade. The grass in the park was extremely well-manicured, like what you would find surrounding a central gazebo in a quaint village square. No weeds, no dandelions, no loose branch sticks lying around. It was like the landscaping crew had just left the premises five minutes before.

Bordering the sidewalk immediately to my right lay an open expanse of rolling grassland that ended at a forest line maybe a mile or so away. Like the grass in the park, the grass of the adjacent prairie was a lush green, reminiscent of the famed grass football field at the Rose Bowl stadium in Pasadena, California; only whereas the grass in the park was neatly trimmed and low, the grass on the prairie grew wild and was much taller—maybe as high as a couple feet in some places—and swayed gently in the breeze.

The sky, meanwhile, was a magnificent blue—the kind of deep blue you would see on a sweltering afternoon in the dog days of summer—with puffy, white clouds that seemed as if they were made of cotton. The temperature was ideal, maybe in the mid-seventies, with a very light breeze that was just enough to rustle the leaves. The entire scene could have been lifted from a Chamber of Commerce marketing campaign.

I continued on the sidewalk, surveying the idyllic landscape around me. The park area to my left was enormous; it seemed to go on and on in front of and behind me, as did the grassy expanse to my right. In fact, this large sidewalk was a stark dividing line between the two settings: to my left, from horizon to horizon, the park; to my right, from horizon to horizon, the prairie with the forest behind it. There was no end in sight to either. I didn't know why I was here, or where "here" was. Even so, I was enjoying the beautiful day and scenery that surrounded me. It relaxed me, and I basked in its warmth as I walked.

After continuing for a while—I wasn't sure exactly how much time passed, but it seemed like I had covered a lot of ground—I could see something far ahead in the distance that appeared to be just to the right side of the sidewalk, the side that bordered the grassland. I couldn't quite make out what it was, but it appeared to be stationary.

It was then that I noticed animals: specifically, squirrels and chipmunks playing in the park, as well as birds flitting about in the trees and soaring over the expanse. Their familiar chirps relaxed me even further as I continued onward—toward what, I didn't know.

I soaked it all in as I walked: the trees, the sky, the prairie, the warmth and the critters. I had never been in a more peaceful place in my life. I again looked to my right and marveled at the great, sweeping vista of the endless grassland and forest behind it, then casually glanced back to my left toward the park area.

And was instantly jolted out of my serenity.

Dad was walking right next to me!

He hadn't been there a few moments ago. He had just suddenly appeared without a sound. Needless to say it startled me, because until now—save for the animals—I had been alone in this wonderful place. I was in shock. Dad was walking almost in stride with me and, noticing my surprise, looked at me and smiled.

"Hi, Bear," he said cheerfully.

"Dad! I didn't know you were here, I didn't see you," I said incredulously, my heart pounding from the shock of unexpectedly seeing my dead father walking right next to me—dead, yet seemingly very alive. There was nothing "ghostly" about him: He was in solid form, appearing every bit as he did in life. I couldn't see through him, he didn't shimmer, there was no aura or glow about him at all. He was … real. It was Dad.

And he looked fantastic. From his appearance, I pegged him to be in his mid-forties: His hair was still mostly black with just a touch of gray sprinkled in, and while he seemed to be strong and vibrant, he also appeared very relaxed. Dad was wearing a dark blue polo-type shirt and jeans; I was in shorts and a white T-shirt, my customary summer attire. We were both wearing tennis shoes.

"I've been waiting for you, Bear. I have something to show you," he said.

I stopped walking so I could gather my thoughts and attempt to size up the situation; he stopped next to me. My mind was racing. This had all happened so fast: First I'm walking alone in a place I've never been and don't recognize, and then Dad—heretofore deceased—appears next to me out of nowhere.

"Where are we, Dad?" I asked, continuing to study every detail of his appearance as he looked at me. It was hard to get past the fact that he was *really there.*

"Let's keep walking," he said. "You'll see."

I knew full well that Dad was dead, yet here we were, together. I was confused.

"What are you doing here, Dad? Aren't you dead?" I inquired.

He smiled and answered the second question first. "No, I'm not dead, Bear," he said gently. "This is where I live now."

I thought his choice of words to be rather odd, because he was, in fact, dead. I knew this; I had seen the top of his head as he lay deceased in front of that love seat in his living room while the paramedics gathered around his body, preparing to remove him from the house and take him to the morgue. I had seen him in his casket and even touched his cold, lifeless body, patting him gently on his chest and telling him through tear-filled eyes that I was sorry and I loved him. So the fact that he didn't consider himself to be dead in this place we were in—whatever it was, wherever it was—piqued my curiosity.

Even more, his statement that this is where he lives now gave me the impression that his life had somehow continued past 7 p.m. Eastern time on Friday, July 1, 2005. As impossible as the idea sounded in my head, Dad had just told me that he is alive. Here. Now. In this place. I knew that he shouldn't be alive, yet here he was, talking to me. I was looking right at him. It was Dad all right, and he certainly seemed to be alive ... but, his calling hours, his funeral, his grave ... They were real; I had experienced them and felt the soul-crushing grief and anguish and sadness associated with them.

But now, I was standing next to him in this strange, beautiful place where somehow, some way, Dad was alive again. Or still alive. I wasn't sure which. Either way, it was wondrous and nonsensical at the same time.

All that truly mattered, though, was that I was with my father. Again.

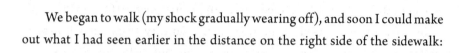

We began to walk (my shock gradually wearing off), and soon I could make out what I had seen earlier in the distance on the right side of the sidewalk: black, steel-grated park benches.

And there were people sitting on them. There were also people standing between the benches or milling about on the sidewalk. Some were in the park area as well. The entire place was fairly crowded but not jam-packed.

Seeing people up ahead was the first time I had noticed another human being here aside from Dad.

As we reached the first of the people in the park area, something seemed a bit off. Each person appeared to be completely oblivious to everyone and everything around them, and nobody was saying a word. With the exception of chirping birds, it was eerily silent. The people here were from all walks of life, races of every kind, male and female, young and old, some men sharply dressed in business suits, others disheveled in tattered clothing as if they were homeless, women dressed to the proverbial nines, others wearing regular day-to-day garb. I studied these people closely as we walked by, observing their facial expressions and their clothing. They seemed completely unaware of my existence as I walked past, most of them staring at the ground or straight ahead. They didn't look at or talk to each other; each was in his or her own little world, the same way that people close ranks around their personal space inside a packed elevator. I was struck by the fact that many, if not most, of these people actually appeared to be stunned, like they weren't quite sure what was happening and were trying to make sense of their environment. They looked tired and confused.

The benches lined up ahead of us as far as I could see, one after another, each filled with three to four people. The people on the sidewalk didn't seem to actually be walking anywhere; they basically just stood in place, maybe taking a few aimless steps from time to time, and they were never in our way as we walked. Two of the people stood out to me for some reason. Maybe it was because they seemed to come from opposite ends of the societal spectrum, yet here they were in the same place.

One was a sharp-dressed man who looked like he could have been CEO of a Fortune 500 company. He seemed physically fit and appeared to be in the prime of his life, maybe somewhere between forty and fifty years old, with short, perfectly trimmed black hair, parted on one side and slicked back. He wore a black suit jacket, white dress shirt with red tie, black slacks, shiny black shoes and black socks, clutching a tan briefcase to his side. He was expressionless and cast his gaze downward, never making eye contact with me or anyone else. He also had the whole bench to himself, which added to his air of importance.

Another guy resembled the destitute man on the album cover art of British rock band Jethro Tull's *Aqualung* LP, minus the beard and scraggly long hair. This man was clean-shaven and had very short hair, something of a buzz-cut, but otherwise appeared similar to the forlorn fellow on that iconic album cover: dingy brown trench coat, dirty beat-up jeans and very worn-out brown boots that looked a little too big for his feet. He was thin to the point of his face appearing gaunt, with slightly sunken eyes and pronounced cheekbones. He was about my height (I am 5-foot-10) and looked to be in his late sixties or so. Based on his scruffy appearance, I guessed that, like the man in the portrait on the *Aqualung* album cover, he was homeless. He was standing on the sidewalk to my right, and even though I passed within a couple feet of him, he did not make eye contact with me. He just stood motionless and stared blankly in the direction of the interior of the park as I walked past. Like many of the others, he appeared stunned, like he wasn't sure where he was or why he was there.

He wasn't the only one. I was wondering the same things:

Where am I? What is this place? Why am I here?

Dad and I walked in silence as I continued to study these people standing on the sidewalk and sitting on the endless line of park benches. Immediately behind the benches lay the grassy expanse, which began at the sidewalk's edge; the benches faced the park interior with its large cluster of trees that stretched ahead of and behind me; all manner of birds continued to fly amongst the trees and soar across the prairie; squirrels and chipmunks raced to and fro in the park interior.

Whatever this place was, it was wonderfully serene.

As we walked, I began to notice that some of the people had tears rolling down their cheeks. They still looked shocked and confused, but now they were exhibiting emotion for the first time. I felt badly for them and wondered why they were so sad. They were in such a tranquil, beautiful place; what could they be upset about?

Dad didn't say a word as we walked. More and more people were crying, for reasons I could not determine. None of this made sense.

We walked some more, and now every single person was crying. This dichotomy of great sadness in the midst of such natural beauty confused me. It didn't jive. What *was* this place?

I had no idea how long I had been here. I got the sense that time didn't matter, or didn't even exist at all. Maybe I had been here an hour, maybe an entire day. I had no way of knowing. The sky was as bright and beautiful as it had been when I first found myself here. Time had either stood still or was irrelevant.

All I knew for sure was that I had no idea what was going on.

But that was about to change.

It was about this time that I realized it was getting harder for me to walk. We had been walking for quite a while—again, how long a period of time I didn't know—and earlier I had walked by myself for some time before Dad showed up. So maybe I was just getting fatigued. My legs must be tired, I thought.

But they didn't feel tired. I played ten years of football and have done plenty of hiking with Kim on our vacations and in the parks near our house. I knew what tired legs felt like, and this wasn't it.

This was different.

It wasn't so much that my legs were fatigued, it was more like I was walking against some kind of current, such as you would experience in the ocean when facing the beach in water a foot or two deep as it rapidly receded around your legs while another wave gathered momentum behind you. Only here, there was no water to make walking difficult. I wasn't struggling to walk; it was more of a minor annoyance where I had to work just a little harder than usual to take each step, almost like increasing the level of difficulty on a treadmill by one level.

I looked down at the sidewalk and saw nothing that would impede my progress in any way. This current, or whatever it was, was invisible, but it was there nonetheless—another mystery in a sea of mysteries.

I trudged on.

It was more of the same as we walked: people crying, my steps slightly impeded by this invisible force, not a word spoken between Dad and me. I kept waiting for him to tell me where we were and why we were here; after all, he had said that he had something to show me. But he said nothing.

The people around us were crying harder now. I could see their bodies heaving as they cried. Their sadness overwhelmed me. I pondered, "Why would Dad show me this?"

It was also getting a little harder for me to walk, like the difficulty on the treadmill had been cranked up another notch. Whereas before it was an annoyance, now it was beginning to strain me somewhat. My legs did not feel tired at all, but this invisible current was beginning to distract me from my people-watching. I wasn't sure what Dad needed to show me, but it was turning out to be a lot of work.

Meanwhile, the people were now crying demonstratively, but Dad didn't seem to notice. He just kept walking, and it was getting harder for me to keep up with him.

Then it hit me: Why was it harder for me to keep up with him? Shouldn't it be hard for him to walk, too? I mean, we were walking right next to each other on a flat surface. It only made sense that what was affecting me should be affecting him. I looked down at his gait as he walked, and he wasn't struggling at all. It was just me. He was walking with ease, while I labored to some degree to put one foot in front of the other. I thought about asking him why this was but figured I would find out in due time. He probably wouldn't tell me anyway.

The level of walking difficulty gradually went up yet another notch. Now I could feel the force of this current pushing strongly against my ankles and lower legs. I again looked down, and this time I saw it: Some sort of translucent material, maybe plasma of some type, was rushing by my legs on the sidewalk. I could see it moving, yet I could see the sidewalk underneath it. I could actually see its current and even the mini-currents within it that swirled around my legs from the lower part of my shins on down; this water-like translucent material rose as high as anywhere from six inches to maybe a foot up my legs. I couldn't feel anything tangible, like the wetness of water pushing against my legs or whether it was warm or cold, but I could feel the force of whatever it was I was seeing below me.

I could walk in this translucent material, but it wasn't easy. Dad, on the other hand, was completely unaffected, walking without any trouble whatsoever even though this current was rushing past his legs as well. It had no impact on him at all.

I noticed that this "water" was only on the sidewalk, and only in our walking path. If it was elsewhere, either I couldn't see it or no one was affected by it, the way Dad wasn't. I began to get the sense that maybe I didn't belong here with everyone else.

Again, I estimated this translucent material, or plasma, or pseudo-water, or whatever it was, to be somewhere between six and twelve inches deep at the most. But it was strong. I was working hard to walk against it, but walk against it I did. I had to see what Dad needed to show me. Curiosity spurred me onward.

By this time, the people had gone from crying to sobbing, their entire bodies shaking as they wept. Some sat back on the benches, their eyes closed, their faces twisted as they cried. Some hunched forward, head in hands, sobbing. I wanted to help them, say something to them, do something to console them, but I got the distinct feeling that they were not aware of me. Not one of them, in all this time, had looked at me or acknowledged me in any way. By this point, I doubted they could see me even if they did look at me.

Something wasn't right. Finally, I broke our long silence.

"Dad, why are all these people crying?" I asked.

He didn't answer.

But I was going to get one. If he needed to show me something, as he had said, then he needed to start delivering some answers.

"Dad, all these people are crying. Why are they so sad?" I implored.

Dad stopped walking for a moment, giving my legs a brief respite from this strange current that had continued to rush past us. He looked at me, then toward the bench near where we had stopped.

"They're not sad, Bear," he said. "They're crying because they know they're loved."

Dad's answer caught me completely off guard. This possibility had never occurred to me. These people had appeared to be emotional wrecks, and it turns out that love was the reason they were so emotional?

I pressed him further. "But it looks like they're upset, Dad."

"They're not upset. They're happy," he replied. "They're crying out of love."

I looked at the people on the bench next to me and thought about all the others I had seen, and it began to make sense—some sense, anyway. They were crying because of an immense love that they felt.

But this left me with more questions.

"Why are these people crying so hard, Dad?" I asked. "They're really sobbing."

"Because they're overwhelmed by the love they feel," he answered. "They've never felt love like this before." His tone was gentle and dripping with compassion, yet he spoke with authority, like not only had he seen this before, he had experienced it himself.

I was completely taken aback. I had never seen anyone react this way to being loved. This must be a truly amazing kind of love.

"What love are they feeling to be crying like this?" I asked.

Dad abruptly went back to being cryptic. "You'll see," he said. "Let's keep walking."

And off we went, Dad moving effortlessly while I struggled against the current. Apparently, I still hadn't seen all that he needed to show me.

And I had already seen a lot.

———

The emotions of the people intensified as we walked. They were now wailing, many of them clutching a hand to their face as they sobbed loudly and uncontrollably. Some had even come off the benches and knelt next to them, practically moaning as their bodies almost convulsed as they wept. If what Dad said was true—and I had no reason to doubt him—then the love these people felt bordered on miraculous.

Meanwhile, it became harder and harder for me to walk. I strained mightily with each step, as if I was walking through wet concrete. It took nearly everything I had to pick up one foot, put it down, lift up the other foot and put that one down. It was becoming very problematic. I wasn't sure how much further I could go.

Suddenly, I noticed something bright up ahead in the distance. I couldn't quite make out exactly what it was, but it seemed to be a building of some kind. It looked to be beyond the end of the sidewalk, which we were nearing but I couldn't yet see, and set off slightly to the right. The grassy expanse wrapped around the end of the park and continued on to the horizon—and, for all I knew, into infinity. This bright object appeared to be situated out in the open expanse.

I battled against the translucent current to get a better look at this bright structure; slowly but surely, we made our way closer and it came into better view. It was a magnificent white, the purest white I had ever seen, whiter and brighter than freshly fallen snow glimmering in the sunlight. This brilliant white building sat atop a gently sloping hill on the prairie; I estimated this hill to be around one-hundred feet high and maybe two-hundred feet wide at the top. The hill sloped uniformly upward at about twenty degrees to the flat top where the building sat, and there was nothing else on the hill. No trees, no bushes, no flowers, no people. The grass on the hill was a dark, lush green and perfectly manicured like that in the park. The imposing white building towered over the landscape.

We continued on and, as we did, more details of the structure began to emerge. It appeared to be made of finely polished marble or some other highly reflective material. The center of the building bore a structural resemblance to the Jefferson Memorial in Washington, D.C., with high, round pillars situated at what I deemed to be the front of the structure, except there was no open area that you could actually see into. In fact, you couldn't see into any part of the building. There were no windows, at least from my angle. And its scale dwarfed that of the Jefferson Memorial. It had a large rotunda in the middle, surrounded by the main portion of the edifice, which was roughly three to four stories high and could have encased countless rooms, hallways and staircases. This great mansion was generally circular in shape, taking up nearly the entire top of the hill on which it sat, with the large dome atop the rotunda dominating this incredible building. Its architecture was reminiscent of classical Greek or Roman, although I could discern no ornate designs or inscriptions on any part of the building. It was a solid white; no other color was present. Its stark simplicity contributed to its majesty.

By now, I almost couldn't walk anymore, but I had to get a better look at this breathtaking citadel. I could now see where the sidewalk ended up ahead; immediately beyond was the expansive grassland on which the hill and building sat. I judged the distance from Dad and me to the bottom of the hill to now be around one-hundred-fifty yards; it was situated a little to the right at about the one o'clock position from where the sidewalk ended. I had an unobstructed view of it, and the closer we got, the more impressive it appeared. It was difficult to look directly at it from this range due to the structure's radiance. It was dazzling and imposing at the same time, yet despite its size and appearance it didn't feel cold or unapproachable. Quite the opposite: It exuded warmth and compassion.

Finally, we stopped. We hadn't yet come to the end of the sidewalk, but I could walk no further. It wasn't that I had become fatigued and didn't have the energy to continue. The current—which I could still see rushing past us on the sidewalk—had become too strong for me to keep going. It was now impossible for me to move my legs at all. I was, in essence, stuck.

I stood there, mesmerized, and surveyed the scene before us. We had reached a point where there was no sound except for a light breeze that occasionally rustled the trees of the park to our left. Directly ahead was the end of the sidewalk, which was maybe twenty yards away, and just past it sat the prairie that stretched endlessly in front of us, giving the sensation that I could see forever—and maybe I could. Shifting my gaze slightly to my right, I stared at the majestic, shimmering palace that was now about one-hundred yards or so from our position on the sidewalk. It was the only structure I had seen this entire time, and it was obvious that it was there for a reason. Someone of great importance must live there or be associated with it in some way. Its power was palpable.

I still saw no activity around it. It stood alone, a solitary sentry standing guard over its surroundings. I was awestruck.

"What *is* that?" I asked Dad. It was the most beautiful building I had ever seen.

"That's what I wanted to show you," he said, his gaze also fixed on the gleaming structure.

"Who lives there?" I asked.

Silence.

The building's brilliance was enhanced from this close range. It almost seemed to glow.

"Who lives there, Dad?" I asked again.

He remained quiet for several more seconds. Then he spoke—and what he said transformed my life forever.

"God," Dad said softly, still staring out at the building on the hill. Then, turning to look at me with a warm smile, he said, "This is Heaven, Bear."

My initial reaction to Dad's revelation was stunned silence, followed by astonishment, followed by wonderment. I was standing in the presence of the Creator, actually laying eyes on His temple, and it was overwhelming beyond words.

An awesome warmth and love welled up inside me, washing over me in waves. Yet, it was far more than that. Yes, I was awestruck and humbled as I stood gazing upon His temple on the hill, but that doesn't even begin to fully capture what it was like to witness His power and His glory. No words can. What I felt transcended the human condition. The closest I can come to accurately convey what I experienced is this: Not only was I in God's presence, He was part of me. I could actually feel the Holy Spirit inside me.

I cannot describe this incredible sweet sensation of the Holy Spirit consuming my soul other than to say it was divinely uplifting and fulfilling. It filled my lungs and took my breath away at the same time. I could literally feel my heart swell. My entire body tingled. It was a transcendent euphoria—and knowing that this is what's waiting for us when we die is mind-blowing.

But it is. I felt it. We become one with God.

I desperately wanted to get closer to this wondrous building. It was so tantalizingly near; there was nothing between me and His temple except for the end of the sidewalk and the beautiful green grass that lay after it. I wanted to walk right up to it and admire it, study it, touch it, peer inside it.

And see God.

There was nothing standing in my way. From the looks of it, I should have been able to walk across the open grass in front of me and up the hill to the building. It was a walk I easily should have been able to make in a few minutes. But I couldn't. The incredibly strong, fast-moving translucent current was unrelenting around my shoes, ankles and lower part of my shins. It was like I had stepped in wet cement and become encased in it. This was as close as I was going to get. It was frustrating to be so close yet so far away from God and his palace, but the feeling quickly passed as I continued to marvel at the building on the hill.

I knew I was in the presence of the Lord; I could feel Him. But I hadn't seen Him.

After another period of silence, I posed the obvious question to Dad.

"Can I see God?" I finally inquired.

"No," Dad said. "You can't see Him until you die."

I hadn't died, yet here I was in Heaven. I didn't understand it, but at this point, understanding what was happening was secondary to the fact that it *was* happening. What I was experiencing, what Dad was showing me, was extraordinary and overwhelming. The radiant white light of the building, its majesty, its magnificence ... this indeed was God's temple, and Dad had taken me as close to it as my mortal soul was allowed to get without actually dying.

As I gazed out at the resplendent structure, I wondered if God was there right now at that moment. Or if He was somewhere else. Or everywhere else. It seemed like the more answers I got, the more questions I had—and by this point, I had so many questions for Dad that I didn't know where to begin. But I knew this wasn't a time for questions; it was a time for truth. And there was another truth I needed to know.

"Is God in there?" I asked.

"Yes, Bear. God is there," he replied.

I had felt God's love and the Holy Spirit inside me, but I needed to hear that God was there at that moment. And He was. But that raised another question for me: Was God only inside the building on the hill, or was He actually everywhere?

All I knew was that this entire place—the animals, the trees, the sky, all of it—exuded an otherworldly peace and serenity. Everything about it was absolute perfection. And it finally clicked in my mind: All of Heaven, every aspect of it, was love. God's love. I was immersed in it by being there. This was where I had always belonged, and I never wanted to leave.

My eyes remained transfixed on the stunningly bright building on the hill—so bright that it almost seemed to shimmer and glow. And then I realized: Maybe what I was seeing wasn't an actual physical structure at all. Maybe it was pure light, the light of the Lord, and that was God on top of the hill in front of me. Maybe I *was* actually seeing Him, but I could only see Him in this manner since I was a mortal being and not yet an immortal soul. Since I wasn't actually dead and ascended to Heaven, I couldn't see God as He truly appears. This great regal building, then, represented mortal ideals of God that I, as an Earth-bound human, would readily understand and recognize: Beauty, elegance, strength, power, majesty, grace, awe and love.

In other words, the building was presented to me as a metaphor for the Creator. I could feel God's awesome presence and intense love emanating from it, but I could not see Him—just as Dad had said.

Dad had also said that "God is there" when I asked him if He was inside the building. It was now clear what Dad had meant: It was God that I was seeing on the hill. What was presented to me as a grand structure of light was, in fact, our Lord. It all made sense now. It was like Dad was giving me the pieces of the puzzle, and I had to assemble them in the right configuration for them to make sense.

I couldn't help but wonder what God truly looked like. A great light? A man? Something I couldn't readily recognize or define? What was that building I was seeing hiding from my eyes? Since the Bible says that God created us in His image, I figured that if I was able to see Him on the hill, He would look like a man. But a man in solid form like a human being, or a figure of light in the form of a man?

Of course, those questions were secondary to the fact that however He truly appears, I was in His presence and I was looking at Him, our Creator, if only indirectly. Just knowing I was that close to the Almighty was staggering. I just couldn't believe it. *He's right there,* I thought. *He's right in front of me. How did this happen? How is this possible?* Never in my wildest dreams did I think I would be—or could be—in this position, in this moment, so close to our Heavenly Father that it would only take me a few minutes of walking to reach Him. I wasn't dead; I should not be able to get this close to God. But I was. I was in complete awe.

I still had a myriad of questions to ask, but one was most pressing at the moment.

"Dad, have you seen God?" I asked, turning my head to my left to look at him.

"Yes, Bear, I've seen Him," he answered softly, almost wistfully, his gaze still fixed on the great temple before us. Dad hadn't looked at me in several minutes; his demeanor seemed reflective, like he was deep in thought. Finally, he turned his head toward me and said in the same tender tone, "You will too, someday." Dad then turned his head back toward the shining temple, and once more we stood in silence.

Earlier, after revealing that we were in Heaven, I had thought that Dad's primary purpose was to show me God's temple. I now knew that wasn't the case.

Dad was showing me God Himself.

As we stood there, my mind went back to the sobbing people in the park. They were still there, behind us a little ways, but out of earshot. Dad had said that they were crying because they were loved, and now another puzzle piece fell into place: The overwhelming love they were feeling was coming from their Savior, Jesus Christ, who died on the cross for their sins so that they could live for eternity in Heaven. Christ's ultimate sacrifice and love for them was borne out in their unbridled emotions that I had seen in the park. Without Him, Heaven would have been unattainable; Jesus was the way. Their tears were evidence not only of Christ's existence but also of His presence in Heaven. He was there. They could feel Him and His love, and so could I.

Dad had referenced Jesus indirectly by telling me that the people were sobbing because they knew they were loved. While I had since realized that all of Heaven was love, it was clear that these people had all been crying for a specific reason, and I now intuitively knew that reason was because Christ had given them salvation. That's what Dad had meant when he said, "They've never felt love like this before." It made perfect sense.

I had not seen Christ in our visit, but I assumed that I was not able to see Him for the same reason that I could not see God. And thus, I assumed that Dad could—and had—seen Christ, especially since he knew why the people were crying; at some point, Dad had probably been one of those people sobbing in the park, and for all I knew he maybe would again. So I saw no reason to ask him any further questions on the subject; his previous answers spoke for themselves.

Instead, I stood there and absorbed it all: Heaven was real. God was real. Jesus was real. Everything I had always hoped for, believed and suspected had been confirmed for me by my dad. I now knew for certain that death was not the end, it was only the beginning—the beginning of eternal life in the Kingdom of Heaven.

More questions raced through my mind, particularly about God and what He looked like, but I knew by now that if Dad had additional information, he would tell me. Throughout our walk in Heaven, Dad had kept me on a need-to-know basis and hadn't offered much in the way of details and specifics—which were irrelevant to the purpose of our visit, anyway. This was about higher truth. The finer points would have to wait.

We stood there silently, basking in the presence of the Almighty and surrounded by the wondrous love and peace that is Heaven. Dad and I stood side by side, experiencing it together yet differently. Whereas Dad and the people in the park were immortal, having shed their physical shells and now living forever in God's Kingdom, I was here as a mortal, getting a sneak preview of what awaits when I join Dad and my other loved ones. This deeply humbling visit had confirmed the existence of God for me and that I would be with Him in Heaven someday, filled with His divine love for eternity.

I soaked in the breathtaking sight of the beautiful shining building on the hill. I was standing on the edge of forever. And I could have stayed there forever.

Then Dad broke the silence.

Turning to look at me, he smiled gently and said, "Well, I have to go now. I'll see you later, Bear."

As soon as Dad finished saying those words, I saw a light. But this time, unlike the intense brightness of the magnificent white mansion on the hill, this light was soft and diffused. I blinked a few times and glanced at the surroundings. The sights were familiar: a nightstand, a closet, two dressers, a television.

This wasn't Heaven. It was our bedroom.

I was waking up.

CHAPTER 10

A MATTER OF FAITH

Immediately following Dad's final words, I awoke. He didn't walk away, he didn't vanish in front of me, he didn't go anywhere. He just said, "I'll see you later, Bear," and my eyes opened. I was back in our bedroom in Stow, Ohio. Dad's words had abruptly ended our visit, transporting me from his dimension to mine in an instant. I went from standing next to him in Heaven in the presence of God and Christ, to lying in bed, in the snap of a finger.

I lay there trying to sort out what had just happened. Even though I was still coming to and groggy, I instinctively knew I had just experienced something profound. As I yawned and stretched, I began to replay the images in my mind: the sobbing people on the benches, the beautiful park and open grassy expanse, the sparkling white building on the hill, Dad walking next to me, his poignant words throughout our visit.

After a few moments of putting it together, I gasped:

I had just walked in Heaven with Dad. I had no doubt of this whatsoever. It had been another visitation, but it was unlike all the others. This time, I was the one doing the visiting. Somehow, whether by Dad or a higher power, I had been summoned to Heaven to be with him. I could clearly recall every detail of it, every word Dad spoke to me, even the sounds of the chirping birds in the park.

I lay there absorbing the magnitude of what had just happened. I didn't know why it happened, I just knew that it had happened and it was real. I was awestruck. I almost couldn't move, and I didn't want to move. I was in some kind of stunned paralysis, trying to get my mind around this extraordinary experience I just had with my dad.

After a minute or two, my head still on the pillow, I looked up at the ceiling and smiled.

"Thanks, Dad," I said, and climbed out of bed to start my day.

Dad had shown me Heaven. And my life has never been the same.

It has been several years since that experience, and there isn't a day that goes by when it doesn't cross my mind at least once. Sometimes it is a fleeting thought; sometimes I ponder it for a while. Every detail, every sound, every color are as vivid today as they were then. It changed my life forever.

I have analyzed this remarkable experience in just about every way it can be analyzed. I am no theologian or Bible scholar, so my analytical skills as they pertain to this event are rooted in one simple fact: It happened to me, and I interpret it accordingly.

And maybe it's better that way. I don't have any kind of deeply involved religious background to steer my thinking in any particular direction. I take my experience in Heaven and compare how I felt immediately after it happened to how I feel about it now. And I can say that nothing has changed. What I felt then is what I feel now.

I didn't see things that are traditionally associated with Heaven: the Pearly Gates, a magnificent city with streets paved of gold, people "walking" through a dreamy cloudscape. I also didn't experience anything related to a near-death experience: There was no dark tunnel with a light at the end of it, no loved ones waiting for me to cross over.

Of course, I didn't actually die, so it makes sense that I wouldn't see things that so many people who have had near-death experiences have seen. And as such, it also makes sense that there's much of Heaven that I did not or could not see—particularly since the powerful translucent current on the sidewalk had prevented me from getting any closer to God's temple (and, by extension, God Himself). I clearly was being blocked by an unseen force, and I was being blocked for a reason: It wasn't my turn to get closer to that incredible white building and see more of Heaven ... yet. Those sights apparently are only for Heaven's permanent residents.

However, I have taken the liberty of searching for descriptions of Heaven in the Bible to see if anything matches what I saw. And I did see enough of Heaven to know that it exists, it's real, and that what I did see is close—real close—to some descriptions in the Bible that I never read or heard until after my experience. Here are a few examples:

From The Apocalypse of St. John The Apostle (also known as the Book of Revelation) 22:5:

And night shall be no more, and they shall have no need of light of lamp, or light of sun, for the Lord God will shed light upon them; and they shall reign forever and ever.

It was a bright, sunny day the entire time I was in Heaven, except I never actually saw the sun. The lighting also never changed; it was as bright when the experience began as it was when it ended. I also never noticed changing shadows. I have no way of knowing how long I was there. I slept for about seven to eight hours, but that doesn't mean I was in Heaven for that same amount of time. Maybe it was longer, maybe it was seven to eight minutes, or maybe it was seven to eight seconds. As I stated earlier, I got the feeling then, and I feel this way now, that time does not exist in the afterlife. It's a function only of this dimension. Therefore, the words from this verse of the Bible ring true with what I saw. There was no night, no sun, yet it was consistently daylight. "... for the Lord God will shed light upon them." Meshing this verse with my experience in Heaven, Dad and I had been walking in God's light, which illuminated all.

This is echoed in The Apocalypse 21:23-25:

And the city has no need of the sun or the moon to shine upon it. For the glory of God lights it up, and the Lamb is the lamp thereof. And the nations shall walk by the light thereof; and the kings of the earth shall bring their glory and honor into it. And its gates shall not be shut by day; for there shall be no night there.

Again, it was a beautiful, bright "sunny" day when I was there, but there was no sun.

From The Holy Gospel of Jesus Christ According to Saint John (also known as the Book of John) 14:2-4:

In my Father's house there are many mansions. Were it not so, I should have told you, because I go to prepare a place for you. And if I go and prepare a place for you, I am coming again, and I will take you to myself; that where I am, there you also may be. And where I go you know, and the way you know.

These three verses haunt me, because as Jesus told His disciples, my dad was doing for me by showing me Heaven. I believe that Dad took me to where he was, in part, to show me that it indeed exists: "... *I will take you to myself; that where I am, there you also may be.*" This is exactly what Dad did for me. And because of this, there isn't a shred of doubt in my mind that Heaven is real.

Apocalypse 7:9 mentions:

... a great multitude which no man could number, out of all nations and tribes and peoples and tongues, standing before the throne and before the Lamb ...

I saw people of all races and all walks of life while walking past the endless row of benches at the park, so this phrase matches what I experienced. (I have used the word "park" for lack of a better term; it took the entire visit to Heaven to reach the end of the park, so my best guess is that it was a few miles long. I could not determine its width since I couldn't see through the thicket of trees that comprised its interior.)

And, in my mind, the most poignant Biblical verse in relation to my visit in Heaven is Apocalypse 21:22, which is in reference to the Heavenly Jerusalem:

"And I saw no temple therein. For the Lord God almighty and the Lamb are the temple thereof."

This verse flat-out states that God *is* the temple and cements for me that what I saw as a great temple on the hill was, in fact, God. The image of the temple that I saw, and this verse, are virtually one and the same: I saw a temple that I quickly realized, and that Dad confirmed, was actually God, and this verse says that God is the temple. So I did see God, but since I wasn't dead, I literally saw Him as a temple—a metaphor for God. When I die and ascend to Heaven, I will see God in His true form. This verse confirms to me beyond any shadow of a doubt that the great temple on the hill was God.

There are other Bible verses that are relevant to my experience, but the ones mentioned above carry the most significance. The Bible does say that only Jesus can take you to Heaven, which, to me, explains how I was able to see it.

———

Much of my analysis has been supposition. I ask myself a question and then try to answer it through connecting the dots, educated guess or common sense. As long as I'm still on Earth, I won't know if my answers to these questions are correct, but I'll know soon enough.

Below are ten questions that I have contemplated following my visit to Heaven:

Question 1: *How am I, or anyone else, able to visit Heaven before dying?*
Answer: My feeling is that Jesus allows this for people whose souls are troubled for whatever reason. Everyone has problems of some kind, but not everyone has a tortured soul. And those with tortured souls who are also believers narrows down the list even further. In my case, I could not get over my feelings of guilt regarding my dad, the fear that he died thinking I did not love him. I believe Jesus allowed me to visit Dad in Heaven to show me that Dad did, in fact, know that I loved him, and Dad took me to God to prove this. The entire journey was about love: The people crying tears of joy, the pristine white building on

the hill, the existence of God and Christ ... the theme from top to bottom was love. Dad was telling me that he knew I loved him by showing me the perfect love that awaits us in Heaven.

My feelings of guilt were gone the instant I woke up from the visit, and I've never felt them since. Dad has also never visited me again. There's no need; he put my mind at ease. His work here is done.

Question 2: *Why did Dad wait so long to tell me we were in Heaven?* I didn't know where we were until we neared the end of the sidewalk and I could no longer move my legs, with the magnificent white mansion looming on the hill in front of us. **Answer:** I think Dad wanted me to experience what I was seeing without context, so that I would focus on the moment rather than on where we were. If I had known immediately that we were in Heaven, the message of the visit may have been lost on me.

Question 3: *Why didn't everything I see jive with all the Biblical descriptions of Heaven?* **Answer:** I wasn't dead, so I wasn't able to see everything (thus the "current" that prevented me from walking further when we neared the end of the sidewalk). If I had walked on streets of gold, or seen Christ and God, etc., that would have meant that I had died. But it wasn't my time, so therefore I wasn't privy to experience all of Heaven. I was simply afforded a glimpse of it.

Question 4: *Why didn't Dad tell me right away why the people were sobbing?* After all, he had waited until I asked. **Answer:** My best guess is that if Dad had told me the reason immediately, I wouldn't have paid close attention to the profound emotion they were feeling. By not telling me, my heart went out to those people because I thought they were crying out of sadness. This empathy connected me to them on a deeper level, so that when Dad told me the real reason for their crying, I had a better understanding of the overwhelming joy that consumed them.

Question 5: *Why was Dad's personality different in Heaven from what it was when he was alive on Earth?* This is something I haven't touched on, but the difference in his personality was noticeable. In life, Dad often was in a hyper or agitated state, particularly around Mom and me, and he generally had a tendency to talk loudly (as do I). His voice was sharp. In Heaven, his entire demeanor was warm and mellow; he seemed almost like a different person.

He talked softly and his tone was gentle; the overall quality of his voice was tender and reassuring, which it usually wasn't when he was alive save for solemn occasions such as Christmas or funerals, or our late-night conversations about the deep topics that I enjoyed so much. **Answer:** As an eternal soul in Heaven, Dad is forever immersed in the Lord's love. Therefore, Dad *is* love, as are all souls in Heaven. So the Dad I saw in our visit was pure and righteous, the perfect version of himself.

Question 6: *Why didn't I see all my other loved ones, or at least some of them?* **Answer:** If I had actually died, I believe I would have seen and interacted with them all. But I was still alive, so again I wasn't able to see and experience all that Heaven is. This visit was for the specific purpose of allaying my guilt by showing me that Heaven, Christ and God do exist, so it was just between Dad and me.

Question 7: *Why wasn't I overcome with emotion the way the people in the park were?* While I was filled with the Holy Spirit as I gazed upon the great building on the hill and experienced feelings and sensations that I never knew existed, I never broke down emotionally. **Answer:** Once again, I was only there to observe. The people I saw had died and ascended to Heaven. They were eternal souls bathed in the love of our Heavenly Father and thus could feel the depth of His love in a way that I could not.

During my many analyses of my visit to Heaven, I stumbled onto an interesting observation about this aspect of my experience: The amount of emotion exhibited by the people in the park was directly related to their proximity to the building on the hill. Their demeanor, particularly the shocked and stunned looks on many of their faces, has convinced me that the people I saw at first were the "new arrivals" in Heaven, recently deceased on Earth. They were trying to make sense of their situation, perhaps not realizing that they had died and not sure where they were. They were confused and trying to figure out what was happening to them. The further Dad and I walked, the more we began to see people crying. These people further down the park sidewalk had realized that they had died, were now in Heaven and were feeling Christ's love. And the closer these people were to the building on the hill—in other words, closer to God—the harder they were crying. So it would make sense, then, that these people toward the end of the sidewalk had been in Heaven longer than the people we had seen earlier. My best guess is that every person I saw was on their way to meet God and Christ, and the people nearest the mansion on the hill were next in line.

I also did not see anyone on the hill, either walking up it or at the top near the temple. After pondering this at great length, I have determined that there probably were people there, but I was not able to see them past the point on the sidewalk where I could walk no further. That seemed to be a line of demarcation for me of some kind. If I wasn't allowed to walk past that point, or see God how He truly appeared on the hill, then it also makes sense that I could not see the people heading toward and up the hill to come face-to-face with their Creator.

Question 8: *How could I not know I was in Heaven and in the presence of Christ and God until Dad told me?* After all, you would think that someone would know if they were near our Savior and the Creator. **Answer:** Again, I was only there to observe. Dad was just giving me a glimpse of Heaven, proving to me that Heaven, Christ and God are real. So if Dad had not told me where I was and who was there, I would have had no way of knowing. I wasn't a permanent resident.

That said, the instant that Dad did tell me where we were and that we were near God, I absolutely did feel His presence in ways that are virtually indescribable; it was like my soul was instantly opened up to His love. Without a doubt, my knowing where I was flipped a switch. Why this was the case, I'm not sure. My working hypothesis is that I possessed no ability to experience those feelings as long as my mind was closed to them, and the moment that I was aware of where we were, my mind opened like a floodgate and the waters of God's love rushed in.

Question 9: *If the people I saw were souls in Heaven, why did they look so "human" and why were they wearing clothes? Shouldn't they have appeared more ethereal?* The people I saw in the park area were solid-form human beings, no different than anyone you would see walking down the street or sitting in a restaurant. **Answer:** The Bible tells us in the Book of Genesis that God created us in His image, so it makes sense that we retain that image when we go to Heaven. We appear in His kingdom as we appeared on Earth: As human beings.

As for why the people in the park were wearing the particular clothing they had on, I believe that's what they were wearing at the time of their death. They ascended to Heaven as they were. Dad, who had been dead several years by the time of our visit, was not wearing the same clothes that he wore the day of his death, which leads to the obvious conclusion that our appearance in Heaven does change, at least superficially.

Question 10: *Why did Heaven appear so Earth-like with trees, grass, benches, the sidewalk, etc.? Isn't it supposed to be more of a supernatural realm than a terrestrial world?* **Answer:** In the Bible, Jesus and the apostle Paul both use the word "paradise" as another term for Heaven. The portion of Heaven that I experienced certainly was a paradise; it appeared to be the perfect version of Earth. The radiant colors of the sky, trees, grass, etc. overwhelmed my senses, and the landscape of the park area, spacious prairie, thick forest and God's temple on the hill was sublime. What the rest of this paradise looks like and whether it remains Earth-like in appearance or is more celestial, I don't know, but I am certain that it is resplendent in whatever form it takes.

I have more questions, of course, maybe hundreds. But they, like the ten detailed above, cannot be fully answered—or answered at all—until our souls go to Heaven. And while I can't help but analyze every aspect of my visit in an effort to make better sense of it and satisfy my natural human curiosity, I have also been careful to accept it for what it was: a miracle. I was temporarily called to Heaven to be with my dad for an extraordinary journey of love and confirmation. From the moment I awoke from that journey, my life has never been the same. It was like a dark cloud had lifted from my psyche. It was freeing; my emotional and psychological shackles had been removed. I was able to fully enjoy life again, to live with joy in the moment and hope for the future.

It was literally a gift from God.

So how has my life been different following this divine experience?

Aside from erasing my feelings of guilt regarding my dad and thus being generally happy and feeling self-assured again, there is one fundamental difference in my life since my visit with Dad in Heaven: I know that life is eternal. Thinking it, hoping for it or believing it is one thing; *knowing* it is another. It changes everything. Of course, I can't present evidence to support that my experience happened and that Heaven is real, but I don't need evidence. Others might, but I don't. It happened to me, and that's all the evidence I need. If I could present hard scientific evidence, then it would have been an Earthly, human experience and not the divine miracle that it was.

I have a different perspective on life now that I know it is eternal. My visit to Heaven has given me a macro outlook on life instead of getting bogged down in the micro; I know that regardless of what happens in this realm, bigger and better things are in store in the next existence. No matter how bad a day I might be having, knowing what's waiting for me when I die helps to take the edge off. I don't sweat the small stuff or get as exercised about some things as much as I did before; I'm able to maintain a more even keel.

I also appreciate things more. When I first open my eyes as I'm waking up and see the bedroom bathed in the light of a new day, I thank God for giving me just a little more time on this Earth. Hearing the birds chirping outside, the breeze rustling through the trees, the rain beating against the windows or even seeing a blanket of thick snow covering the landscape make me feel lucky to be alive. While our time in Heaven is forever, our time on Earth is but a cosmological blip so I try to enjoy as much of it, and get as much out of it, as I possibly can before I take the next journey.

To that end, I'm reminded of the wise words of my hospital roommate after I underwent anterior cruciate ligament reconstruction surgery on my left knee in the summer of 1992, when I was twenty-four years old. I was in utter agony upon waking up in the recovery room following the intricate, hours-long operation and had a torturous night's sleep after being wheeled up to my room. My left leg was tightly wrapped with several layers of bandages, tape and other items that I could feel but not see. I could barely move, and the only position I could sleep in was on my back—which, even in the best of times, doesn't work for me; I'm not a back-sleeper, preferring instead to sleep on my sides or stomach.

As if my position on the bed wasn't uncomfortable enough, the pain was excruciating. The only relief I could get was when the night nurse came in periodically to replenish the water pack that was wrapped against my knee for pain management. The soothing feeling of the fresh, ice-cold water in the pack pressing against my throbbing, pounding, surgically repaired knee was absolute heaven—and as far as I was concerned, the nurse who administered it was an angel. I never did get a good look at her that night due to my shaky state of consciousness and the darkness of the room, but even through the drug-induced haze of the pain medication I could see that she was wearing a white nurse's cap, white top and white skirt. All white, like an angel. She may have had short to medium-length dark hair, but I couldn't be sure; it could have just been the shadows. Also, from what I was able to discern, she didn't appear to be much older than I was. She came into the room several times throughout the night to check on my condition and make sure my water pack stayed fresh and cold; I wondered if she knew that her night-long monitoring of the cold-water pack was the only thing that prevented me from being in abject misery. The last time I remembered her being in the room, I uttered "Thank you" to her as she left; she softy replied with, "You're welcome. Hopefully you can get some sleep," and was gone. I never saw her again.

After a fitful night's sleep, I woke up the next day moaning in pain—and only then did I realize that I had not been alone in the room since arriving there from recovery the night before. I had the bed closest to the window, and the curtain to my right was pulled to partition the room, indicating that I had company on the other side of the partition. I had not noticed this partition earlier in the darkness and my medicated stupor. I had no idea who the patient was on the other side of that curtain; I couldn't see them at all. I was in too much pain to care anyway.

Apparently, though, the continuous moaning emanating from my side of the curtain caught the person's attention.

"How you doing over there, young man?" a voice called out from the other side of the curtain. "You sound like you're in a lot of pain this morning."

I could tell from his voice that it was an older man, perhaps in his seventies.

"Yeah," I answered, "I had knee surgery yesterday. I'm in a lot of pain. It's going to be a long day."

It was a chore just to make my voice loud enough to be heard on his side of the partition—especially since I had to talk over whatever equipment he was connected to over there.

"Well," the voice said, "it's like an old Army buddy of mine used to say: Any day above ground is a good one. You don't have too many good days below ground."

We made small talk for a while, and later that night I was released to go home to start my rehab and recovery. I never met or even saw the older gentleman I had spoken with in my hospital room that day, but I have always wondered which war he fought in. Based on my guess that he was somewhere in his seventies, he must have served in World War II, and his mention of the Army made me think he probably fought the Germans in the European theater of war since the Marines saw the lion's share of the ground action in the Pacific theater (although the Army certainly was involved as well). Either way, I was embarrassed to have been moaning and groaning after a knee surgery in Akron, Ohio, when this man surely had experienced the horrors of war in cramped, muddy foxholes and bombed-out towns throughout Western Europe, fighting arguably the most highly trained, highly motivated, and best-equipped foe in American history.

I have never forgotten that older gentleman's statement that morning in the hospital room all those years ago, and it assumed even greater meaning following my visit with Dad in Heaven. The man's point was well taken back then: Enjoy life while you have it, because it can be over tomorrow. But after my walk in Heaven with Dad, that point was hammered home in a far more poignant way than it had been when I was twenty-four with most of my life still ahead of me. Now, at fifty, I know that the majority of my life is already behind me and, as such, my hospital roommate's Army buddy quote hits closer and closer to home all the time. I don't think T.S. Eliot's eternal Footman is holding my coat or even reaching for it yet, but he sees it in the closet. He knows where to find it.

Even so, as I stated earlier, I no longer fear death now that I know we never actually die. Yes, our body dies, but our soul survives to live in glorious eternity in Heaven. I'm not looking forward to physical death and hope that it is still far off in the future, primarily because I want to squeeze every last bit of life out of my existence here on Earth before I move on. There is still much of this beautiful garden planet God created that I would like to see, there is still a lot that I want to accomplish in this life, and I'm nowhere near ready to say goodbye to my loved ones and even my own body. But when my time does come, I know what is waiting—and who is waiting—on the other side of the veil.

Of course, even armed with this knowledge of what awaits, I'm still human and can't escape the frailties and imperfections that come with it. I get angry, I get sad, I get upset, I get frustrated, I have bad days, I have bad moods, I have regrets, I have stress, I have worries and concerns, I dislike certain things and certain people, I get wracked with grief when a loved one dies; negativity is not erased from this life just because you know that a better life—a perfect life— lies beyond this one. There are things in life that can make you miserable and people in life who can make you miserable, circumstances and individuals that drain your energy and your optimism; day-to-day life can be a battle, a survival of the psychologically fittest. Not everyone is on your side or in your corner, not everyone has your best interests at heart; there are people who will try to drag you down and prevent you from reaching your potential. As long as we are alive on Earth, these challenges will present themselves to us on a regular basis. It's part of being human. We are emotional creatures, and part of our nature is such that emotions often control our thought process and behavior. It's unavoidable.

But I have found that knowing life is eternal prevents the darkest of those emotions from taking hold of your psyche; it stops hopelessness and despair from consuming you when they otherwise would have devoured your soul. It opens you up to God's love, which protects you from the dark recesses of your own mind. It gives you the inner strength to withstand assaults on your character and to rise above the daily noise and reach for something higher. When you know that not only do you survive your body's death but you also live for eternity in Heaven, there is nothing that can defeat you.

It is a triumph of the soul.

There is another element to my experience that I have only slightly touched on: the concept of, or existence of, Hell. As I said before, I am a Christian, though I am not what many people would consider to be devout; I do, however, believe in the basic tenets and principles of the Bible. And that includes the existence of Satan, demons and Hell. What I saw and experienced in Heaven was the intense love of God and Christ. I am sure that the opposite exists: the intense hatred of the devil. Everything has an opposite—light and dark, night and day, right and wrong, good and evil—so it only makes sense that there is a Hell and that Satan is a real figure.

I couldn't possibly determine (in other words, judge) what offenses someone must commit to be condemned to the lake of fire. We all sin, most of us repeatedly, because we are human; Jesus died on the cross in part to absolve us of our sins so we could, in fact, go to Heaven. So it can't just be the fact that someone sins that puts them on the fast track to Hell. It has to be something deeper, something worse, something far more insidious.

It has to be something that tarnishes your soul, something that can't be forgiven through any amount of repentance. What could some of those things be? Well, we can surmise that horrid things like murder in cold blood, rape and child abuse would be high on the list. It would seem that those who commit such heinous crimes against humanity, against God's children, could not possibly hope to redeem themselves and gain access to Heaven. But then again, we're not in a position to judge so we can't be sure, can we?

We always hear stories and see documentaries about hardened violent criminals on death row who allegedly find God and become saved. Is this enough to erase, or at least outweigh, their misdeeds of the past and allow such criminals turned born-again Christians to walk in Heaven with Christ? Could Adolf Hitler have allowed Jesus into his heart while he cowered in his bunker in Berlin at the end of World War II and thus been allowed into Heaven, regardless of the fact that he orchestrated the mass murder of six million Jews? Would salvation trump something as dastardly as the Holocaust? These are questions that mere mortals like us can't answer.

But Hell must exist. It must, because Heaven exists. There can't be one without the other. The Bible says Hell exists, and it says Satan is real, a fallen angel who was cast out of Heaven. Evil certainly exists; we see it every day on the news, we see it all around us. Mass shootings, bombings of innocent civilians, acts of unspeakable cruelty, all of them are the manifestation of evil. All of them are signs—some would say evidence—of Satan's influence and existence.

The belief in the existence of an underworld and evil entities is nearly as old as humankind itself. Various cultures and religions over millennia have embraced the idea of an underworld—of a Hell—of some type, some more terrifying and permanent than others. Even the ancient Egyptians believed that the spirit had to journey through a dangerous underworld before reaching the afterlife. The fact that the concept of Hell, like the concept of Heaven, is so pervasive in the human condition over such vast stretches of time is not trivial. This belief comes from somewhere. The cynics and non-believers among us would say that the belief in an underworld of evil spirits is simply humanity trying to make sense of its existence—or, even more cynically, a superstition nefariously designed by oppressive rulers and religions to keep their followers in line. To scare them straight, if you will.

But if that is the case, why has this belief in a Hell of some type and the evil entities that accompany it persisted almost since the dawn of man? If it is just a flimsy ploy to trick people into behaving, well, we can't even get strictly enforced laws with punishments up to and including death to achieve that purpose in our society today. So it's highly doubtful that using the idea of an underworld as a Jedi mind trick to make people toe the line would last across the ages in all corners of the globe.

There has to be something more to it than simple population control, because people eventually would catch on to the chicanery—probably in relatively short order. No, the concept of a treacherous, terrifying underworld is a deeply rooted, fundamental aspect of the human condition that is not bound by geographical or philosophical constraints.

The simple answer of why it has endured so long is because it is real. Some near-death experiencers have reported seeing and visiting Hell the way I have related my experience in Heaven, saying that what they saw in their visitation changed the way they lived their lives. They can give highly detailed individual accounts of their experiences like I can. And after my visit with Dad in Heaven, I don't doubt for one second that they are telling the truth and what happened to them did, in fact, happen. I know that Heaven and God are real, and I have no doubt that Hell and Satan are real.

In fact, I have had indirect exposure to evil entities—or maybe it's just the same entity over and over—in the dream state. I'm not sure these would be called visitations in the same sense as the others I have had, but they were something more than just dreams because I could actually feel the dark nature of these demons—and my fear of them—to the point that I would force myself to wake up to get away from them. I have had several of these occurrences, where I know something is lurking in my dream state, watching me, then starting to follow me. I instinctively know that it is trying to get me, but I can never discern exactly where it is and what it looks like. I can just feel it; I know it's there because the hate and evil emanating from it are palpable. It's absolutely terrifying. It always seems to come out of nowhere: The dream will start out innocuously enough, then suddenly I will become gripped with fear when I sense that the demon has returned. I can't tell if it's the same demon chasing after me every time, or if it is a series of them, but it's a demon nonetheless.

I also don't know in exactly which realm I am encountering the demon. Is it infiltrating the dimension that my subconscious mind is in as I sleep and attempting to ambush me, or does my subconscious mind sometimes slip into another reality that these entities occupy—perhaps even being tricked into doing so since my conscious mind is temporarily shut off? I do get the overwhelming sense that its purpose is to harm me, possibly even kill me.

The demon's appearance in my dream state has happened often enough that I now recognize immediately when it's under way. It used to take me by surprise, but now I can sense its presence as soon as it shows up. There's no way to predict when, where and how it will show itself in the dream state (it doesn't actually show itself per se, the most I can see is a shadow or an outline at times, but it does make its presence known through the intense evil it gives off)—but apparently my subconscious mind is on to it.

I'm sure I haven't had my last dream-state experience with the demon—in fact, I even encountered it during the writing of this book. But fortunately I have been able to evade it by making myself wake up and thus escaping whatever dimension I was trapped in with it.

So far.

———

One more thing: Throughout my visit to Heaven, I noticed animals, particularly birds, squirrels and chipmunks. I'm sure I saw these three creatures in particular because of where I was in Heaven: a park-type area bordered by a large grassy plain. This also confirmed something that I had long suspected: Animals have souls. It makes sense that they, too, go to Heaven. After all, they, like us, are created by God, so they are God's creatures. And when their time on Earth is done, they are called to Heaven to be with their Creator like we are.

In fact, I have always believed that animals are closer to God than humans: They are without sin, so their souls are pure. Humans, on the other hand, do not have pure souls, which is the very reason why Christ died on the cross: to give us a path to Heaven.

There are several compelling verses in Scripture that refer to animals in Heaven, particularly horses, but a few stand out:

From The Prophecy of Isaias (also known as the Book of Isaiah) 11:6-9:

The wolf shall dwell with the lamb, and the leopard shall lie down with the kid. The calf and the lion and the sheep shall abide together, and a little child shall lead them. The calf and the bear shall feed; their young ones shall rest together; and the lion shall eat straw like the ox. And the sucking child shall play on the hole of the asp; and the weaned child shall thrust his hand into the den of the basilisk. They shall not hurt, nor shall they kill in all my holy mountain, for the earth is filled with the knowledge of the Lord, as the covering waters of the sea."

From Apocalypse 4:6-11:

And before the throne there is, at it were, a sea of glass like to crystal, and in the midst of the throne, and round the throne, are four living creatures, full of eyes before and behind. And the first living creature is like a lion and the second like a calf, and the third has the face, as it were, of a man, and the fourth is like an eagle flying. And the four living creatures have each of them six wings; round about and within they are full of eyes. And they do not rest day and night, saying, Holy, Holy, Holy, the Lord God almighty, who was, and who is, and who is coming. And when those living creatures give glory and honor and benediction to him who sits on the throne, who lives forever and ever, the twenty-four elders will fall down before him who sits upon the throne, and will worship him who lives forever and ever, and will cast their crowns before the throne, saying, "Worthy art thou, O Lord our God, to receive glory and honor and power; for thou hast created all things, and because of thy will they existed, and were created."

Apocalypse 4:13 even begins: "And every creature that is in heaven"

These verses and many others seem to explicitly acknowledge the existence of animals in Heaven. With my own confirmation of seeing birds in flight in the "park" and the grassy expanse, along with chipmunks and squirrels darting about, I have no doubt that we are joined by animals in Heaven.

And that includes our pets. I think I can speak for many, if not most, people when I say that if my beloved pets won't be with me in Heaven, then it won't be much of a heaven. I wouldn't want to live for eternity without them. If our cats Sylvia, Halen and Nookie, plus all our family's dogs, won't be in the hereafter with me, then I'm not sure I would want to be there at all. But I think they will be, because there were many animals during my visit in Heaven. I saw them, and Scripture refers to them.

That's good enough for me.

How has all this resolved my feelings about Dad and our relationship when he was alive? I'm not naïve enough to think it makes every last bit of negativity go away, but it does soften my stance on most things. As I said before, we didn't have a bad relationship; it was just complicated with some rocky spots, like plenty of parent-child relationships. Things I thought were important before now seem trivial. I will always be frustrated that he didn't get more out of life, frustrated that he held himself back and didn't get to do and experience the things that he deserved.

Am I now certain that Dad knew I loved him when he died? Yes, I am. I believe that was the central reason for our visitation together in Heaven. It was about pure love, and that included my love for Dad. He was telling me that he knew I loved him. That has not been an issue in my mind since I woke up the morning following our Heavenly journey.

Yet, there are a couple things between us that I am still working on trying to forgive. I'm not sure if I ever will. I know I should, but maybe I'm not mature enough, even at age fifty, to take that step at this point. Of course, that doesn't mean I don't love my dad and appreciate everything he did for me. It has nothing to do with that. Our time together in Heaven freed me from that emotional prison and allowed me to separate and compartmentalize my feelings; they are no longer interconnected. My love for my dad stands above all else. Whatever issues we may have had are secondary to the love I have for him. The fact that I haven't been able to forgive him for certain things doesn't mean I won't, nor does it stand in the way of my feelings about him as a father. He wasn't a perfect dad, and I wasn't a perfect son, but he was the perfect dad for me. I wouldn't trade our time together for anything. I only wish it had been longer.

Then again, our time together is only just beginning. I know he's always with me—after all, he said so himself—and I know he is waiting for me in God's Kingdom along with all my loved ones and pets. We will all be together for eternity, basking in the light, love and glory of the Lord.

I can't prove that for a fact, but I know it in my heart.

Because I got a glimpse of Heaven.

EPILOGUE

A couple nights after we had to have Sylvia put to sleep in March 2003, I was standing at the sliding door that leads to our back deck, looking up through the glass at the starry night sky. It was my first pet death since my dogs Mo and Boomer died nearly ten years earlier. My first instance of dealing with the loss of a pet came when I was eleven years old. It wasn't a dog or a cat, but rather a fish. A little white fish we had in a bowl in the living room of our apartment in Mogadore. It was my first fish, and I wasn't aware that their lifespans were so short. I was always sure to feed him, and I would watch him zip about in his bowl, studying his coloring, his eyes, his little fins, everything. He swam so gracefully and seemed so happy in his own little world. I named him Casper because of his beautiful white coloring.

I would feed him and visit him as soon as I got up every day. At school, I would think about him and couldn't wait to come home and see him in his watery play land. He was fun to observe and I loved him.

One morning, Casper didn't seem as energetic as usual. He was listless, just kind of sitting on the bottom of the bowl. His fins and gills were moving, but that was it. I asked Mom if something was wrong with him, and she said maybe he just wasn't feeling well and needed some food. I'm sure she knew what was about to happen but didn't have the heart to tell me.

I fed him, but he made no effort to eat. His status remained unchanged throughout the day, and I had trouble sleeping that night. When I woke up the next morning, Casper was clearly struggling, floating at an odd angle near the top of his bowl. He wasn't quite on his side, but he was closer to being on his side than he was to being straight up and down. I got a sick feeling in my stomach. I asked Mom if he was going to be OK, and she said that we would pray for him to get better. This lifted my spirits; after all, with Jesus on our side, what could go wrong? I went to bed that night optimistic that Casper would pull through.

When I went downstairs the next morning, to my horror I found him floating at the top of his bowl, motionless. I pushed him with my finger, and he didn't move. He just floated with the current made by the motion of my finger. I knew he was gone.

I had Mom come over to make sure, and she looked at me sadly and said, "I'm sorry, Tommy, it looks like he died."

I stood there gazing forlornly at his lifeless little body floating at the top of the bowl, tears streaming down my face. And I couldn't stop crying. I cried the rest of the day and cried myself to sleep that night. I cried some more the next day, and nothing Mom and Dad said to console me helped. I had never experienced pet death before, and I was devastated. I don't remember how long we had him, maybe a couple months, but I thought it would be years. I was shocked it was so short.

I felt betrayed by Jesus. I had prayed to Him to save my beloved little fish, and He didn't do it. Instead, He just let Casper die. It made no sense to me. It seemed cruel and left me confused: Why hadn't praying worked? Why did Jesus ignore me? Was I being punished for some reason, and if so, why take it out on Casper, who had done nothing wrong?

I asked Mom why Jesus hadn't answered our prayers, but of course she didn't have any answers, saying only that everything happens for a reason. I would sob in Mom's arms, continuing to ask why Jesus would take Casper from me, why He didn't let Casper live longer, why Jesus would do this to me. Unable to console me and provide me with answers that would pull me through my grief, Mom bought me a book about turning to Jesus to cope with death and grief. Seems like heavy reading for an eleven-year-old, but then, I had read legendary World War II correspondent Ernie Pyle's book *Brave Men* about the European theater of war when I was only five. I've always loved to read and could handle heavy reading at a young age, so Mom thought I was ready for it. And nothing she said to me was helping anyway.

I can't remember the name of the book or exactly what it said, but it addressed the fact that just because people and animals we love die doesn't mean Jesus doesn't love them or us. In fact, quite the opposite: Jesus is calling them home to be with Him in Heaven. It took a long time for me to get over losing Casper, and even when I think of him now I have to fight back tears. Childhood emotions are deep-seated and often never leave us, and the sight of my poor Casper floating at the top of his bowl was traumatic. I wasn't ready for it. After reading the book Mom got for me, it made a little better sense and helped me grieve. Most people would say it was only a fish, but to me Casper was my friend. I saw him and talked to him every day, it was my responsibility to care for him, and when he died I took it personally. I felt that it was my fault to some degree, even a large degree, and I had let him down.

Slowly, the words in the book began to comfort me. I knew Casper was with Jesus, and I would see him again someday. I was thankful for the time I had with him, and I've never forgotten him. He will always have a special place in my heart.

A couple months later, I was making my usual rounds as a lieutenant on the School Crossing Patrol at O.H. Somers Elementary in Mogadore when someone tracked me down to tell me that my parents were in the parking lot waiting to take me home. It was only late morning; we were barely halfway through the school day on Nov. 30, 1979.

This had never happened before. I could only remember one other time when either of my parents had to come get me at school. It was back when I was in first grade at Betty Jane Elementary in Akron, right before we moved to Mogadore. It was recess, and I had found an open swing on the playground and was in hot competition with a kid next to me to see who could go higher on the swing set. The kid then upped the ante, taking his hands off the chains he was holding onto and putting them on his thighs. He somehow maintained his balance in the swing seat despite not holding on to anything, and to my even greater amazement, continued to swing just as high. He looked over at me, his hands resting in his lap as he swung, and smiled broadly as if to say, "Gotcha!"

Being the competitive kid that I was (and still am), I couldn't allow myself to be bested. I released my grip from the chains that connected my seat to the structure of the swing set above and put them on my thighs, as he had done. My momentum carried me forward, then back. I looked to my right and smiled at him as he had done to me—then flew backward off the seat, did a full flip in the air and landed squarely on my chin on the asphalt surface of the playground. I lay there in a heap as horrified students looked on before a supervisor rushed to my side. I knew by the sheer terror on her face that whatever my face looked like, it wasn't good. I was immediately whisked away into the school building for first-aid treatment on my bloody mess of a face, and soon afterward a frantic Mom showed up to take me to the doctor. Much of my sympathy capital was lost when Mom asked me what happened and I told her I was trying to swing as high as I could with no hands.

"Why the hell would you do that, Tommy?!" Mom exclaimed.

"Because the kid next to me was doing it," I answered, my chin throbbing with pain. "I thought I could do it, too."

"Well, don't ever try anything like that again!" an exasperated Mom said. "You're lucky you didn't really hurt yourself."

My injury (and stupidity) was the reason for Mom's trip to the school that day in 1974. But on this day five years later, there was no obvious reason for both Mom and Dad to be at the school, and especially to take me home. It had been an uneventful morning, and I was fine. What's more, both of them should have been at work.

Something is wrong, I thought. *Terribly wrong.*

I quickly gathered up my things and, with a lump in my throat, walked out to the parking lot.

Dad hadn't even bothered to pull into a parking space, instead waiting for me in the middle of the parking lot to make a quick exit. I got into the back seat behind Mom on the passenger side, and the air in the car felt heavy and still. Both of them were sniffling as Dad began to drive off.

"Tommy," Mom began, her voice quaking. "We have some real bad news to tell you."

To this day, I don't know why I knew this or how I knew this, but I just knew this:

"Did Frisk die?" I asked. Frisk was my dog, a three-year-old wire haired terrier mix. We had gotten him as a puppy in 1976, about a year after we moved to Mogadore, and he and I had been attached at the hip ever since. We were literally growing up together. He slept on my bed with me every night, followed me around the apartment everywhere I went, curled up next to me on the couch when I was reading or doing homework; wherever I was, Frisk was there, too. He was like my shadow. Going on our annual family summer vacations to the beach in North Carolina was excruciating because I missed Frisk so badly and was terrified that something would happen to him; I knew that as long as I was home, he would be safe. Being an only child, I saw Frisk as more than my dog; he was the brother I didn't have. He filled a lot of gaps in my life.

I could tell that my question caught my parents off guard. They looked at each other, then there was silence for several seconds. Finally, Mom spoke.

"Yes, Tommy. Frisk is dead. We're so sorry," she said, her voice barely above a whisper. "He was hit by a car today."

My blood ran cold, I went numb—and then I burst into tears. We all sobbed heavily as Dad drove us back to our apartment. It was one of the longest, saddest days of my life. We had been preparing to move from the apartment to a house in another part of Mogadore in a few days, and we had someone come to the apartment to do some minor repairs that the landlord requested we do before moving. This person had left the back door ajar, and Frisk had gotten out. Usually when he had gotten loose before, he would just run around the parking lot of the apartment complex until he got tired, at which point he would just let me catch him. This time, though, he had taken off in the other direction, toward the heavily traveled road in front of our apartment building, and tried to race across to the other side.

A neighbor friend of ours across the street found Frisk lying motionless in her yard a few feet from the road. The person who hit him never stopped the car to check on him and see if he could be saved. Maybe he could have been if quick action had been taken, or maybe he died instantly. I have always wondered if Frisk saw it coming at the last instant or had no idea he was about to leave this Earth. I hope it was the latter and that he didn't suffer at all, that death came instantly. It tortures my mind to wonder if he lay in agony in the grass of our neighbor's yard, whimpering in pain, waiting to die. I hope that Jesus took him humanely.

Mom, Dad and I spent much of the rest of the day sobbing in our darkened living room. I had never seen Dad cry like that. He was sitting in the chair in front of the living room window, his head buried in his hand, heaving. He hadn't even cried like that at Clar Clar's funeral. Mom and I sat on the couch, crying uncontrollably. I repeated loudly several times through my tears, "I WANT MY DOG BACK. I WANT MY DOG BACK." But I knew he wasn't coming back. He was gone. Forever.

The last time I saw Frisk, his body was covered in a blanket in the trunk of our car. I could make out his shape underneath the blanket and a few tufts of his fur were visible, poking out from under the blanket. I asked to see him one last time, but my parents refused; it was undoubtedly better that I didn't see Frisk in his final condition. We closed the lid of the trunk and made the short drive to Grandma and Grandpa's house in Brimfield, where Dad and Gramps buried him in the family pet cemetery just behind their house.

Frisk's death destroyed me. For several weeks, I couldn't eat, I couldn't sleep, I vomited often, I could barely function. We had just moved, I was in a strange new house, and my best buddy was gone; my whole world had been turned upside down and inside out.

I had just come to terms with Casper dying, and now Frisk gets run over by a car. It was a lot to absorb in such a short time frame. The world suddenly seemed like a scary, unfair place. I had come to realize that Casper was in Heaven, so I knew that Frisk was there too, but it seemed like Jesus had either turned His back on me or had forgotten about me altogether. The grief book Mom had gotten for me to deal with Casper's death helped in the case of Frisk as well, but it took a long time to fully accept why Jesus would take my dog, my best friend, from me in such a cruel, painful fashion.

Nearly a month later, a dog wandered onto Grandma and Grandpa's property—it was fairly common for ingrates to dump their unwanted animals out in the country near their house—and Grandma enticed him onto their porch. It was late December, a dangerous time of year for a homeless animal to be wandering around outside in Ohio. She fed him and cared for him for a few days, then she and Gramps decided to give him to me to replace Frisk. I came home from school one day and saw their car in the driveway, which was strange since Mom and Dad were still at work. I walked into the living room of the new house wondering what was going on and Grandma and Grandpa were sitting in there, smiling at me.

"Look behind me, Tommy," said Grandma, sitting in the rocking chair.

I walked over and peeked behind the chair. Lying there on the floor and looking up at me with big brown eyes was a snow-white dog with curly hair—a Cockapoo. I could tell he was young, just barely out of puppy stage. I was in shock.

"He's yours, Tommy!" Grandma said. "We found him at the house."

I named him Mo, and he became my best friend for the next fourteen years. "I know you still love Frisk and you miss him," Dad had said that day when he got home from work, "but you'll learn to love this dog in your own way. It will be different, but that doesn't mean it will be worse." It wasn't. Mo was one of the best things that ever happened to me.

I still think about Frisk often, the good times we had together, playing and racing around the house, him chasing me up and down the stairs, yipping and barking while I laughed and shrieked as I tried to get away from him. I tear up often when I think about him, wondering what it would have been like to have had him in my life for his full lifespan. I would have been in college by the time he had lived out his life; instead, he was taken from me when I was in sixth grade. I can't help but feel like we got cheated.

I have visited his grave often at the property in Brimfield in the decades since he was killed. It's been a while now since I went out behind the house to see him—years, actually—but just being inside that house on our visits with my aunt and uncle make me feel close to him. My visits with him at his grave are intensely sad; I never got to say goodbye to him as you would when you have to put an animal down. I went off to school the morning of Nov. 30, 1979, like I did every other morning, not knowing that when I closed the door behind me, I would never see him alive again. Our parting was so abrupt, his death so tragic, that it left a hole in my heart to this day. I talk to him as I stand over the large rock that serves as his makeshift headstone, telling him how sorry I am about what happened to him, that I miss him and that I'll see him again someday.

And I will.

So here I was again, twenty-four years later, staring up at the clear night sky, mourning and contemplating the death of another beloved pet, wracked with guilt that Sylvia might be alive if only we had gotten her to the vet sooner to diagnose and treat her kidney failure. Of course, nothing we did could have saved her at that point, but you always play the "what if" game in that situation, beating yourself up that you didn't act sooner and could have done more. Death, though, is in God's hands, and there's nothing we can do about it.

As I gazed up at the stars through the sliding glass door, tears streaming down my face, feeling empty and alone without Sylvia, I wondered if she could see me where she was or knew the depth of the sadness I was feeling. Looking up at the clear night sky, I said through tears: "I love you and I miss you, Sylvia. Daddy will see you again someday."

At that moment, a shooting star streaked across the sky, starting almost directly above our house and hurtling toward the east, giving the effect of it angling downward out of the sky—like it was sent from Heaven. It caught me completely by surprise. It was late at night, actually the wee hours of the morning, and I thought there was a very good chance that I was the only person to see it.

As if it was meant just for me.

The timing was impeccable—it occurred during the time of night when I was usually still up, and immediately after I had said those words. It was one coincidence too many.

"I saw that, Sylvia," I whispered through bleary eyes. "Thank you."

The next day, I told Kim about the shooting star. Before I even mentioned my thoughts on a connection to Sylvia, Kim said, "That was Silly. She was telling you that she's OK."

Yes, I, too, believed that Sylvia had sent me a message from Heaven.

And now, I know she did.

A FINAL NOTE

Our beloved cat Ashton passed away during final production of this book. Ashton was diagnosed with congestive heart failure in early December 2018, bounced back strongly for several weeks on medication, then went downhill rapidly in mid-January. Despite the best efforts of several veterinarians, Ashton did not recover. By this time he was also in kidney failure, and we made the gut-wrenching decision to have him put to sleep on January 18.

Ashton was somewhere around ten or eleven years old and was the youngest of our group of four cats. Considering his age, I thought he would be the last one standing. Instead, Kim and I found ourselves saying goodbye to this gentle, loving soul far sooner than we ever expected.

Ashton was the classic fat cat. He was a large—very large—Russian Blue/Chartreux mix with a thick, beautiful double coat of slate gray fur with paws and feet the color of cinders (thus his name). I have never seen a bigger housecat than Ashton; he was about the size of a full-grown bobcat. He was a stray who just wandered up to our front door one night in April 2011 and never left. He trusted me immediately, and we developed a special bond. But there was a problem: We had five other cats at the time and weren't sure if adding a sixth was a good idea; we didn't know how the other five would accept him—if there was enough room at the inn, so to speak.

I sat outside with Ashton just about every night for more than a month. I worked nights back then and usually didn't get home until midnight or later. Upon my arrival, Ashton would materialize out of the darkness and dutifully wait for me near the front door, anticipating another night of companionship with his new friend. On nights when I got home and didn't see him right away, I would begin to worry that something awful happened to him. With a pit in my stomach, I would continually look out our front storm door and scan the immediate surroundings for any sign of him, hoping to see his familiar gray shape making its way toward the house. I would think to myself, *"Well, that's it. He's gone. Something happened to him. I'll never see him again."* But then, sure enough, on one of those trips to the front door I would turn the corner and see Ashton sitting calmly on the stoop, peering through the glass door into the living room as if to say, "Hey, I'm here! Where are you?" Waves of relief would wash over me, and I would grab my coat and step outside as he greeted me with a loud, friendly meow and rubbed against my legs; another quiet, peaceful night together was about to begin.

Usually, though, Ashton was already there waiting, sometimes even skittering excitedly across the driveway and toward the front door as I pulled in. I kept bowls of fresh food and water for him on our front stoop; I put a radio on the stoop and kept it tuned to my favorite program, Coast to Coast AM, for us to listen to through the night; I set up a lawn chair adjacent to the stoop so I could hold him in my lap, snuggling him against my coat as we tried to keep each other warm in the chilly April night air; and I stationed my car in the driveway for weeks to clear space in our garage for "Ashton Central," which consisted of a lawn chair, a little table stand with the radio on top, food and water bowls, and a makeshift cat bed comprised of a cardboard box with a blanket inside. The garage became Ashton's safe haven from the elements—it seemed to rain or storm almost every night in that month we sat outside together—and I lost count of the number of times I fell asleep holding Ashton in my lap while sitting in the lawn chair in our garage. The comforting warmth of his body against me, combined with the soothing cadence of his purr—and with the dulcet tones of Coast to Coast AM emanating from the radio next to us—often had me dozing off in no time.

Although he was a stray, Ashton appeared to be in very good condition; he wasn't dirty, his fur wasn't matted, and there were no telltale signs of having been in a fight such as scratch marks on his face or tattered ears. I got the feeling that he either had been dumped on our quiet little side street or left behind when someone moved. I felt badly for him, especially when he got caught out in the rain and storms. Usually he made into the garage just in time to avoid the inclement weather, although once, after he had jumped off my lap in the garage and wandered out into the night, he came racing right back in moments later, soaked, after the skies had opened into a sudden deluge. More often than not, though, we managed to stay warm and dry together as the hours clicked by toward morning.

Ashton and I spent every night just like that, on the front stoop if the weather was tolerable or in the garage if it wasn't, the two of us huddled together in the wee hours of the morning while the rest of the neighborhood slept. It was as if we were the only living souls on Earth. I will cherish those nightly hours of solitude with Ashton for the rest of my life.

After at least a month of this and unable to find him a home, we decided to take him in. Keeping him outside any longer was no longer viable. He had been front-declawed and therefore had no ability to defend himself if attacked, and it was only a matter of time before he contracted a fatal disease, was hit by a car, or suffered abuse or worse at the hands of a heartless human being. In good conscience, Kim and I just couldn't continue to leave him to fend for himself outside.

So Ashton became the sixth member of the Hardesty cat family and proceeded to give us eight unforgettable, glorious years of unconditional love and unbridled fun. All our other cats took to him immediately—he was a true gentle giant—and he went out of his way to, well, stay out of everyone's way; he quickly found his own niche in the house and fit right in. He was my buddy; he slept right next to me nearly every night for eight years, and he often lay by my side in his favorite spot on the family room couch while I sat at the laptop writing this book, keeping me company in the wee hours night after night, month after month.

That spot is empty now as I write this final segment of the book. The comforting, familiar sight of Ashton sound asleep in his spot as I type is gone, replaced by an unoccupied pillow and bedsheet.

But while that sight is gone, Ashton is not. He continues, just like Clar Clar, Grandma, Gramps, Uncle Billy, Sylvia, Uncle Denny and Dad continue. None of them are gone, and neither is Ashton.

'Til we meet again, Ashy Boy.

And we will meet again.

Printed in the United States
By Bookmasters